AGAINST ODDS

Against Odds

Reflections on the Experiences of the British Army, 1914–45

Dominick Graham
Emeritus Professor
University of New Brunswick
Canada

First published in Great Britain 1999 by
MACMILLAN PRESS LTD
Houndmills, Basingstoke, Hampshire RG21 6XS and London
Companies and representatives throughout the world

A catalogue record for this book is available from the British Library.

ISBN 0–333–66858–8 hardcover
ISBN 0–333–66859–6 paperback

 First published in the United States of America 1999 by
ST. MARTIN'S PRESS, INC.,
Scholarly and Reference Division,
175 Fifth Avenue, New York, N.Y. 10010

ISBN 0–312–21591–6

Library of Congress Cataloging-in-Publication Data
Graham, Dominick.
Against odds : reflections on the experiences of the British army,
1914–45 / Dominick Graham.
p.   cm.
Includes bibliographical references and index.
ISBN 0–312–21591–6 (cloth : alk. paper)
1. Great Britain. Army—History—World War, 1914–1918.   2. Great
Britain. Army—History—World War, 1939–1945.   I. Title.
D546.G47   1998
940.54'0941—DC21   98–17691
                                                          CIP

© Dominick Graham 1999

This book is printed on paper suitable for recycling and made from fully managed and
sustained forest sources.

10   9   8   7   6   5   4   3   2   1
08   07   06   05   04   03   02   01   00   99

Printed and bound in Great Britain by
Antony Rowe Ltd, Chippenham, Wiltshire

I dedicate this book to my friend and colleague

Shelford (Ginger) Bidwell

who died in 1996. Much of the material for it was researched while we were preparing *Firepower: British Army Weapons and Theories of War, 1904–1945, Tug of War: The Battle for Italy,* and *Coalitions, Politicians and Generals: Some Aspects of Command in Two World Wars.*

Contents

List of Illustrations

All photographs are reproduced by kind permission of the Imperial War Museum.

List of Maps

Preface

Above the stairs leading down to the Monet exhibition in the Musée Marnottan at La Muette, in Paris, is engraved Louis Gillet's comment on Monet's *Nympheus* hanging in the salon below.

> Etonnante peinture sans dessin et sans bord ... Cantique sans parolles ... ou l'art ... sans le secours des formes. Sans vignette ... sans fable ... sans allegories ... sans corps et sans visage ... Par le seulle vertu des tons ... N'est plus qu'effusion ... lyrisme ... ou le coeur se raconte ... se livre ... chante ses emotions.

I cannot communicate my personal response to a painting or musical composition beyond a generality widely shared. An attempt to build a bridge of words from the ideal to the real trivialises the former. But painting and music recall glimpses of the drama of battles much more vividly than literature, although poetry narrows the gap. Poetry is music and painting in words. Prose is usually too linear for the complexity of the subject: it is best represented by anthologies which have been compiled without apparent design or limits. Of his anthology, *Vain Glory. A Miscellany of the Great War, 1914–1918*, Guy Chapman wrote: 'There is no truth about the War.' Those of us who seek its parts are like painters in oils. We keep adding to our picture in search of the truth; an impression here, a colour there. Looked at closely the details make no sense: at a distance the sense appears as art.

In this book I have attempted to combine a factual frame of events with personal retrospect at a distance of half a century. I have tried to paint scenes without a beginning or an end and yet to retain historical truth. An analogy is the making of a multi-media disk. The editor farms out many thousands of topics to his authors. He gives them the sources for short paragraphs on each. Like pre-factory piece-workers, authors are not told how their contributions will be used. They are not responsible for connecting them into thought sequences. The functions of combat soldiers and the authors of disks are similar in that the former contribute paragraphs in battle after battle. Neither knows what he has contributed to the whole picture until the author receives a shiny disk and the soldier reads a regimental history, probably years later. Then he is curious to discover how his own experience corresponds to what he reads. Has the editor's linear text bridged the gap between thousands of experiences all over a battlefield and higher matters that provide a frame for his narrative?

I have attempted to explore the gap, knowing that it can never be closed completely.

DOMINICK GRAHAM

Acknowledgements

Much of my material was collected for the three books that Shelford Bidwell and I wrote together. So I must again thank my friends in many places for their help in the past. On this occasion I thank the staff of the Public Record Office for being unfailingly patient, helpful and efficient. The Imperial War Museum's Annex staff produced tapes of interviews and their wonderful collection of photographs. Mr J. Atkinson, the Librarian of Bovington Tank Museum, whose phone is seldom silent, found time between calls not only to show me his collection of interviews with combatants but also to offer me his considerable technical knowledge. Garry Watts and his staff at Teesside University Institute of Design scanned and adjusted the maps. I owe a debt to General Playfair, whose photograph when Chief of Staff in Ceylon I would have included in the illustrations had there been space, for the hours of pleasure his official historians' files on the Mediterranean Theatre of operations gave me at the PRO.

My intention to balance historical accuracy and human experiences required readers with experience of war, or at least serious students of the subject, and historical sense as well. My thanks go to Sydney Jary, who was not only encouraging but also corrected my errors. Terrence Coverdale's service with the King's Own Scottish Borderers and with General Montgomery in Northwest Europe overlapped the subject. Rea Leakey provided vivid incidents from his remarkable career, particularly in the Desert, recorded in his own memoir which we discussed under his hospitable roof. Marc Milner, of the University of New Brunswick, read early drafts which he criticised ruthlessly to my advantage. Sebastian Roberts, Irish Guards, at present concerned in army operational research, read and circulated a draft among present-day regular soldiers.

Dominick Graham   DOMINICK GRAHAM
East Rounton
North Yorkshire

List of Abbreviations and Technical Words

Arms   Used to describe divisions of the army, for instance infantry, artillery etc.

CAB   Documents from the cabinet series at the Public Record Office, Kew.

DAK   Deutsches Afrika Korps.

DSO   Distinguished Service Order. Usually awarded for superior performance in the command of battalion-sized units. In special cases it is awarded for gallantry in action.

DCM   Distinguished Conduct Medal. Similar award for senior ranks below commissioned officer.

GSO   General Staff Officer. Describes an officer of the general (G), as opposed to adjutant (A) or quartermaster general branches of the staff.

HE   High explosive. Filling of various kinds for shells designed to disintegrate the shell casing into many small fragments. Fuses of various degrees of sensitivity determine the nature of the shell-burst.

IWM   Documents, tapes and photographs from the Imperial War Museum, Lambeth.

MC   Military Cross. Awarded to officers for gallantry.

MM   Military medal. Similar award for privates, ncos and warrant officers.

NCO   Non-commissioned officer. Various ranks from lance corporal and below warrant officer. Divided into junior ncos and sergeants and above who are senior ncos.

OH   Books of the official series of war histories published by HM Stationary Office

RA   Royal Artillery. Private soldiers are called gunners, corporal ranks are bombardiers. Gunner is used to describe someone representing the artillery Arm.

RE   Royal Engineers. In the Army called Sappers. Responsible for a wide variety of tasks at all levels.

Sigint   Signal intelligence at various levels from high grade Enigma intercepts to Army field intercepts by the Y service.

WO   Documents from the War Office series at the PRO.

Introduction

Initially, this book had two purposes. First, to clear up some of the themes that Shelford Bidwell and I developed in our books and bring them to a conclusion: secondly, to examine how the conclusion was influenced by my own war experience. As this work proceeded I decided to add a postscript about Britain's association with continental Europe in the light of her performance in the war.

Although I was born two years after it ended, the First World War was a powerful presence over my shoulder while I was growing up. It was a frequent subject at the dinner-table. Later, the senior leaders under whom I served in the Second World War, Generals Wavell, Auchinleck and Montgomery, were influenced by their experience in the First. The same was true of the Americans Marshall, Eisenhower, Patton and Bradley. These considerations reinforced my inclination to treat the wars as a single historical unit and to focus my study on the leaders.

Douglas Haig was the outstanding British field commander in the First World War and Montgomery in the Second. Both were proud of their troops and were determined that they should shine in comparison with their allies. It was not until the second half of 1917 that the comparative weakness of the French allowed Haig to take the initiative with his armies. His tactics in Flanders were then unsuitable. When he urged his commanders to push forward patrols with machine guns and cavalry, at Messines for instance, his conception of the fighting derived from 1914, when he commanded 1st Corps at Ypres with distinction. On the same battlefield, in the conditions of 1917, the cavalry could not comply and the infantry were not organised or trained for spontaneous action. The novel use of artillery and tanks by his Third Army at Cambrai, in November, was not of his devising. He was never able to match his strategic ideas with suitable operations and tactics.

Haig's major fault was his authoritarian style. His instructions re-iterated general principles found in military texts without explaining their relevance to the matter in hand. His style kept his army commanders at arm's-length and gave them neither firm direction nor liberty to operate on their own. On the Somme and at the 3rd battle of Ypres Rawlinson, Plumer and Gough were disconcerted by his manner, which left them in doubt as to his purpose. During the German offensives of 1918 he allowed his subordinates more latitude than previously because his enemy had seized the initiative. In the final months, when General Foch was supreme allied commander and the British played a prominent part, there was a balance of power between the three allied armies. Haig no longer needed to convince the French of British competence, as he had formerly, and gave his army commanders the intellectual liberty he had denied them earlier.

Although Haig complained to his diary about his ally, he never openly quarrelled with Joffre, Foch or even Nivelle, as Montgomery was to quarrel with Eisenhower. Unlike Montgomery, who was autocratic not authoritarian, Haig was a compromiser, much less positive in his style than some have supposed. He was shrewed, though, and well aware that by working well with his French allies he would keep British politicians from interfering in operations. In the autumn of 1918 he understood that it was essential to end the war before the Americans were strong enough to dominate the peace negotiations, although the Germans were not forced to capitulate unconditionally.

Haig was not recognized as the victor of an Alamein or a Falaise Gap, but he emerged from the war as a tough leader credited with the final victory. It was only after his death that his weaknesses as a field commander were exposed and, with hindsight, his reputation questioned. His armies remained his faithful supporters, nevertheless, and there was no credible replacement for him during the war. Montgomery, too, was admired by his soldiers but better known to them. Haig was remote: he would not have appreciated a friendly wave instead of a salute from a soldier on the road as he passed them in his car. And that he would have distributed cigarettes to them and gathered them round his vehicle to tell them how the battle was progressing would have been unthinkable: he had neither the verbal skill nor the inclination.

Montgomery explained his methods in the field so clearly, to officers and men alike, that he was unwilling to accept challenges from less clear minds. Trained as a staff officer, and as an instructor at the staff college, he was didactic to a fault. He enjoyed refining his ideas and expressing them in his clear, round, rather childish hand. In contrast, Haig's contemporaries wondered how he had managed to pass the staff college course as a student. He was unable to argue a point clearly without resting his case on assertions. His written work was cliché-ridden. He avoided frank examination of his plans by distancing himself from potential inquisitors.

The field commanders-in-chief in 1914–18 were allowed more political and military liberty than their Second World War successors – except, perhaps, Douglas MacArthur. Montgomery never had the strategic independence from London enjoyed by Haig. On the other hand, as a subordinate coalition commander, Haig did not have the operational independence of Montgomery commanding the 8th Army in the Middle East and Italy under General Alexander and in Normandy as Commander-in-Chief. Haig served most of the time and Montgomery finished his war under foreign supreme commanders. As military subordinate Haig was to be preferred; Montgomery was the preferable superior.

The relationship between the service chiefs of staff in London and Washington and their political chiefs was closer in the second than the first war. Brooke and Marshall served in their respective national joint chiefs of staff committee and the international Combined Chiefs of Staff Committee with which the Prime Minister and the President worked closely. With the exception of Marshall's relations with MacArthur, they kept tight control over their field commanders. Neither joint nor combined staff committees existed in the First World War.

British weapons in both wars, while they improved in the course of each war, remained inferior to their opponent's. Mongomery took that into consideration; Haig did not. His men had to advance into withering defensive fire until the end of 1917, when tanks were used in large numbers at Cambrai, with new artillery methods. In Normandy, vastly superior allied artillery fire was still unable to master the German infantry's suppressive fire and the superior gunnery of their tanks. In that respect the situation there resembled that on the Western Front.

The army of 1914–18 retained cohesion despite its casualties and repeated disappointments. It was drawn from a society that accepted the authority of the officer classes and followed young leaders who had a strong sense of duty and honour, and sometimes misplaced confidence. Haig accepted their service without question, and without comprehension. Montgomery, when he came to command in the Second World War, had learned from the First. He realized that he had to work for the trust of his men: he could not expect self-sacrifice from a citizen army that had come through depression and pacifism in the 1930s. He did not expect it to perform like professionals or the previous generation of volunteers and conscripts. He was never explicit about its limitations, naturally, although his generals understood them implicitly. The morale crisis in Normandy, partly the result of shortage of infantry replacements, showed that commanders were right to accept limits to the endurance of their infantry and tanks advancing with inferior arms, albeit supported by artillery which, alone of the Arms, believed itself to be the master of its opponent. They were also right to rely on high explosive to bludgeon their way forward.

A delicate contract between men and their leaders, like the live and let live practice in some units on the Western Front, was implicit by 1944. It showed in the limited, set-piece operations which were seldom pressed to a decision by committing fresh troops to achieve a further advance. Limitations were necessary not only to protect morale but also to preserve the infantry reserves. Thus limited resources, relatively inferior weapons and delicately balanced morale resulted in a tactical symbiosis which was natural but, at this distance, looks unimpressive. It was not seen in the ranks as an indication of national impotence let alone relative national decline. In the highest echelons, necessarily, it was.

In the army's daily struggle in Normandy, a few outstanding men set an example which maintained morale and the myth that most men did their duty to the limit of their capacity in the face of extreme danger. Actually, men performed according to a norm acceptable to their consciences and their friends. Examples of gallantry raised the norm in most units to an acceptable level. The connection between casualties, success and time in action is still difficult to establish but a successful action was judged to be one in which casualties on reaching an objective were relatively few. With experience and economy in manpower a few divisions earned a reputation for success and high morale and were used more often than others.

A comparison of the morale of fighting men in the two wars suggests that in the earlier one society was more cohesive. The men of the Kitchener and territorial armies drew their corporate spirit from their town, district, occupation, social and recreational connections and were, in many ways, best handled with that in mind. The army had to join them rather than the reverse. The regular army's strong corporate spirit, on the other hand, was based on its common professional training and standards, its language and social customs, and its history. The making of such a spirit has been analysed and studied, and carefully maintained, particularly by regular NCOs and Warrant Officers. When units were decimated, time after time, and their civilian connections were cut by wounds and death and the mixed provenance of reinforcements, the regular army was the model for their reformation. Yet, although the army gradually became more homogeneous, it was disconcerting for a man to be posted to a strange unit, in which people spoke with a different regional tongue and wore unfamiliar headdress and buttons.

Each arm of the army had a distinct view of the battlefield. The sappers and gunners were rather like defencemen on the ice hockey rink. They saw the game as a whole, set up the plays and destroyed the opponent's offensive moves. Gradually, as the wars progressed, the gunners dictated the shape of operations. This required the peacetime pecking order, in which social standing and tactical importance were once related, to be revised. In peacetime exercises the guns were seldom heard and the devastating effect of artillery fire had to be left to the imagination. It took until 1942 to restore artillery to the dominant position that it had gained by 1918.

Since 1945, the idea of winning battles by weight of high explosive has been derided by some writers. They have tended to revert to a view, common in peacetime, that battles should be won by subtlety and tactical skill, preferably from an inferior position. This is wrongheaded for a reason other than the obvious one that 'God is on the side of the big battalions.' For that matter, God was not on our side through much of the course of either war, with calculable results. We started not only from a position of technical and numerical inferiority but also professional inferiority. We only won our battles when we learned to concentrate our forces and do what we did best, which was burying our opponent under tons of high explosive. In the Second World War the Germans replied by stopping our poor bloody infantry, at a distance, by suppressive fire from their MG 42s and 34s. When closing with them was impossible, blowing them apart with high explosive was the obvious counter.

From the point of view of the young man in an infantry battalion, a cavalry/armoured or gunner regiment, both wars were struggles to catch up which were never quite won. Furthermore, we entered the second war from a Britain whose morale had been undermined by miserable leadership, high unemployment, an inferior education system, which had been inferior in 1914, too, and serious shortcomings in our industry. My generation, of whatever class, started out with fragile morale. It is essential to judge our performance and that of our military leaders with that in mind. Montgomery had served in combat divisions throughout the First World War and understood not only the importance of high morale but how to achieve it in the British

Army. He remembered that recruits entering the pre-1914 army often had to undergo six months of physical exercise and special feeding before they were fit to start their training. The 1939 conscript was little better: his standards of education and physique were inferior to those of the Germans, as they had been in 1914. Montgomery endeavoured to enable his men to overcome these disadvantages.

Montgomery was an outsider. I remember my father speaking of him in that way when they were both serving in Egypt in 1933. Introspective, a teacher by vocation, he was quite clear that the tasks that he set his men should be achievable, and that they should see for themselves when they reached the goals he set, and be pleased with themselves. He was not a clever tactician and he knew that his army was not clever either. Simplicity, direct methods, endurance, obstinacy and emphasizing the positive, if necessary beyond the point of reason, were his hallmarks. They struck a response from soldiers who, like football fans, wanted to win and be on the winning side. The more sophisticated officers reacted less well to Montgomery, as have a later generation unable to understand the mood of those times.

The flavour of class war in it made Montgomery's leadership Cromwellian. Many of his cavalry and some of his Black-Button (Rifle Regiment) subordinates, led in the style of the First World War, when the relationship of the classes was quite different. A friendly, familiar, paternal companionship between officers and men, like that between a landowner and his farm staff, did not work so well when most of the men in the ranks came from industrial cities. Many Territorial officers with whom I served were restricted by the sort of restraint country people naturally applied to their farming methods, their relations with wild life and their employees. Such officers could not easily conceive the battlefield as a place where industrial tools were applied efficiently and dispassionately to kill the enemy. Montgomery's enthusiastic references to 'a killing ground' or 'killing match' were regarded as 'rather common' by some and 'public school' by others. Actually, though, most of the army subscribed to that 'Gotcha' mode of thought well expressed by the *Sun* newspaper when the Argentinian battleship *Belgrano* was sunk in the Falklands war, or by the partisan spirit of a football crowd at a local derby. To Montgomery fighting was an industrial process: he concentrated on technology, detail and process. Fairness had nothing to do with it. It was a mechanical view of the battlefield and his army's success depended largely on confidence and familiarity with his methods. They had to be explained, however, and to be simple. They were really a refinement of the methods of 1918.

Montgomery learned his command style from the mistakes of 1914–18 and his realization that commanders could no longer rely on unquestioned trust and soldiers' willingness to follow leaders into a meat grinder, unless they were sure of winning. His methods matched his means and achieved a relative success.

The difference between the pre-Montgomery 8th Army and the 2nd Army was striking to me, a young officer who had been removed from the battlefield and the Army to a prison camp for over a year between July 1942 and the end of 1943. The moratorium in my life made me more aware of change than if I had been in the UK throughout the previous years of preparation, or even had I served in the Eighth Army during the Montgomery period. Before it the army was amateur, friendly, and fought as though it were playing a game. Failure was accepted almost as a matter of course. Our generals seemed to us to be about what we deserved. Afterwards, their shortcomings were less obvious. They managed a machine of immense power. Battles were routines repeated until the enemy was battered into defeat. We expected to be successful, simply by keeping on keeping on. It became an artillery war and I understood it. But it was never enjoyable even to the extent that the Desert had been enjoyable.

During the gap in my battle experience the Army had perfected its drills following Montgomery's urging to 'keep it simple, stupid!' To the extent that weapons made possible, its leaders correlated military strategy in the form of plans, the operational execution of them and the tactical methods used in the operations. Montgomery did not repeat Haig's mistakes in that respect. However, his co-ordination of strategy, operations and tactics was not entirely beneficial, for ironing out eccentricity in conducting operations dampened initiative, and spontaneity disappeared. But it was necessary – to produce many Wittmans required Tigers and Panthers, MG 42s, Panzerfausts and machine pistols. We lacked them.

If the British army did well without those particular advantages, the Germans could claim other handicaps. Until 1942 the odds were against us: afterwards they were against the Germans. The skies then filled with our aircraft, the seas with our ships, and our bellies with food. 1917 had been a less obvious turning point than 1942, with which Montgomery was soon associated, and the surrender of the German armies in the autumn of 1918 was a surprise after their spring and summer offensives. Indeed, neither we nor the Germans absorbed the switch in fortune between the wars. The latter came to believe that they were stabbed in the back by their own people and deceived by

Allied politicians. We preferred to stress our earlier failures than our success in the last 100 days in which the war was won.

Since 1945, the reverse has been true. We exaggerated our success while the Germans turned their back on their political and military failure and made an economic success of the peace. We have been reluctant to accept the full implications of the Russians and Americans having concluded the Second World War with our help. We have saddled ourselves with a British myth about our role in the Second World War which has affected adversely our relations with Europe.

The myth has its roots in a particular interpretation of British historical relations with continental Europe. In previous centuries we acquired allies on the Continent to oppose whichever powers dominated. We acquired the Austrians, the Prussians and the Russians at various times in the eighteenth century to defeat the French. Later the French and the Russians helped us against the Germans and the Austrians. Then the Americans and the Russians played the decisive role between 1941 and 1945. That marked the relative decline, not only of Britain, but of Europe as a whole, for it had, in effect, torn itself apart in two civil wars. We never won a major war on our own. When we imagined that we could, the failure of our diplomacy and our earlier successes caused us to be so unpopular that we were defeated by the American colonists with the help of the French and the Dutch.

When Germany had been defeated in 1945, not by France or even by us but mainly by our American and Russian allies, Europe had lost its relative dominance in global politics and the balance of global power had changed. We ought to have continued to involve ourselves in the Continent, not, as previously, to build an alliance against the dominant power, but to restore the relative power of Europe in the world. Within Europe we had to help to build a political system in which war between its members would be unthinkable.

A narrow-minded Britain failed to attempt this task. It had not, and still has not, accepted its relative decline, as Europeans have accepted the decline of their own powers. The end of the Cold War, which has changed the role of the United States in Europe, has made closer ties between Britain and Europe logical and even more necessary. The form of those ties is the subject of debate today. Continental Europeans have far more serious historical skeletons to bury than have we, but they have come to the correct conclusion that the experience of two wars unites them. Had we been physically overrun or suffered the trauma of national socialism we would have no hesitation in surrendering some independence to a European Union. The implications of our post-war economic defeat and military dependence on the USA has been harder to grasp.

How then may our unbalanced view of the Continent be corrected? First, by accepting the truth about the wars, and then adapting our old strategy to the new conditions. When our allies on the Continent had been defeated in 1940 we were impotent to defeat the Germans. We were only saved by Hitler's mistakes and the New World redressing the balance of the Old. Awareness of the true situation motivated the policy of appeasement and those who would have made a deal with the Germans in 1940. Now that Europe is united at last it would be madness to treat its members as enemies or rivals. Yet, when politics take over from wars allies are still necessary, although none will be an ally for all seasons. We do not want Europe to be divided by balance of power diplomacy, although we must ensure that no European state becomes too powerful within the Union. Political differences will continue, as in the past. We must not allow the European Commission to enforce agreements on the grounds that equality and uniformity are necessary for union: European union should not require agreement on all points. Social and cultural differences are desirable and they should permit political and economic differences. Like difference in blood grouping, they are a fact of life. They can be lessened, perhaps, but that is not necessarily desirable. Variety in European culture is our strength as Europeans. We must prevent the bureaucracy of the European Commission treating it as tiresome and undesirable, let alone unnecessary.

That point reminds me that I spent over 30 years in Canada, where German, Dutch and Scandinavian, among other cultures, have merged easily with anglophone. Most of us rejoice in the strength of French culture, although political conflict continues between francophones and anglophones. Trouble has occurred only when separatist Quebecois insist on having a separate political identity as well as retaining their provincial and cultural one. Religion and law, and of course language, are part of the latter, granted after the 'Conquest' of 1759. In practice political but not economic power has been shared since Confederation in 1867, although the French have been outnumbered.

The British in Europe are, in some respects, in a similar position to the French in Canada, but they have less reason to fear being absorbed. The English language and culture are strong enough to withstand absorption. The Europeans have many languages; ours is the primary world language. As regards politics and economics we have been engaged with the rest of Europe for centuries. A *modus vivendi* that acknowledges the relation between culture, economics and politics must be found. Lines may have to be drawn, but without rancour.

Prologue

Britain's Royal Navy was the more important of the services in the imperial era. In 1911, it was the Admiralty that determined that Britain could not hold her Eastern empire together without a friendly Japan. As her ally, Japan enabled Britain to concentrate her forces in Europe and the Mediterranean in the 1914–18 war. The alliance collapsed in the 1920s. In the 1930s Germany and Italy, allied with Japan, made a formidable axis that had to be appeased. Indeed, by 1939, faced by Japan in the East and Germany and Italy in Europe, Britain was caught in the knight's move she had avoided in 1914. Divided by the rival ideologies of left and right her ally, France, was not motivated by a desire for revenge against Germany for the defeat of 1870, as in 1914. Indeed, she dreaded another blood bath. Britain feared the Soviet Union, which was not an ally as Russia had been in 1914, and she could not count on an isolationist United States for help. It is easy to see that Britain had more reason to stay out of a European imbroglio in 1939 than in 1914.

'Business as usual' was Britain's political slogan in 1914 when she joined France and Russia in the war against Germany and Austria–Hungary. Indeed Britain would not have had the means to pursue her initial plan to support Russia with funds and possibly arms unless she continued her trade with the rest of the world. So Britain's main effort was to be on the industrial and financial fronts and on the high seas. She planned to provide a small regular army of six divisions and a cavalry division as a token force to fight beside the French on the Continent. After six months a territorial force would follow the regular army divisions.

The 1914 plan went adrift. First, the Russians absorbed all the money that Britain could spare but were still unable to defeat the Austrians and Germans. The plan to have the great Russian steamroller do the main work against the Germans ended finally when the Anglo-French attempt to open the Dardanelles route to Russia and to defeat Turkey failed in 1915. Secondly, the French, hell-bent on recovering the provinces of Alsace and Lorraine that they had lost in 1870 and on defeating the German invaders of Flanders and Artois, demanded more and more British troops to fight beside them. Field Marshal Earl Kitchener, made minister of war in 1914, anticipated the need for larger British forces to administer the *coup de grâce* to Germany when she and the French had exhausted each other by 1917. He raised a volunteer, citizen army immediately but hoped to preserve its strength until the decisive phase of the war. When the French demands that Britain shed her blood equally beside her French comrades could no longer be resisted, the Western Front became the major theatre of war for the British Army. From then onwards Britain was fighting for her life, her overseas credits exhausted, her industry at full stretch, her merchant fleet decimated and her manpower over-stretched. The Kitchener armies were almost destroyed on the Somme between July and November 1916.

In 1939, the British Army was less prepared for modern war than in 1914. Only a year earlier its role was still the protection of the Empire. The policy of rearmament between 1935 and 1939 was based on business as usual – for a strong economy was considered the first line of defence – on the preparation of an industrial and administrative infrastructure, on preparing the Royal Navy for its traditional role and on the Royal Air Force. The air force was to be used as a deterrent force against Germany and a defensive force to protect the United Kingdom. The army came last in the pecking order. Conscription came only in April 1939, the first time it had been instituted in peace. But men had to be armed and trained, and time lost could not be regained – if it ever existed, given the resources of the country, its lack of political will and its social state after years of deprivation.

In preparing this book about the British army, my focus was concentrated on a few questions. The army was efficient and comparatively well-armed in 1914. That it fought as well as it did in 1915 and 1916, when its regular cadre had been virtually destroyed in the opening months of the war, is remarkable. That it ended the war in 1918 as the most effective force on the Western Front is astonishing. Its story in the Second World War seems less creditable, although less often criticised. Routed in its first campaign in 1940, after which it was deprived of its French ally, it was given time to arm and train behind the shield of the Royal Navy and the bravery of the pilots of the RAF. Unlike the Old Contemptibles in 1914, it did not leave its cadres in Continental graves – although its weapons were largely surrendered.

Two general questions arise from these observations. First, how did the BEF of 1914–18 manage to emerge as the fine army that it apparently became despite the slaughter it had undergone? The second is whether, after its defeat in 1940, it performed in the rest of the war as successfully as its predecessor. Can it be said of it that in 1945, when the Second World War ended, it was at the top of its form?

Part I
1914–18

1 The Army Prepares

The 1906 reforms of Lord Haldane, the minister of war, had accorded with some, although not all, of the ideas of Jacky Fisher, the First Sea Lord.[1] The balance of power in Europe required the friendly co-operation of Britain and France. The *Entente Cordiale* of 1904 cleared the way for it. A defence treaty with Japan allowed the Royal Navy to concentrate on the Western Approaches and the North Sea and to share responsibility for the Mediterranean with the French. On land, the huge French Army would play the main part if war came with Germany and Britain were involved. In that event, a small force of six infantry divisions and a cavalry division could cross from England at once and six months later Territorial divisions could begin to join them. The formation of more regular divisions, the 7th and 8th and the 27th, 28th and 29th would require the withdrawal of some units from their imperial posts and their replacement by Territorials.

All of this signified the transfer of British attention to continental Europe. In the years before 1914 the training of the regular force in England was directed to fighting in a continental war. Yet, it was not assumed that Britain would necessarily fight on the Continent if war between Germany and France occurred, for Britain had not agreed to that. Nevertheless, arrangements were made with the French general staff for an expeditionary force to cross the Channel to a deployment area. Britain had guaranteed the neutrality of Belgium, whose security had always been a British concern. Were either France or Germany to invade Belgium, Britain might be dragged into a war. The fear of members of Asquith's Liberal government was that a major war would involve Russia and France on one side and Austria and Germany on the other and that Dutch and Belgian territory would be invaded. Haldane was at pains to show that his measures for the British Army would provide economies but should not be regarded as a provocation to Germany or a commitment to France.[2]

Nevertheless, the understanding in the Army was that it had entered the 'Big League', and professional standards rose. There was a change of emphasis from imperial policing and small wars to continental war. There had already been a tightening of standards after the exposure of the Army to Boer talent in South Africa. Marksmanship and infantry fire-control were improved. The QF[3] 18-pounder, a new field gun, appeared in 1904 and the 4.5 howitzer in 1908. British liaison staffs at the Manchurian war front between Japan and Russia had brought back new ideas, particularly about the management and effect of modern fire-power.

The War Office General Staff was extended to the rest of the Army between September 1906, when Haldane signed the order, and 1908. An Imperial Conference was held in 1909 and the 'Imperial' General Staff was extended to India in the following year under the direction of Major-General Sir Douglas Haig. Haig had been Haldane's right-hand man in the measure of 1906, and in reforms of the Territorial Force until he left the post of Director of Staff Duties for India. The post of commander-in-chief was abolished as part of the Esher reforms of 1904 so that the Army was no longer divided between a largely civilian war department and the military establishment at the Horse Guards. However, the Chief of the Imperial General Staff (CIGS) did not replace the commander-in- chief but was the first among equals on the Army Council, of which the chairman was the civilian minister of war. The General Staff was 'general' only in the sense that its Chief was head of the operations, intelligence and staff duties (co-ordination) divisions. They were the G as opposed to the Q and A divisions. The supply or Quartermaster General's division and the personnel or Adjutant General's division had equal access to the minister. In this respect the British differed from the German General Staff, in which the Operations branch was in control and the minister was often a soldier himself.

The German arrangement would have been unacceptable in Britain. The Adjutant General's branch was concerned in many questions of political importance: recruiting and morale, pay, discipline and military law were some of them. The Quartermaster General's department was responsible for supply in the Army and concerned with the civilian finance branch at the war office and the annual grant of money from parliament. Necessary though it was for the politicians to control the Army, it had military disadvantages. Sir Frederick Maurice commented at the end of a lecture given by Sir Herbert Miles after the First World War:

> I have never been able to see that any system in which there were three, four or five military members of Council, each separately responsible to the Secretary of State for War, had any principle of military organization behind it. That system, it seems to me, has been solely due to political exigencies ... to ensure that there shall be a reasonable amount of dissension in the Army Council.[4]

The first years of the war were coloured by hindsight, in that deficiencies were attributed either to incompetence or Treasury economies in the years before it, notably over machine guns and shells. Yet Haldane's experience with his colleagues was made uncomfortable by resistance within the Liberal Party to any military reforms that were not economical. Members of the Army Council were habitually forced to trade innovations in one area for concessions in another in the name of economy. Money between 1906 and 1914 had to be shared with the Navy, which was involved in the Dreadnought programme and, in the last two years, with the newly created Royal Flying Corps. Haldane spent less each year from 1907 until 1914 on the Army alone. Yet considerable advances were made in weaponry, clothing and field supply as well as in tactics.

The Moroccan crisis with Germany in 1911 drew attention to the Army's ability to fight on the Continent and made the staff put a time-scale beside the numerous measures it was considering for its modernization. Thereafter, it seemed wiser to take what was available than wait for weapons that might not be delivered in time.

One of the principal debates within the Army concerned the effect of infantry fire-power on tactics. At the Staff Conference in 1910, Major N.R. McMahon, from the Small Arms School at Hythe, recommended a scale of one light machine gun in each infantry company. Neither light machine guns nor automatic rifles were in service. Experiments had shown that the existing scale of two medium machine guns per battalion was probably adequate in defence, provided there was a clear field of fire of at least 400 yards. Defenders could probably cause up to 60 per cent casualties on attacking lines unless the attackers could generate significant fire and the defenders' fire be suppressed by artillery. If the attackers carried light machine guns they could keep down the heads of defenders in trenches. Hythe could then 'formulate new ideas about frontages and formations' based on the known effect of their fire. A huge volume of accurate light machine gun fire from a narrow front at short range from within the company would make possible the instinctive action and reaction between men, some of whom gave covering fire while others advanced. That co-operation was lacking at the time. Fire and movement – that is movement forward by one sub-unit – should be covered by fire from another. The small-unit battle would be speeded up and be comprehensible to reservists and easier to control.

Automatic rifles and light machine guns, the agents of these tactics, were in various stages of development in Western armies at this time.

Tactics manuals included statements like: 'The assault is made possible by superiority of fire.' Yet Major General Lancelot Kiggell, Haig's
successor as Director of Staff Duties, contradicted McMahon and this
statement in *Field Service Regulations* when he asserted:

> Victory is won actually by the bayonet, or by the fear of it, which
> amounts to the same thing as far as the actual conduct of the attack
> is concerned. This fact was proved beyond doubt in the late war. I
> think the whole question rather hangs on that; and if we accept the
> view that victory is actually won by the bayonet, it settles the point.[5]

Confusion between the effects of volume versus accuracy of fire
showed itself in the common belief that more machine guns, and particularly automatic rifles, meant less accurate fire. The high performance of British riflemen would be lost, it was argued, if they could
generate more fire with automatics. Actually, machine guns were
more precise in their effect than many riflemen scattered about the
field, whose fire was difficult to control. In fact, for many purposes
machine guns were *too* accurate. A more dangerous, but paradoxical,
argument about fire-power was that defensive fire had become so
lethal that men would not advance against it. Rather, they would
attempt to shoot the defenders out of their positions. That would slow
up the attack. Men would go to ground in front of an enemy position
and suffer higher losses than if they advanced. The answer, it was said,
was to raise morale so that men kept going, despite casualties, until
they reached the enemy trench and settled matters with the bayonet.
The paradox was that this argument recognised that the decision was
decided by gaining fire superiority. How to achieve it without slowing
up the battle was the question. McMahon believed it lay in fire and
movement using light machine guns and automatic rifles.

The army remembered the argument of MacMahon and that of his
opponents on the morning of 1 July 1916, when it suffered 57 000
casualties following the latter's policy, although light machine guns
had been in service since early 1915. None the less, new weapons were
not usually introduced in peacetime merely as a result of scientific tactical trials at Hythe. A more cogent argument proved to be that the
existing British rifle and machine gun were inferior to the German
weapons. The Maxim machine gun had been in service since 1893. A
new Vickers, weighing only 38 pounds instead of 60, was available but
awaited the provision of new ammunition for the rifle for which a light
.276 or .256-inch cartridge with a superior nitro-cellulose propellent
was on trial. Its performance would be superior to the .311-inch

German Mauser or the new French Lebel. However, until the trials for the new weapon were completed it was unwise to bring in a new machine gun that ought to be of the same calibre as the rifle. Assuming that the trials were successful, the new rifle would go into production in 1913 and issue would be completed in 1916.

The first indication that the Germans were increasing the scale of machine guns in their infantry battalions led to the decision to adopt the short Lee Enfield .303 rifle resighted for new Mark VII ammunition which gave a flatter trajectory even than the German Mauser, whose bullet's highest point at 700 metres was 6.23 feet. In the middle of the Morocco crisis in 1911 the programme for its issue was expedited and regular divisions received it in 1913. That decision allowed the programme for the Vickers machine gun to go forward and in 1912 it was issued first to cavalry regiments. In October 1913 the .276 programme was postponed owing to over-heating and extraction problems. The same problem delayed trials for an automatic rifle and a light machine gun which had been underway since 1910. Trials with the .303 Lewis light machine gun had taken place in 1912 but it had not passed the rugged tests necessary for infantry use in the field and it was not to reach the troops until 1915 on a scale of one per company.

Disagreements within the Army about fire-power in defence and attack continued until the war broke out. Hythe concluded that the difficulty was attacking dug-in infantry with a good field of fire. This was why McMahon wanted light machine guns to accompany the attack. The existing two Vickers machine guns were considered adequate for the defence of a battalion provided it had a good field of fire. Additional fire in attack and defence would come from field artillery but there was disagreement about its deployment and role too.

The French 75-mm QF gun had a high rate of fire and a flat trajectory. The French employed it over open sights or from semi-concealed positions – that is, on reverse slopes from which the guns were not visible to the enemy although their flash and smoke probably were. The infantry knew that the direct fire of field guns was decisive and that this usually required the guns to be close to them. The artillery had doubts about this, for their observers in Manchuria (in the Russo-Japanese war of 1905–6) had seen how effective the Japanese artillery had been, firing from completely concealed positions. They had also seen artillery visible to enemy observers being destroyed. However, for observers to direct the fire of guns in concealed positions required that they had telephones and cable to order the bearing and distance from the guns to the target. The Royal Artillery did not have sufficient cable or phones to control the fire of their guns in this way in a mobile battle.

The destruction of targets required many rounds of ammunition and much time, so the artillery's intention was to neutralize the enemy's fire rather than to destroy him. That task was best achieved at short range by shrapnel from 18-pounders, particularly over open sights. It should be remembered that only 4.5-inch howitzers and 60-pr guns had high explosive in a division. Counter-battery fire against concealed guns was not expected to be very effective because the fall of shell could not be observed. All in all, battery commanders felt that they could serve the infantry best from gun positions from which they could fire direct, although they were hazardous. At the battle of Le Cateau, in the first days of the war, 3rd Division used concealed positions, but their fire was not very effective. 5th Division used direct fire with great effect but they suffered heavily as a result. Surviving guns had to be retrieved under fire with great gallantry.

When Sir Douglas Haig returned to England from India he took command of 1st Corps at Aldershot. In that post he had much to do with the tactics of the Expeditionary Force. While in India he had corresponded regularly with Kiggell and urged him to oppose those who wanted to increase fire-power at the price of speed of application. He favoured what was termed the French 'Allez! Allez!' school, whose tactics centred on the 75-mm and opposed attempts to shoot the enemy out of his positions. In fact, his conception focused on the advance to contact when the speed with which available fire could be brought to bear would decide an engagement. He thought much less about the build-up for the decisive battle that would follow the first contact of the opposing armies. Here he opposed those who relied on weapons still in the pipeline and insisted that existing weapons must shape tactics.

Haig was a cavalryman. He viewed the battlefield from the back of a horse. He esteemed machine guns, accurate rifle fire and guns that galloped into action and swamped the enemy with a hail of shrapnel. Despite the scorn that has sometimes been levelled at the cavalry of this period, it was no longer devoted to the lance. Although some units were slow to shape their tactics around the rifle, the machine gun and the 13-pounder field gun, most did so. They shot straight and used their horses to carry men and weapons to decisive positions. When Haig came to review the course of the struggle on the Western Front in 1919, he saw it as a protracted build-up battle after the first engagements. The mud, the blood and the huge investment in heavy weapons were necessary and inevitable in order to open the front to the last phase of the war. That was, like the first, a mobile battle of small units employing fire and rapid movement tactics. The long period of bloody stalemate in the middle prepared the way for the final victory, Haig argued.

In this conception of the war, Haig was not so very wrong if you accept that there was nothing that he could have done to prepare the army, and indeed the whole country, for the huge material struggle that took its course between 1915 and 1917. The Government had not developed a chemical industry capable of producing high explosive in large amounts, nor the engineering industry to turn out rifles and machine guns and heavy howitzers or guns and fuses and grenades in time for their use decisively until 1917. Even when the war started, politicians were not prominent in furthering the provision of arms, leaving it to the Master-General of the Ordnance, General Sir Stanley von Donop, and Lord Kitchener.

Haig, who was commander-in-chief of the British Expeditionary Force from December 1915 until the end of the war, has been heavily criticized for the role he played. His critics, though, must offer viable alternatives to the way he fought. The material superiority of the German Army for much of the middle years cannot be laid at Haig's door. He ought to be judged by his handling of what was available to him, by his management of subordinates, the way he conceived military strategy and applied it to operations, and the suitability of his operations to the tactics for which his army was equipped and trained. These are the lines on which his performance shall be judged here.

Winston Churchill was not an admirer of Haig's intellect or judgement but did admire his courage. He wrote of him in two passages of inimitable prose:

> Sure of himself, steady of poise, knife in hand, intent upon the operation; entirely removed in his professional capacity from the agony of the patient, the anguish of relations, or the doctrines of rival schools, the devices of quacks, or the first-fruits of new learning. He would operate without being affronted; and if the patient died, he would not reproach himself.[6]

> But the Great War owned no Master; no one was equal to its vast and novel issues; no human hand controlled its hurricanes; no eye could pierce its whirlwind dust-clouds ... But ... the fact remains that no other subject of the King could have endured the ordeal which was his lot with the phlegm, the temper, and the fortitude of Sir Douglas Haig.[7]

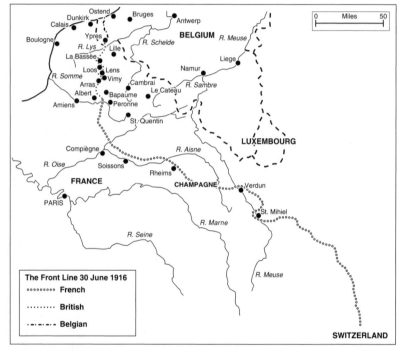

1   The Western Front

2 Learning the Ropes

The German armies had swept through Belgium and reached the Marne in August 1914 when a French counter-blow, in which the BEF took part, forced them back to the Aisne (Map 1). The front consolidated there while the Germans advanced out of Belgium towards Boulogne and Calais. Replaced on the Aisne, the British moved north towards Ypres to block this advance and to outflank it if possible. The front stabilized in November with the Belgians on the coast, a small French army on their right and then the two British corps in front of and to the south of Ypres.

During the autumn, winter and early spring four more regular army divisions, made up of overseas battalions, an Indian Army corps, the 1st Canadian Division and territorial battalions and cavalry regiments, joined the BEF. Later in 1915, territorial divisions joined and at the end of 1915 the first Kitchener volunteer divisions. In March the Royal Navy attempted to force the Dardanelles passage and in April British, Australian and New Zealand troops landed at Gallipoli and French divisions on the southern shore of the straits. The struggle there continued until the end of 1915 when Gallipoli was evacuated.

On the Continent the British were subordinated to French plans to defeat the German invaders. The BEF attacked at Neuve Chapelle and other places in Artois, south of Ypres. Their design was to divert German attention while the French mounted much larger operations against Vimy Ridge and in Champagne. The year ended with the major battle of Loos, in which the British used gas for the first time. None of these battles achieved what they were intended to. The Germans had used chlorine against the French and the Canadians in April in the Ypres salient. They continued to reduce the salient in 1915 and 1916 so that they held the higher ground. In fact, they generally held better ground tactically elsewhere, and since they intended to stand on the defensive opposite the British, their trenches were better engineered for defence.

In 1915, the BEF lacked the weapons and numbers to break up the German trench system, which was being strengthened continually. At Neuve Chapelle it was a single, strong line of trenches with machine gun positions behind it and a third zone which contained reserve battalions. Communication trenches connecting these zones were constructed and they, in turn, were made defensible to enable allied attacks to be taken in flank. Switch lines could be occupied and used as jumping off positions for counter-attacks if a front trench were lost. Cellars in villages were used for rest and cover from bombardments, and in areas where the water-table was not near the surface extensive shelters were dug underground. Villages and towns were road and track centres. Their defenders brought up reserves and counter-attacked down the roads. As shelling destroyed soil drainage the possession of roads was an advantage. Roads were, of course, magnets for shells. From higher ground the Germans could observe stretches of the British front and observe British preparations. Their own were concealed on the reverse slopes.

Lines of barbed wire in front of trenches prevented their being taken by surprise. Wire had to be cut by hand or by artillery fire. The former was slow and dangerous and the latter required well-aimed shrapnel fire or sensitive fuses that enabled high explosive shells to burst on the surface. It was not until 1917 that the BEF possessed such fuses. Wire accumulated in some places to such a depth that it was impenetrable. Machine-guns firing on fixed lines enfiladed gaps in the wire and made attacks converging on them suicidal. At the beginning the British were short of wire, duck-boards, revetting material such as metal posts and sandbags, and the Territorial and New Army units were untrained in digging trenches and dug-outs.

The bombardment of continuous trench lines, particularly those on forward slopes, made holding them so expensive in lives by the middle of the Somme battles in 1916 that the Germans manned their front trenches lightly and with a high proportion of machine guns. The main defensive zone consisted of a series of strongpoints. By 1917, concrete pillboxes and natural strongpoints from which fire could be brought to bear on attackers replaced continuous trench lines. Most of a unit lay in a counter-attack role in support trenches on reverse slopes. Whole divisions lay a few miles behind the main trench system, out of range of field guns, ready to mount counter-attacks when the attackers had lost their momentum. The Germans adopted what has become an orthodox defensive method: namely fighting for an area, rather than for individual points, by counter-attack with fresh forces against disorganized and weakened attackers.

At the height of continuous trench warfare in 1915, once attackers entered a trench, bombers worked their way down it from traverse to traverse. The traverses divided a trench into defensible sections which could be blocked off if part of the trench were lost. The few unreliable bombs that the BEF had before the war were handled by engineers. In 1915, workshops behind the lines designed and made bombs for the infantry, but they were dangerous to use. Eventually specialist bombers were trained in battalions but keeping throwers supplied required bombs to be carried in sacks across fire-swept zones between trenches. Factory-made rifle grenades, the powerful Mills bomb, smoke and chemical grenades appeared in 1916 and 1917.

The mention of bombs introduces one of the more important trends in the infantry story between 1914 and 1945, namely the increase in its fire-power. In 1914 a battalion had two Vickers medium machine-guns but otherwise was armed with rifles alone. In the following year the Vickers were organized in a company for each brigade and eventually into divisional machine gun battalions of 64 guns. The Canadians had 96 guns in their divisions. The Machine-Gun Corps, separate from the infantry, was formed. The Lewis light machine-gun replaced the Vickers in battalions on a scale of one per company, later one per platoon and by 1918 two per platoon. In the Second World War that was increased to one in each of the three sections in the platoon and one in platoon headquarters. The increase in battalion fire-power was extended to include anti-tank, mortar and carrier platoons in the Second World War. The manpower of the rifle companies was reduced to supply men for these support sub-units although a sub-machine gun replaced the rifle as the personal weapon of many men.

Before the fire-power of the infantry had been increased, an engineer, Lt-Col E.D. Swinton, acting as a military observer in 1914, proposed that a tracked and armoured vehicle was needed to flatten wire and trenches and carry fire-power forward. The Naval Division, which had been employed at Antwerp in 1914, had armoured cars and the vehicle Swinton envisaged would be a cross-country version of their vehicle, like an agricultural tractor. Remarkably, the result was the first tank, which saw action in September 1916 in the Somme campaign.

The employment of weapons manned by teams, from tanks and guns down to the Vickers, introduces special problems. It has been commented that while the army arms the man the navy mans the arms. There is an element of truth in that slick observation but it ceased to be a true distinction in this century. A gun or a tank, a mortar or a medium machine-gun is 'fought' by its crew. It is their home and the centre of their lives. Serving it cements friendships and loyalty. Each member fights under the stern and critical, if friendly, stare of his mates. Four or five tanks work together tactically as a troop and 12 to 16 as a squadron. The individual actions of tanks can usually be seen by others in the unit. The field gun troop of four guns and the battery of eight is a team bound together by technical training and common knowledge and the occupation of a piece of territory. Line and radio signallers, command-post computers and surveyors each plays a different part in delivering shells accurately where and when they have been demanded. They each help to support tanks and infantry in their defence of a position or their attempt to occupy one held by the enemy. That sentence introduces the problem of combining the work of several Arms in a common end. It was not a new problem but modern arms and organization and the size of the battlefield made its solution more complex.

There is a paradox to explain here. The First World War is often described as a war of material and mass armies, their units advancing in lines against overwhelming fire-power. In one respect that is a correct description. Simultaneously, the inevitable process of point and counter-point was developing a response. Smaller units, well-provided with fire-power, working in conjunction with others, sometimes of the same and sometimes of other Arms, were coming into existence. The process was delayed because it demanded new weapons and, above all, educated leaders – and we are not referring to officers, but to junior NCOs and private soldiers who had to make decisions and act on them.

This dialectic at work in both wars demanded better educated and trained soldiers. The Germans had an advantage in that their conscript soldiers were selected and were better educated, on the whole, than their British opponents. The British regular, in his years of service, was taught to carry out the duties of other men fighting beside him and to think in terms of teams. In wartime there was little time to teach volunteers, let alone conscripts, to think in that way. It is not difficult to draw analogies from civilian life. Today's member of the staff of a large farm can put his or her hand to the care of stock, of machinery, of arable crops and grassland, if not financial questions of prices, or chemical ones concerning fertilizers and herbicides. After seven years a regular soldier's peripheral knowledge was considerable and he could take to small unit tactics without difficulty. But by 1917, there were not many pre-war regulars left in the ranks.

Before the war Brigadier (later Lieutenant-General) Ivor Maxse, Director General of Training in 1918, instigated the break-up of infantry companies from a left and right component into platoons, commanded by subaltern officers, and sections commanded by corporals using fire and movement tactics. An obstacle to the development of this idea was that battalions were homogeneous rifle units, except for two medium machine guns. McMahon had proposed an answer in light machine guns and semi-automatic rifles. Trench warfare pushed this organisation aside for a time so that platoons ceased to be tactical units. Specialists like bombers, snipers, and Lewis gunners were the bricks of battalions. Small permanent sub-units with nominal roles of their men and tactical and social cohesion started to re-appear half way through the Somme battles. The changed nature of German defences, itself the result of British artillery action and the need of the Germans to economize in NCOs, and the arrival of the necessary weaponry to make British sections into viable fire-units brought about this change. At the same time the centralizing, mass attack philosophy still prevailed so that two schools of thought co-existed and conflicted. The artillery and the tanks, essentially Arms organised in teams, and infantry divisional commanders who had learned from the Somme, were on the 'progressive' side. Corps commanders and their superiors, further from tactical reality, tended to be the conservatives.

Within what may be described as the 'progressive' school there was a problem that continued to be difficult to solve in the Second World War. Although the infantry acquired rifle grenades and short and longer range mortars as local artillery, they required support from the weapons of other Arms – the 4.5-inch howitzer and 18-pounder batteries' high explosive and shrapnel and the heavier 60-pounder gun, and the 6-inch, 8-inch and 9.2-inch howitzers, and eventually the machine-guns and 6-pounder guns of the new tanks, which by 1943 carried 75-mm guns. Communication between infantry and artillery was initially confined to telephone cable, flags and helio, runners and direct contact. At first it seemed that to render reliable support guns should be in battalion areas in sections of two guns. Observation of the battle from close to the guns and within call of the infantry seemed necessary despite the casualties that the guns suffered from the enemy's observed fire. As the front congealed, the guns were further back. Medium machine guns in the hands of companies of the Machine-gun Corps operated like artillery by firing indirect, using artillery methods to create 'beaten zones' behind the enemy front. Lewis guns moved forward with platoons to cover the advance of its sections.

Naturally, this team-work was sometimes well done and sometimes not done so well. When the latter was the case, the mass attack methods seemed more advantageous and, from the point of view of senior commanders, easier to use. However, as the nature of German defences changed to less dense defence in depth, barrages and lines of attackers became less efficient and more expensive in lives. Thus the dialectic moved on to favour not only the progressive method in attack, but also the German method in defence. Indeed, in 1918, it was the Germans who developed loose attacking tactics as a natural answer to their own defence methods, which, by then, had been superficially imitated by the British.

Air support had been developing in the meantime. German air observers had directed artillery using radios on the Aisne. The Royal Artillery followed them. First it was necessary to re-map the Western Front by a combination of aerial photography, oblique and vertical, and traditional ground survey. Artillery was enabled to survey its own position and its targets'. Gradually the two gun-laying elements required to strike a target, line and range, were fixed, together with ballistic elements such as meteorology and those associated with individual guns, like muzzle velocity. It was not until late in 1917 that the ballistic qualities of shells, the reliability of their explosives and fuses, and the variety of the latter brought the artillery to a reasonable level of efficiency. Communications between observers and guns and between units and the artillery continued to be a headache, for cable was often cut by shellfire, and wireless was still developing.

Meanwhile, the radio links between aircraft and the guns had developed remarkably by 1918. It was possible for pilots to radio guns and direct them by artillery codes to targets in pre-arranged zones. Networks of telephone lines were used to direct several batteries. As important was the artillery intelligence that aircraft supplied. Enemy gun positions could, of course, be bombarded by heavy guns. As important was the indication that their positions gave of the intentions of the enemy. Forward movements of guns indicated an attack. Photographs taken at regular intervals provided a record of the changes being made in their locations. It was difficult to hide gun positions from photographic aircraft.

These activities that linked artillery and Flying Corps units required increases in the artillery staffs and brought them, at times, into conflict with the General Staff. In 1914, artillery commanders had small staffs, for artillery was decentralized. At Army level the Major-General Royal Artillery travelled with his Royal Engineers equivalent in one staff car and they were known as Tweedledum and Tweedledee. They were advisers, not commanders. By 1917, counter-battery staffs and batteries, the sound-ranging and flash-spotting organisation, heavy mortars, and corps and army artillery required artillery staffs and commanders: the Royal Engineers had survey and mapping units, road-makers, bridge builders, railways and postal units besides many other activities beyond those envisaged before the war.

It is to the command and staff aspects of these developments that we shall now turn.

3 Politicians, Commanders and Battles

Naturally, the growth of the BEF increased the burden of its commanders-in-chief. Sir John French's BEF of two corps initially totalling five infantry divisions and a cavalry division became two armies of several corps. Haig's BEF of 1916 had five armies of 19 corps and 53 British divisions, two ANZAC corps and a Canadian Corps. Co-operation with the French was an inescapable political as well as a military task for both men. After Kitchener died at sea in June 1916 and Asquith ceased to be prime minister at the end of that year, the political dimensions of Haig's operations increased with the military importance of the BEF relative to the French.[1]

Kitchener briefed Haig on the Cabinet's view of continental operations. When the French were fighting for their lives against the German offensive at Verdun and planning a counter-stroke on the Somme at the junction of the BEF with the French armies, Kitchener advised Haig not to commit himself to fighting a decisive battle.

Haig's position was difficult. Sir John French had been told by Kitchener to co-operate with General Joseph Joffre unless he considered that Joffre's orders endangered the BEF.[2] Like all such instructions, their interpretation in changing circumstances was the problem. French proposed to withdraw the BEF to refit in the last stage of the retreat from Mons when Joffre was planning his counter-stroke on the Marne. Kitchener overruled him. When their losses at Verdun compelled the French to hand the main role on the Somme to the British, they asked Haig to press his attack until the Germans were forced to desist at Verdun. That could have become an open-ended commitment. Although tactical judgements were properly left to Haig, this one concerned longer-term British strategy, which was a political responsibility. Kitchener again urged caution and advised General Sir Henry Rawlinson, whose Fourth Army was to be responsible, to be wary.[3]

Kitchener had not intended his new armies to be committed to operations that might gravely weaken them early in their careers. So his advice was to satisfy the French with a series of limited attacks to wear down German resistance but not to attempt a break-through. But

Kitchener's influence was waning, even if his argument remained cogent. Until the withdrawal of Allied forces from Gallipoli at the end of 1915, he and his Cabinet colleagues agreed that Britain should encourage the Russians with money, and if possible arms, to divert German divisions from France to the Russian front. They did not approve of French demands for more and more British troops to help them oust the German Army from French soil. It was not possible for the British to fight the war at sea, finance the Russians and provide them with arms, and also fight a land war *à outrance* on the Continent.[4]

Here we come to the alleged disagreement between Easterners, who believed that Britain should seek a military and political solution in the eastern Mediterranean, and Westerners, who wanted the French to be fully supported on the Continent as the only decisive front. At first the Cabinet were Easterners. After the withdrawal from Gallipoli, the Eastern fronts withdrew to Salonika to fight the Bulgarians and to the Suez Canal to face the Turks. The French had had prodigious casualties in 1915 and were arguing that the Russians would be best supported indirectly by fresh British divisions fighting on the Western Front to divert German divisions from Russia.[5]

Kitchener was drowned on his way to Russia before the Somme battles opened on 1 July. By then he was paying the political price of the Gallipoli failure, largely laid at his door. In Cabinet, his disdain for political manoeuvring, his inability to persuade and sometimes to explain what he was trying to do in the language of politics, and his lack of a political base, had made his replacement imminent. And yet his policy was not superseded when David Lloyd replaced him at the War Office.

Haig himself had been disinclined to follow Kitchener's advice about restraint, but under Lloyd George he lacked a friendly, apolitical adviser, let alone a soldier of stature, as Kitchener had been, whom he respected. Henceforth, he resisted political intervention in military operations, preferring to co-operate with Joffre to avoid the need for political referees. Indeed, the prime minister, Anthony Asquith, always disinclined to intervene in military matters, did not want to restrain the commanders at a time when the French still trusted Joffre and the BEF had not yet been fully engaged. The situation would change a year later, when Joffre had been removed and his successor, General Nivelle, caused a mutiny in the French armies in the spring of 1917.

There was a solution of sorts for the British Army on the Somme (Map 2). Kitchener had proposed its general principle – a limited

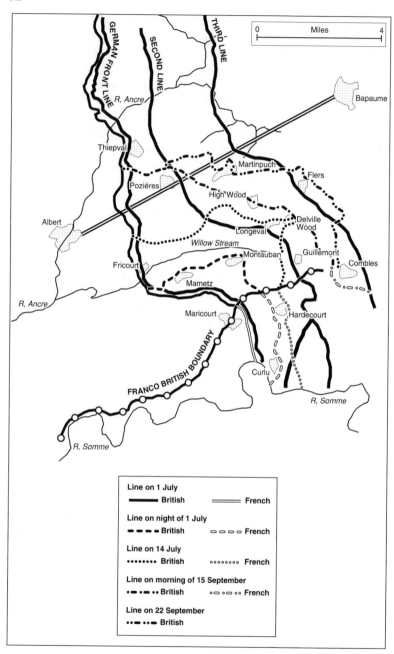

2 The Somme, 1916

tactical operation that could be terminated when required. Here operational theories in June 1916 must be briefly explained. Ferdinand Foch commanded the group of French armies to the right of the British Fourth Army under Rawlinson. Foch and Rawlinson agreed that to achieve a break-through, the base of the thrust had to be sufficiently broad to prevent the enemy on its flanks from pinching it out. The centre of the thrust had to be out of artillery range from the flanks. Road communications had to enable fresh divisions to move forward and renew the assault before the enemy's railways and roads brought reinforcement. It was their opinion that the Allies had not sufficient reserves or heavy artillery for this and that the front was not broad enough. Furthermore, German defences had been steadily improved since 1914 and were very strong. Whereas the high water-table in Flanders required trenches to be built on the surface where they were vulnerable to heavy bombardment, deep dug-outs in the chalk and clay sheltered trench garrisons in comparative safety in Picardy. Consequently, Foch and Rawlinson intended a series of limited attacks, and only if and when all available German reserves had been absorbed would they attempt to break through. Foch, volatile and sanguine, believed that this moment would eventually arise; Rawlinson did not. He wanted the limited operations to be broken off when they ceased to be profitable or had forced the Germans to desist at Verdun. Rawlinson retained this view in opposition to Haig in all his battles.

Indeed, Haig intended to make a lodgement on the left from which to thrust towards a corresponding penetration by the French when they had crossed the Somme on the right flank. He intended this advance to be rapid. That required reserves to be positioned with a preponderance of artillery on the left, where the German line happened to be at its strongest. He had hoped to use the new tanks for his operation but they were not ready. He ignored Foch's alternative, as it would take too long. An offensive *au fond* or one that continued *sine die* would be equally unacceptable in London. In effect Haig intended to force the Germans to shift reserves to his front by threatening a break-through, even if it did not succeed. He did not intend to pursue his plan to the point when the London politicians started to nag him.

The disagreement between Haig and Rawlinson about what kind of battle to fight blighted the first few days of the Somme. Reflecting the confusion, GHQ's initial directive to Rawlinson lacked that all-important element, a frank statement of the aim. When Haig and Rawlinson conversed they discussed details, never fundamentals.

Questions remained unanswered and often unasked. Why were divisions placed uniformly across the front in conflict with Haig's intention to break through on the left? Why was the method of crossing the gap between the trenches left to the individual divisional commanders, modified by corps commanders? Why was patrolling to determine the effect of the preliminary bombardment, which lasted a week, not undertaken systematically? Although Haig discovered this when he visited divisions, he did not pass his findings to Rawlinson. Whereas he wanted a short (hurricane) bombardment in depth to shock and neutralise the defenders to prepare for a surprise penetration, a prolonged bombardment designed to destroy forward defences was used. And yet, General Sir Noel Birch, who became Haig's chief Gunner only in June, told him that there was insufficient artillery, particularly medium and heavy howitzers, for either plan to be effective. He could not persuade Haig of this. Major-General C.E.D. Budworth, who replaced Birch as Rawlinson's Gunner at Fourth Army, also knew that even the front German trenches could not be destroyed unless he concentrated all his guns on them for a week. He wanted the attack on the next line to be launched only after a second bombardment. Budworth had not the authority to change the scheme preferred by corps commanders, who intended a rapid advance, and decided that the bombardment should not be restricted to the forward defences.

To support the advance on and beyond the first trenches a standing linear barrage fell on each objective. It lifted to the next one after a certain time. Whether the infantry had reached it or not, there was no provision for halting the advance of the fire because it was assumed that the advance through the Germans' 'devastated' lines would be rapid.

Gunners were treated as advisers, not commanders, in all this. Divisional and corps commanders feared an untidy advance, improvised actions and, hence, loss of control. What was termed 'the great wall of chinagraph' which showed the objectives on maps, had to be drawn and maintained in headquarters by staffs. It acquired comforting authority by being there. The lack of flexibility disallowed spare guns to fill in gaps in the fire-plan and discounted the need for Gunner observers to recall the advancing line of shells when they outstripped the advance. The only action that battery commanders could take was to overrule their superiors by taking their guns out of the fast disappearing barrage. They seldom had the information and the telephone cable to send orders to the guns to that effect, and perhaps they lacked the moral courage.

After the first few days the Rawlinson–Foch conception of a series of limited advances prevailed. From the 14th July, when the second great battle began, until early December when the battles ended, a cruel learning process continued in a series of limited corps battles. Nevertheless, the duration of the campaign was decided by Joffre with the agreement of a compliant Haig. Both men believed, with some justification, that they could grind down the Second German Army if it stood and suffered huge punishment from allied artillery. In fact, Second Army's chief of staff, Colonel von Lossberg, changed its methods to avoid it.

We should understand that commanders had not yet grasped the limitless scale of the war on the Western Front. At Loos, the autumn before, it was obvious that more guns, heavier guns, more reliable ammunition and more of it had to be found and committed if a breakthrough were to be made. More trained divisions were essential. At Loos, a bitter dispute between French and Haig occurred over the commitment of two reserve divisions which Haig was convinced would have achieved a break-through at Hill 70 had they been released to him in time. French was removed largely as a result of Haig's complaint. Haig had had the same conviction about imminent success at Neuve Chapelle in March 1915, where he disagreed with Rawlinson, then one of his corps commanders. His cavalry mind was convinced that speed and timing were the keys to success in 1915 and 1916, as they were in 1914, when the density of troops on the ground was so much less. He was wrong. Coming from a small army and a non-technical Arm he had not yet grasped the huge mass of men and material needed to ensure significant results and that his limited means could offer only limited success. That was why Kitchener, and later Lloyd George, tried to restrain him.

Every commander carries in his mind a picture of the battlefield and its opportunities based on his last experience, and Haig's was on the Menin Road at Ypres in 1914 when he commanded a corps. Most senior commanders tended to believe that when preparatory bombardments of two hours, unthinkable in 1914, had given way to ones lasting several days and eventually three weeks at the 3rd battle of Ypres in July 1917, no enemy could be alive and competent when their men advanced. It was true that British and French trenches, mainly built for assaults, could not have survived such treatment. And nor did they in the German attacks at Ypres in 1916. But on the Somme, where German mined dugouts had been steadily deepened and their support systems extended since 1914, targets were too numerous and the heavy howitzers too few to destroy them. Nor were the fuses on the shells designed to penetrate the clay and chalk. Even the wire in front of German positions took days to destroy. It was tangled rather than removed by high explosive, and night patrols seldom reported the state of it accurately. Shrapnel had to be used to cut it. Fired at short range from exposed gun positions, wire cutting was a nerve-wracking task for the gun detachments. On the following night German working parties would repair the damage they had done.

In the summer of 1916, artillery equipment and ammunition were still unreliable. Almost half the shells did not explode. The sensitive fuse 106, which destroyed wire and was lethal against infantry in the open, was a year away from service. The 18-pounder recuperator system, not designed for continuous firing day after day, and sometimes ill-maintained, gave much trouble, so that many guns were out of action. Prematures, particularly on 4.5-inch howitzers, were not infrequent. There were few smoke shells, which would have been invaluable for concealing advancing troops; and no gas shells, which were later used to neutralize artillery, whose detachments became casualties if they were caught without respirators or were exhausted if they wore them for long.

The terrible casualties on the first day of the Somme, about 60 000 killed, wounded and missing, had several causes, most of which we have rehearsed above. German shelling on the jump-off trenches was lethal and counter-battery was not yet effective. German machine guns, often depicted as being manned in the front trenches so recently bombarded, were more often used like artillery from 2000 or 3000 yards behind the forward trenches. Others, in the forward area, fired in enfilade from positions not being attacked directly.[6] Battalions were not ordered or even allowed to move into no-man's-land before the bombardment ceased so as to take the opposing trench before it could be manned. A proposal that a creeping barrage should advance across the gap in front of the enemy trench was rejected as being too dangerous. This 'fire-roller' was used in the second phase of the attack on 1 July by 7th Division in 15th Corps and Major-General Ivor Maxse's 18th Division in 13th Corps. In fact, 13th Corps, on the right of the line, reached its objectives. When the attack was resumed towards High Wood and Delville Wood on 14 July creeping barrages were used effectively.

The creeping barrage, simply called a barrage in the Second World War unless it was termed 'standing', used artillery as a neutralizer, rather than a destroyer. On the Somme shrapnel shells were used for barrages. When they were correctly paced and placed and the infantry had learned to 'lean' on them, they were consistently effective in both wars. In a terrain from which most features had been erased by shelling they gave the infantry direction. However, it inhibited infantry tactics based on fire and movement because the infantry followed it in lines rather than sections. They needed, as Maxse and some other divisional commanders observed on the Somme, to move in section 'worms', not battalion 'waves'. Infantry had to learn to advance using their own fire-power, which was increasing. Above all, the enemy's positions had to be accurately located, and barrages were often used as an excuse for ignorance on that score. On the Somme, German infantry learned to withdraw before a barrage began and then to counter-attack – as the Afrika Korps was to do in the Gazala battle of 1942. Point and counter-point.

On the urging of progressive divisional commanders like Maxse the scale of Lewis guns in a battalion was increased from eight to sixteen guns, sufficient for one gun to a platoon, late in the Somme battles. In the winter of 1916–17 the tactics of individual battalions developed but were not expanded into a general policy stating that the mass linear assaults of 1915 trench warfare were inappropriate because German defences had changed. The latter were now deeper and looser knit, depended on infantry fire-power and the counter-attacks of formed bodies up to a division in strength, initially placed beyond field gun range. The front was no longer held by men in a trench line but rather by skirmishers in well-concealed posts with a high proportion of machine guns. Such a line was not markedly vulnerable to heavy bombardment or a creeping barrage: nor were companies advancing in waves an appropriate formation in which to approach it.[7]

In the late stages of the Somme General Hubert Gough could still observe that in some battalions not a single platoon was organised.[8] Companies were run by its officer commanding and his company sergeant major with a nominal role from which they 'told-off' men for tactical duties. Lewis guns were company weapons which could be allotted to platoons as required but were not part of them. Maxse, Stephens and many other division commanders[9] had first to organize platoons into sections capable of independent fire and movement before tackling the new German defence scheme. The fighting unit was to be the section, Maxse insisted. He had made that point in 1913 when platoons replaced 'half-companies' as the tactical subunit.

Despite the vigour of divisional tactical thinking in the spring of 1917, the Arras battles in April and the long 3rd Ypres struggle starting at the end of July inhibited the retraining of infantry battalions to incorporate section fire and movement. The introduction of the No. 23 Mills rifle grenade and No. 24 rifle bomb with a cup discharger, together with the increase in Lewis guns, enabled platoon commanders to turn their commands into fire units but few had the knowledge or time; nor were they encouraged to do so, for in the settings of the 1917 battles, section tactics seemed redundant. Corps were largely responsible for staging battles and their commanders generally continued to believe that the cutting of wire and the destruction of the enemy's front defences by a long bombardment were essential preliminaries to an attack behind a creeping barrage. At Cambrai, on 20 November, this was to change with the introduction of a new artillery methods with tanks that made pre-bombardments redundant.[10]

Until August 1917, the new German defence tactics introduced by Colonel von Lossberg of the Second Army on the Somme seemed to pass the British by.[11] Barrages demanded linear attacks with which Hubert Gough, commanding the Fifth Army, began his operations at Ypres on 31 July. When they soon bogged down, Haig's Brigadier General Staff (operations), John Davidson, circulated a memorandum about the new German methods and asked his commanders for their proposals about how to deal with them. He favoured limited attacks which would go through the skirmishing line and possibly into the first part of the enemy main line and then await the counter attack using artillery defensive fire to repulse it. Gough's attacks had had deeper objectives, in some cases beyond field artillery range. German counter-attacks with fresh troops had found the defenders too disorganised to resist.

Maxse, by then commanding 18th Corps in Fifth Army, wrote two letters on 12 and 21 August, in reply to Davidson's proposals. He agreed that initial objectives should probably be no more than 2500 yards from start lines. He acknowledged the dominant role of artillery, writing: 'ground is gained by artillery, ground is defended by artillery, battles are won by artillery and are lost by lack of artillery'. But he went on to say that infantry in attack or defence should not be crowded and that fresh infantry should be available to counter-attack the enemy's reserves. In his second letter he recommended more extensive use of low-flying aircraft in the attack, more tanks with aircraft working in conjunction with them, more extensive use of fuse 106 to destroy wire and men in the open and ' a more elastic infantry formation for the attack, built up of platoons working in depth rather than battalions stereotyped in waves'. Mechanical carriers should lighten the men's loads.

Some of these ideas were used in the final offensives between August and October 1918. Maxse had not heard of the new artillery ideas about to be used by Third Army at Cambrai in November which obtained complete surprise. The German artilleryman, Colonel Georg ('Break-through') Brüchmuller, had developed similar ideas at Riga on the Russian front. The new artillery survey methods used at Cambrai were available at Ypres but the ground and Haig's battle plan would not have suited the method.

On 9 December 1917, after the 3rd battle of Ypres had sapped the energy and strength of the BEF Maxse wrote to Brigadier Charles Bonham Carter, then responsible for staff duties, tactical doctrine and training manuals at GHQ, when the reduction of the strength of brigades from four battalions to three was being discussed:

> Why not consider the future organisation of platoons in 1918, when we shall be worse off for manpower, *now*. Rather than cut numbers in platoons why not double Lewis guns. Train companies to operate on wider fronts and have intervals between fire units. Scrap the idea of shoulder to shoulder. Substitute waves for worms which deploy quickly to fire or to avoid the enemy's fire. Teach each fire unit to keep together and support its neighbour with fire.[12]

He added some advice to pamphlet writers that their successors in the next war should have noted. They did not grasp what kind of men were commanding platoons, he urged.

> They try to cram a Staff College education into a pamphlet ... It is a fine performance but bewilders our platoon commanders and people like me. If they would be simple and teach a few points in each pamphlet I think they would produce better results.

Battle tactics, like most human activities, cannot be treated discretely. Bound by trench horizons, the subject was treated as though attack and defence could be differentiated. In fact, defence is concerned with fighting over and dominating an area by attack and counter-attack more than with simply holding a point marked on a map. The methods used by the Germans in their tactically successful offensives in March, April and May 1918 derived directly from their looser defensive methods of the previous year, particularly counters to Gough's attacks in August and the 3rd Army Cambrai intrusion in November 1917. In

March 1918 the German task was made easier when the British held the front loosely without introducing the essential corollaries – namely, local and regional reserves able to move and fight tactically in the fashion envisaged by Ivor Maxse and others. Their positions, often visible and marked on artillery maps, were dead ducks. Concealment was easier in the shapeless morasse of the old front lines, but after the German strategic withdrawals in the early spring of 1917, the British Fifth Army positions were in the scorched earth area they left behind, in which every square inch was surveyed by the German artillery, old positions were booby-trapped and concealment required special care.

In the spring of 1918 the Germans had trained selected infantry to work in small units which used their own weapons to penetrate gaps in the front and to fight through and beyond British gun lines. Their artillery used Brüchmuller's methods and a prodigious amount of gas against British artillery. The German advance reached almost to Amiens. Writers have asked why the British could not have done the same. It sounds easy. Actually, against the Third Army defending the well-developed Arras defences with their underground tunnels, the Germans were not nearly so successful as on the Fifth Army front, where the defences on the right had been taken over from the French and were weak. Impressive though the German assault divisions were, those that followed them were frequently caught in closed formations and slaughtered. The Royal Flying Corps attacked men on roads successfully. Exhaustion, and ill-discipline when hungry men were tempted by captured food and drink, was the undoing of some units. Logistics, a problem in all relatively deep advances, was not solved. Short of cavalry, the Germans were restricted to the pace of marching men.

That the Germans penetrated the front again at Ypres in April and on the Aisne in May showed that their artillery and assault infantry could combine to break the old-style rigid defences. With more cavalry, armoured cars and, perhaps, tanks, the conditions of 1914 might have recurred, but that is unlikely. Tanks were incapable of moving long distances for several days on end. Motor vehicles and trains brought reinforcements to the flanks of penetrations more quickly than could the attackers. Aircraft – reconnaissance, artillery observation and assault – were powerful new additions to the advantage of the defence. A lesson of these final German offensives was that the front which could not be unglued by one devastating blow might be loosened by a series of them at different points, each of them employing infantry, tanks, artillery and aircraft combined. This was the method used by the British in the last 100 days of the war.

Haig's policy of fending off interference with operations from politicians was not seriously threatened while Joffre was the supreme commander. He was aware of grumbling from below when he carried on the Somme offensive into early December and agreed to Joffre's proposal to continue it in February 1917. But the French got rid of Joffre and Haig found himself at odds with Nivelle, Joffre's replacement. Lloyd George, who had just become prime minister, supported Nivelle when he proposed increasing his authority over the BEF. The British were directed to take over French line so that French divisions could be prepared for a major offensive in Champagne. Haig was to fight a diversionary battle at Arras. The pattern of previous years was being repeated.

Haig and his army commnders were tired of playing second fiddle to the French. Lloyd George showed more confidence in them than in the British just when Haig was convinced that his men were reaching their peak and the French were over the hill. Haig was particularly upset because Joffre had agreed that when the renewed Somme operation ended he would mount an offensive at Ypres. Nivelle's plan upset that scheme. It would not begin until April when the ground became suitable for tanks. Haig visualized his part at Arras being prolonged into the summer. Casualties there would weaken his effort in Flanders and, unless the French achieved early success, or admitted failure and halted the operation, there would not be time to mount and finish the Ypres offensive before the autumn. He and his commanders had lost confidence in French ability to win the coming battle, particularly after the German withdrawal to a well-prepared line behind the old Somme front during the winter.

Haig's loss of confidence in the French reinforced his determination to fight a British battle, on his own ground and in his own way. All his battles so far had been at French behest. He had supported them loyally. His armies had suffered heavily on the Somme but learned a great deal. It was galling to find that Lloyd George was so prejudiced.

And then the tables turned. Nivelle failed dismally in Champagne: mutinies began and spread in the French Army. General Petain, the hero of Verdun and a defence specialist, replaced Nivelle. The political leadership, pressed by Petain, and unaware, as yet, of the limitations of the Americans (who joined the war in April 1917) decided that there should be no major offensive until the French had recovered. Clearly they thought the British incapable of anything but limited attacks designed to distract the attention of the Germans from the plight of the French. Lloyd George visited Haig to ask for this action on 6 May.

Haig told him that a part of his planned Ypres offensive, an attack on the Messines Ridge, would be ready in early June. A successful assault on such an important tactical feature would certainly cause the Germans to respond. Lloyd George was delighted and, apparently, impressed at the contrast between French depression and British confidence. What followed demonstrated how politics in high places could influence operations.

The starting point is the decision of Lloyd George, his French colleagues and General Petain to cease major offensives in 1917 until the Americans took the field. Messines, though, had been planned earlier as part of the first phase of Haig's Ypres offensive to be fought jointly by Plumer, commanding Second army in the Ypres salient, and Rawlinson, whose Fourth Army had fought on the Somme. These two had decided to fight the 3rd battle of Ypres in phases. First, Messines on the right and Pilckem Ridge on the left would be taken to acquire observation and gun positions for the second phase, an attack up the Menin Road. After three days to shift artillery, dump ammunition and register targets this attack against the key German positions, the toughest nut to crack, would take the front as far as Gheluvelt. After that, Rawlinson would attack along the ridge to Passchendaele village and beyond. Passchendaele was at the north-eastern end of the ridge on which Messines was at the southern, although the high ground continued to the west, around the southern side of Ypres (Map 3).

Haig had other ideas. He had decided that the thrust line should be north-east from the existing line, with Passchendaele as first objective. It crossed the natural German counter-thrust from Menin and Gheluvelt down the Menin Road to Ypres. The important and difficult Menin Road sector would lie at the junction of Plumer's and Rawlinson's armies. Plumer on the right would be pinched out of the fighting during phase two, leaving Rawlinson on the left to continue towards Passchendaele village, his right flank becoming progressively more exposed. Moreover, Haig wanted a one- phase attack with Passchendaele its first objective. Neither Plumer nor Rawlinson thought that to be sensible.

The Rawlinson–Plumer plan (Map 4) originated in March 1916 before the Somme. Then, Haig counted on a quick switch of British divisions to Ypres from the Somme to catch the Germans unprepared so that a rapid advance would be possible. Neither Rawlinson nor Plumer believed that to be likely and their knowledge of the ground made them persist in looking closely at the tactical problems. Hence their preliminary attacks against the key features of Pilckem and

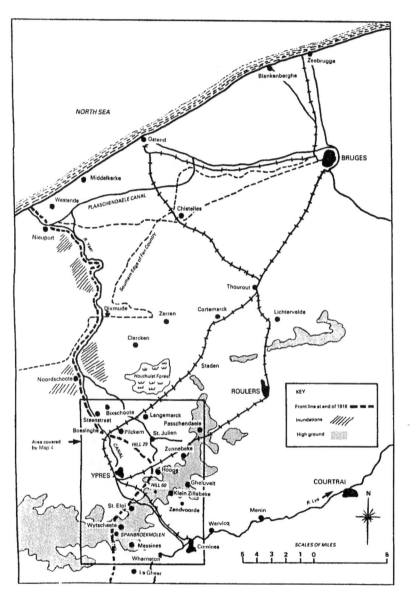

3   3rd Ypres

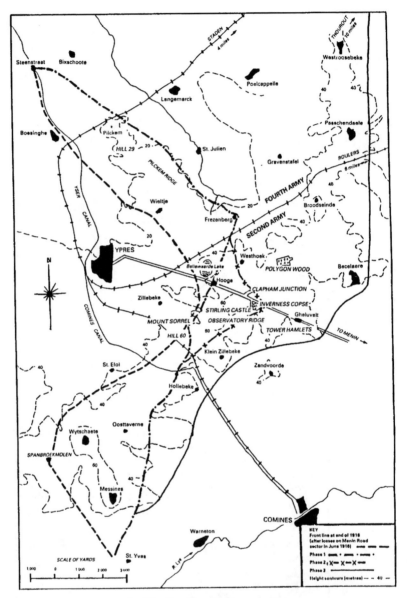

4 The Rawlinson–Plumer plan

After two initial phases (1. against Messines ridge and Pilckem ridge;
2. against the Menin road position) the Second Army pushes its left along
ridge to Broodseinde and Fourth Army north of the Ypres–Roulers railway
takes the Passchendaele–Staden ridge.

Messines, followed within a few days by the main attack on the Menin Road. It was not practicable, they argued, to attack right across the front initially. When the Nivelle regime took over, Haig continued to insist that the combined French and British attacks further south would enable him to switch divisions north and catch the Germans at Ypres unprepared, as before, and allow him to attack from his present positions across the front. He answered Plumer's continued objections by asserting that tanks would settle the matter on the Menin road. When Plumer talked to General H. Elles commanding the Tank Corps he was told, firmly, that the blasted woods on the Menin Road was unsuitable ground for tanks.

On 7 May, the day after Lloyd George had visited him, Haig told the assembled Army Commanders that Gough would fight the battle on the left in July after Plumer had taken Messines in early June. The conditions set by Rawlinson and Plumer, that the main attack against the Menin Road should follow the Messines and Pilckem attacks by only a few days, was ignored. The Germans would have six weeks to recover after Messines had been taken. There could be no surprise.

Haig knew that Gough, a fellow cavalryman, was convinced that deliberate methods had forfeited an opportunity to break through on the first day at Arras. To prompt him to agree with Haig's plan for a rapid advance from the positions at present held he was given the GHQ files, not those containing the objections of Plumer and Rawlinson. He duly produced a plan that suited Haig. Before 31 July, when the infantry advanced, Gough had discovered what was wrong with it, and had his boundary with the Second Army altered to alleviate the problem on the Menin Road, but had failed to persuade Plumer to co-operate in a joint attack to protect his right flank.[13]

Haig's determination to proceed, despite the decision not to launch any more strategic operations, and his obstinacy over the tactical plan need to be explained. The Navy desired him to seize the Channel ports, Ostend and Zeebrugge, to deny them to the short-range German U-boat fleet. He had planned landings from the sea in conjunction with Admiral Bacon, commanding the Channel Fleet, for that purpose. He believed that reaching the Dutch frontier beyond Zeebrugge might unhinge the right of the German front. That could best be achieved by a rapid advance. Brigadier Charteris, his chief intelligence officer, had told him that the Germans were near collapse. As for the tactical plan, Haig was convinced that he knew the ground and was right in overruling Rawlinson and Plumer. Moreover, he did not want another prolonged killing match which he would find difficult to sell to the War Policy Committee in London. Yet, when Sir John French was commanding, John Davidson's very intelligent predecessor, Frederick Maurice, had studied a campaign in Flanders that French was considering and, in an elegant, logical and dispassionate appreciation concluded that it was unpromising either as an attrition battle or as a break-through.[14]

But commanders who believe that they are being prompted by intuition and experience are sometimes being deceived by wishful thinking. For Haig was determined to show what the British Army could do. He believed that Ypres might be the beginning of the end for the Germans but he could hardly have chosen a worse tactical position from which to put his idea to the test – attacking out of an overlooked salient. The battle to neutralise the enemy artillery behind the ridge, which the Germans dominated, had to start seven weeks before the infantry attacked on 31 July. 3rd Ypres was an artillery battle. For every ten infantrymen engaged in the battle there were eight gunners. It was the hardest battle ever fought by the Royal Artillery. Yet H.C.C. Uniacke, Major-General Royal Artillery to Gough, was not consulted before Gough made his plan, let alone when Haig and GHQ evolved the outline that Gough received.

The contretemps over the plan, of which Lloyd George was unaware, might have had political implications, for the prime minister had agreed in Paris that the British would not undertake another major operation. Haig was called before the new War Policy Committee on 19, 20 and 21 June to explain his plan. Plumer had just been successful at Messines Ridge, a notable victory. An item on the agenda was the U-boat crisis and whether an operation to take the Channel ports, first suggested to the CIGS by Asquith in that connection in November 1916, would be helpful. When Admiral Sir John Jellicoe, by then First Sea Lord, declared that the whole anti-submarine campaign would be jeopardized if the U-boat havens at Ostend and Zeebrugge were not eliminated, the Committee was surprised and shocked. Questioned about his plan, Haig managed to suggest that he would undertake a series of limited attacks which, he asserted, would lead to his reaching the Channel Ports but could be terminated at any time. Thus he indicated that he could square the circle; limited attacks and naval satisfaction. He was given permission to continue his preparations but not to start the operation. Considering that the artillery battle was about to begin, with divisions moving into the Salient and due to advance on 25 July, it seemed unlikely that Haig could be told to stand-fast at the last minute. Permission to proceed was given at the last minute, a month later.

Understandably, Haig was on edge when he returned to France on 27 June. Gough explained his final plan at a meeting the next day. Like his outline presented on 14 June, it was for a rapid advance. D-day for 3rd Ypres was postponed until 31 July.

Gough's operations, in wet conditions, were only partially successful at considerable cost. Haig turned to Plumer and had him mount limited operations along the lines proposed on 16 June by Davidson. In dry weather in September Plumer was successful in three limited battles. Then the rain came and operations bogged down, becoming a frightful struggle in liquid mud. The Canadians, who took over under General Curry, built roads through the mud and ended the battle when they captured Passchendaele on 10 November.

4 Necessity Knows No Law

I remember my father, Fergus, dressed in his regimental Greens on his way to a battalion guest night, sitting on my bed to chat. He was smoking a State Express cigarette while he told me about the battle of Neuve Chapelle in March 1915. The pre-bombardment failed to cut the wire facing the brigade on his left and he described how the Scottish Rifles were held up in front of it and shot to pieces. At the time he was commanding a company of the Irish Rifles, which he led into the attack with a hunting horn. A bullet passed through the horn while he was blowing it. I have it now on my mantelpiece.

The Irish Rifles were brought home from Aden in 1914 to join the 8th Division, formed after the war began. Although they suffered casualties in small attacks near Ypres in December, Neuve Chapelle was their first major battle. The Rifles were in brigade reserve and passed through the leading battalions beyond the village which they had captured. Fergus' company was held up in an orchard by machine guns firing from the slopes of the Aubers Ridge which dominated that section of the front. While visiting his platoon positions Fergus was struck in the knee by a ball from a shrapnel burst. After dark he was evacuated through the Advanced Dressing Station to the Casualty Clearing Station and back to England. The labels on his kit sent after him and the huge ball that hit him are here in a show-case together with the shell splinter that hit me 30 years later in the Rhineland.

Fergus married my mother in April 1915. He was still in hospital and on crutches. But he recovered and suffered no ill-effects, although knee injuries were troublesome. Luckily, he never went back to the Western Front but spent the rest of the war in Salonika and Palestine fighting the Bulgarians and the Turks. We were both lucky. Instead of the Royal Ulster Rifles like my father and grandfather, I joined the Royal Artillery. The Rifles' regular battalions were in 3rd Division and 6th Airborne, both of which had 'interesting' wars. I survived several campaigns with only light wounds and was not involved in really horrible tactical disasters.

I found it easy to talk to my father about his experiences and later, in conversations with his contemporaries, I deduced what kind of leader he had been. Thorough and methodical but courageous, impatient and quick-tempered, he was much admired and deserved his

Distinguished Service Order, Military Cross, Croix de Guerre and mentions in despatches. The more informal campaign in the Mediterranean suited him well, for he had spent time in West Africa as a district officer and for the rest of his career, except for commanding his battalion, he headed for places where he could manage but not be managed by others. He was adjutant of the Malay Defence Force in the 1920s and commandant of the Shanghai International Volunteer Corps when the Japanese invaded in early 1937. He retired just before the Second World War, having refused command of an armoured brigade for which, he rightly said, he was not qualified. After the war started he was appointed commandant of the north-west area of the Royal Observer Corps, managing a team of attractive young women in the Carlisle control room and farmers on the posts from Beatock to Shap.

During his service he rode competitively and successfully, sailed boats with skill but not distinction and shot for the social pleasure it gave him. His advice to me after the war was to take the opposite career path from his. I was to attend the Staff College and stay close enough to the War Office that I could throw a stone through the windows. He had, himself, refused a nomination to the Staff College and never served in the War Office. Nor did I, as a matter of fact, although I did attend the Staff College.

When I returned from Norway in June 1940, took leave after the Battle of Britain, returned to England from prison camp in Italy in December 1943 and from the Rhineland where I was wounded in 1945, we talked about recent battles. He never spoke as though his war gave him any right to lecture me, although he asked shrewd questions which made me think carefully before answering them. It seemed to me that we belonged to the same army, with many of the same characteristics and certainly the same men, just a generation apart. But it was not until the final year of my war that I felt that my army was as good as his.

And yet it was his army that I found in 1939 when I joined, and then it was not very good. It had been allowed to run down by the conformist, War Office soldiers who had filled in forms correctly in the years since 1918, and got ahead. And yet, miraculously, sufficient real soldiers survived the years of peace-time stagnation to lead the Army to victory in the second half of the war. They must have kept their wits and courage alive by laughter and calculated disobedience. It was their spark of humour and skill that ignited the intuitive actions of the younger men who were to carry the torch and their example to victory in 1945.

It is unjust and unreal to divide the pre-1914 army into sheep and goats. Yet 'Oh What a Lovely War', Leon Wolff's *In Flanders Fields* and publications of their ilk have stigmatized many fine 1914 commanders and staff officers by depositing alluvium on their reputations. The early death of so many regular soldiers in 1914 and 1915 deprived all the armies of potential innovators by the end of those years. In a disciplined society, in which obedience to hierarchy was *de rigeur*, change had to wait for a critical mass to recognize that the war would last long enough to require every one – regulars, territorials, volunteers and conscripts, general officers down to private soldiers – to take part in an extended learning process. That was a radical idea to set against the orthodoxy that they had to teach soldiers to apply existing texts. In today's society, in which change is continuous, it is a commonplace one. I remember a brilliant young Scottish Assistant Instructor of Gunnery (a warrant officer) at the school at Almaza, in Cairo, admonishing us in 1942 to avoid the 'high priest' mode of instruction. It impeded constructive thought and blocked two-way communication, he told us.

The task in 1915 was to apply new weapons, as they appeared, to the sound concept of fire and movement that existed in 1914, in order to solve the dialectical conundrums facing the army. Some of these were how to balance infantry fire power against numbers employed, to determine the optimum size of small tactical units, the best use of indirect versus direct fire, to judge when neutralizing was more appropriate than destructive fire, and to balance mobility against shell weight when producing new artillery. The problem was no less than replacing the static trench fighting of 1915 by the looser, tactical methods that were to be created in late 1917 and 1918.[1]

There were two obstacles to progress. First was insufficient weapons and ammunition – including high explosive, for which there was no factory in the UK that made amatol, a mixture of tri-nitro-toluene and ammonium nitrate, the best shell filling. Not unnaturally, commanders were convinced that satisfying these needs would enable them to break through the front. The second was that the mass of obedient, trusting and yet sceptical officers and men needed to participate. Necessity had to know no law. There had to be a democracy of ideas. The high priest had to listen to the congregation.

Even the better anthologies, like Guy Chapman's *Vain Glory: A Miscellany of the Great War, 1914–1918*,[2] and few memoirs, can overcome a public impression that the military experience on the Western Front was homogeneous in time and space. The learning process of the armies has only comparatively recently been explored in historical work about the fighting.[3] Records of 'tail' activities are comparatively scarce. Yet, it was military 'boffins', workshops mechanics, munition designers, logistics staffs, radio and telephone technologists, road builders, quartermasters, hospital doctors and nurses, who were conscious of progressive methods because all of them were engaged in functional activities. The platoon, company, squadron or battery soldiers because they were, all too often, short-lived, were unaware of change. It is they who, featuring mainly in the literature, have left the impression that the form of the fighting was homogeneous.

Fighting soldiers of the First World War continue to hold our interest and sympathy because they suffered, we have been told with some justification, in a mismanaged war, but triumphed in the end. They represented the indomitable spirit of 'The People'.[4] A chasm separated them from those who were never 'in the trenches'. The hard times of the 1930s brought them afresh to public notice, not because veterans were being honoured or looked after at the time, but for the subjective reason that the condition of the land fit for heroes had worsened and that it was heading for another war. Emphasizing anew the last war's horrors, its waste and failed peace treaty, was an element in the current mood of appeasement. The poetry of the young dead and of survivors, Siegfried Sassoon for example, who not only fought gallantly but also attempted to revolt against the conduct of the war during it, was popular.[5]

In contrast, the literature of the Second World War was influenced by the public feeling that all that could be said about the fear and the blood on modern battlefields had been said already. Furthermore, as the new war was a 'just war', to present its horrors at the front, as before, was considered inappropriate. New subjects were sought. The psychology of courage and cowardice and advances in life-saving surgery, electronic warfare and its service to Intelligence received attention. They were not only important but bridged peace and war activity. In effect, the experience of combat soldiers in the Second World War was assumed to be different by default, for they were presented differently. This was particularly true of casualties, of which writers of the First World War had made much but those of the Second tended to avoid, or treated unevenly.[6]

The literature of the Second World War celebrated the parts played by civilians and military more equally. Military experiences had varied more widely than in 1914–18. Those of planners, inventors, intelligencers and politicians, and the senior officers responsible for working with statesmen were read with more enduring interest than those of men in units, not because they were typical but the reverse. We had read the soldiers' typical experience in the First World War. Now we wanted something more original than them. So it was the irregulars and specialists, male and female, that attracted most attention, although they were a minority. Civilians were believed to have suffered through bombing and food shortage more than most soldiers, so that the home front's deprivations and achievements were honoured in the record. But here it was not the unique experience that was celebrated, but the universally ordinary ones that bound communities together in a way that was unusual in peace. Indeed, their exposure to danger and death, considered to be against the laws of war, was a source of pride and made their morale as important as that of the soldiers. Thus the manner of presenting the civilian experience in the Second World War was a war behind. It was the typical and the general, rather than the unusual, that was published.[7]

Guy Chapman points out in his Introduction that boredom is the enemy of morale. Even a defeat may raise the morale of the survivors, for it relieves boredom. Ten months in the Ypres salient reduced his battalion to morbidity.

> We had been promised so much, and so little had been achieved. The faith and elan which the will to victory required had been blunted by failure. What the newspapers called victories were known by the men engaged as repulses; and although, as we are now told, these *bataille d'usure* were in fact slowly breaking up the enemy morale, morale is invisible, and it was a visible sign that was wanted.[8]

But its move to the Somme in the March 1918 retreat restored it to health although it lost half its strength there.

The morale of the Home Front was harder to maintain because most people were unable to contribute directly to victory, were bored and had to bear the casualties to their nearest and dearest at the fronts. The winter of 1917, even now, suggests to me 10/10 overcast, chill winds and hunger, and fatigue with war, whether I imagine myself in Russia, Germany, Great Britain or France, on the Eastern or Western Front. Siegfried Sassoon's morale collapsed for a period in 1917, before he resigned himself to death at the front as preferable to accepting his own ineffectiveness in setting an example as a dissident hero at home. He found the mental gap to be unbridgeable between people on the home front and the men he had led on the Western

Front, and preferred to be with the latter. In his review of the second edition of Chapman's book in *The Sunday Times* on 25 July 1939 he wrote:

> People – especially young ones – who assert that they will have nothing to do with the next war will be none the worse for finding out as much as they can about the last one. And those who are willing to fight for their country can save themselves from the dis-illusionment of the 1914 enthusiasts by getting rid of their illusions before the general mobilisation order is issued. The convinced war resister should have a sound all-round knowledge of his subject. He will not help the cause of Peace by condemning war unheard. And candidates for future war memorial lists and total disability pensions will surely be making ultra-modern warfare ridiculous if they enter it in a purely professional state of mind and then, when it is too late, begin complaining of its inhumanity.

This passage helps to explain the difference between the attitude of Sassoon's generation and mine to our respective wars. Today, I am struck by the spiritual uplift felt by so many men in 1914 as they marched off to war. In 1939 many of us went off with the aphorism 'He that expecteth not shall not be deceived.'

> I am setting out in great joy and expectation, not in search of adventure and the spurious excitement of unknown experiences, but in the firm belief and hope that I shall become manly and firm, fully developed, broadminded, full of power and strength, in readiness for the great life which will be waiting for me later on.[9]

The faith and the hope lasted until the autumn of 1916. 1917 and 1918 were gloomy: victory came as a surprise. In the Second World War the greyness was in the early days when the memory of 1917 suddenly returned with the realisation that a long, interminable war interspersed with defeats stretched ahead.

For the Scottish Rifles in the 8th Division, Neuve Chapelle began their pilgrimage from optimism, through the valley of the shadow in 1917 to the exhausted victory and peace of the autumn of 1918. They played their part in the effort to solve an ill-defined military problem in applied science which the army tackled at both ends and in the middle on the Western Front. The infantry tried to occupy the enemy's position or to by-pass it and to keep advancing. The problem then became someone else's – that of the commanders' to reinforce them and give orders where to go next. At the top level, commanders were concerned with finding the means to enable soldiers to advance. When all had been said their action was simplified into destroying the enemy by more and more high explosive. In the middle were the individuals who wrought the details of the techniques of combining infantry, artillery and tanks, the rapier rather than the bludgeon of week-long bombardments, that enabled the infantry to advance in late 1917 and 1918. Their work went forward by trial and error without identifiable leadership from the top. This amorphous movement, for long unrecognized, was progressive. But it would not have been effective without the dour, cheerful courage of the men in hundreds of battalions like the Scottish Rifles.

Neuve Chapelle was fought, in large part, by regular battalions, British and Indian, with the *esprit de corps* of the pre-war army.[10] From the lieutenant-colonel commanding to privates and lance-corporals acting as stretcher bearers, there was much all-round ability in their ranks. Half way through the battle, of which the active phases lasted from the morning of 10 March 1915 until the end of the 12th, the Scottish Rifles were commanded by 2nd Lieutenant W.F. Somervail with distinction. He had been in the army for only about eight months and was later killed as a captain, having won the DSO and MC.[11] Companies under him were being commanded by warrant officers and senior NCOs with equal ability.

The two days of the battle were preceded by a march through the previous night to relieve 2nd Northamptonshire Regiment in the assault trenches. The Northamptonshire Regiment had erected scaling ladders, cut steps in the trench wall and exits through the wire, and built up supplies of grenades and small arms ammunition. They were able to brief the companies on features in the enemy trenches, which included a thick hedge beyond the barbed wire which the artillery intended to cut before zero hour. They were surprised to find that in some places the German trench was only 50 or 60 yards in front of them. It was to be bombarded for 35 minutes before the advance. Indeed, it was so close that casualties were expected from the wire-cutting 18 pounder shells dropping at the short end of their zone, although the 4.5-inch howitzers that would do the physical damage to the trenches were accurate enough.

The march up to the front was tiring, particularly as it was across country and the pace was fast. 'Concertina-ing' then occurred and men had to run to keep up, for being lost in the dark was frightening. Bone-weariness must have been the most lasting battle-memory of the members of the battalion, for it started with the loss of a night's sleep and was followed by two days of battle. In his classic study of morale, John Baynes includes a passage from C.E. Montague's *Disenchantment:*

> For most of his time the average private was tired. Fairly often he was so tired as no man at home ever is in the common run of his work. If a company's trench strength was low and sentry-posts abounded more than usual in its sector a man might, for eight days running, get no more than one hour off duty at any one time, day or night. If enemy guns were active, many of these hours off guard might have to be spent on trench repair ... So most of the privates were tired the whole time; sometimes to the point of torment, sometimes much less, but always more or less tired.[12]

The peak of the battle lasted a short hour and a half from 8.00 a.m. when the half-hour bombardment ceased. By 9.30, the failure of the gunners to cut the wire opposite the Middlesex Regiment, on the brigade left, and A Company of the Scottish Rifles, had had terrible effects. B Company's left was similarly held up and it suffered heavily from enfilade fire from the Middlesex flank. When the C.O. redirected the follow-up companies, C and D, to the right flank, the battalion penetrated 400 yards through the German lines. 'But four hundred human beings lying dead or wounded in a space little more than 200 yards by 100 is almost too terrible to consider.'[13] At 10.30 a.m. heavy guns smashed the German trenches opposite the Middlesex, allowing them to move forward abreast of the Scottish Rifles.[14]

Captain Malcolm Kennedy, a platoon commander in B Company who was wounded twice fighting in the wire and the hedge beyond it, wrote that of the stretcher bearers: '[I]t was impossible to speak too highly. Hour after hour they had worked under fire, bringing in the dead and wounded, till they themselves were near the point of exhaustion.'[15] Baynes advised his readers that a stretcher was an awkward, clumsy thing to handle, particularly with a heavy man to move.

The Scottish Rifles casualties were 469 killed, missing and wounded. The total British casualties were 583 officers and 12 309 other ranks with German casualties 12 000 including 30 officers and 1657 other rank prisoners. Casualties to warrant officers and senior NCOs were serious for the future. In the first stage of the battle 30 out of 50 were killed or wounded. And, even when the less seriously wounded had returned to the battalion later in the year 'the 2nd Scottish Rifles was never again the same battalion that it had been before Neuve Chapelle. It lived on in name, and certainly in spirit, but those men who had gone over the top on 10 March were always in the minority in the years after the battle.'[16]

Mistakes were made and lessons learned by the senior commanders, although not as many as should have been. The enemy had been taken by surprise by the short, violent preparatory bombardment. But that had not been accurate on the left, as we have seen, and it needed to be more intense everywhere. More ammunition was needed and more careful registration to achieve that. In the second part of the battle shells were scarcer on British than on German gun positions. Sir John French complained about the shortage of high explosive; this became a celebrated issue known in the UK as 'The Shell Crisis'.[17] Furthermore, communications between artillery observers and the infantry failed once the advance started, infantry having to withdraw because they were shelled by their own guns. The conclusion was that the infantry would have to comply with the artillery fire plan in future, rather than vice versa. That, of course. restricted their tactical movement. Above all, Sir Douglas Haig, the Army Commander, intervened to continue the battle in the mistaken idea that a break-through was possible. Disagreement about the facts caused bad relations between Sir John French, Haig and Rawlinson.[18]

Sir John's replacement after Loos, in the autumn, was followed by the commitment of the BEF to the Somme offensive, in which the Kitchener armies played a major role. Its first day, 1 July, was a repetition of Neuve Chapelle on a greater scale, except for the decision to use a lengthy instead of a short 'hurricane' bombardment. 14 divisions (13 plus 10 battalions from reserve divisions) advanced in waves in daylight against German trenches on higher ground on about an 18-mile front. Of approximately 700 men from each battalion who went over the top 410, on average, became casualties. At Neuve Chapelle the Scottish Rifles suffered 470 killed, wounded and missing. The 8th division, which experienced conditions approximating to those on 1 July, suffered an average of 400 casualties in each battalion. The four assaulting divisions suffered 11 652 casualties, an average of 242 per battalion.[19]

The shock suffered by the Middlesex, and A Company of the Scottish Rifles, and by the other companies enfiladed by machine gun fire before they could get to grips with their enemy, was similar to that of the many companies on 1 July who never reached the German first trench, either because they met uncut wire, were scythed by machine guns before that, or, if they were in later waves, were slaughtered by artillery fire in no man's land. The men at Neuve Chapelle had watched the Germans being hammered for 35 minutes before they attacked and then were shocked when German machine guns were still able to open on them in the short time it took to advance about 100 yards. On the Somme the bombardment went on, with intervals and periods of merely harassing fire, for a week. The infantrymen had been assured that nothing would be alive when they walked across distances varying between 400 and 800 yards. They had practised the assault, been fed and clothed and been surrounded by friends. They were confident, although naturally frightened. Within minutes of scrambling out of their trench and shaking out to walk towards the enemy trenches they were dead, wounded and in pain, or fighting for their lives alone or with a few others, often strangers. After the first wave those that followed could see what their fate would be. They went forward, none the less.

When men did close with their enemy, for most individuals for the first time on the Somme, they wanted revenge for the killing of their friends at long range from machine guns and artillery:

> We are filled with a terrible hate. Our actions are born of a terrible fear, the will to survive. Some of the Germans were getting out of their trenches, their hands up in surrender; others were running back to their reserve trenches. To us they had to be killed. Kill or be killed. You are not normal.[20]

The opportunities for this occurred on the Maricourt salient and Mametz fronts, on the right, where the German front trenches were overrun and subsequent advances could be made partly over the top and partly up communications trenches. Artillery FOOs were able to accompany the advance and add to its fire-power. The spirit of the young volunteers of these divisions shines out in the accounts in Middlebrook's book. As soon as they were released from the slow, parade ground form of the advance, as the men of the 36th Ulster Division on the Thiepval front were, their initiative showed to good effect. Instead of walking forward slowly in lines, the Ulstermen ran forward and took their opponents by surprise. Elsewhere, the Germans were amazed that they were given so much time to shoot down the lines of men.

Men caught in No Man's Land, the wounded and those thwarted by uncut wire, had to lie out in the heat all that day. Many who were fit to do so sniped at Germans who sat out boldly on their parapets. But that soon brought retribution and many wounded were killed when they moved, or wounded again. Telescopic sights gave the Germans dominance. Shell holes were usually too small for hiding unless they were close to the British trenches. The plight of the wounded even when they were in their own lines, lying at the bottom of a trench, was grisly. The trenches were full of wounded and getting them on to stretchers and out into communications trenches was, in many places, well-nigh impossible. The medical teams were over-borne by numbers and despite Rawlinson's special request for extra ambulance trains, none were supplied until the second day. On the first day five trains had evacuated only 2317 patients. In the next three days trains made 58 journeys carrying 31 214 patients.[21] The delay in retrieving wounded cost many lives. 10 000 of the first day's wounded were still in the battle zone at 10 p.m. on 2 July. 'After being wounded, I walked to Bray, where I spent five nights with only a ground sheet and a blanket'.[22]

> I was brought in from No Man's Land on Monday 3 July and had a rough dressing put on a bullet wound in my foot, but no more. The same day I was taken to a CCS at Corbie and remained there until the Friday night, with no medical attention at all. When I was taken to the Base Hospital at Wimereux, the dressing was removed and my foot and all the way up my leg was completely gangrenous. Within a few hours I had to have a mid-thigh amputation, from what had been a simple wound in my foot.[23]

My namesake, Dominick Browne, a regimental friend of my father's in the Royal Irish Rifles, was one who died of wounds on the battlefield.

Unwounded survivors were heroes to those who had been among the 10 per cent deliberately left out of battle. Their example to re-inforcements was the foundation on which battalions were rebuilt. Curiously, survivors did not immediately return with bitter stories about the errors of the higher command, although middle-piece officers were in some cases angry at the criminally ignorant orders they had received during the afternoon to renew attacks in hopeless situations. Indeed, it was clear that more brigade and division com-manders ought to have refused corps orders on the grounds that they were based on misinformation.

The errors of the artillery have been discussed previously and there is no doubt that had the German trenches been engaged, as later was done, until the attackers were within 50 or 100 yards, German casual-ties would have been considerable. The corps commanders were not in favour of that and the training of the gunners was thought not to be up to it. Brigadier-General Budworth, Rawlinson's IV Corps gunner at Neuve Chapelle and Loos, wrote a trenchant report after the failure of the Loos attack. He said that ideally a short, violent bombardment, as at Neuve Chapelle was best, but at Loos the gunners were not well enough trained, he had not sufficient heavy guns for it, too few rounds and too many of them proved to be duds. He did not recommend another major attack until there were sufficient heavy guns to destroy the enemy defences, which was not the case at Loos and would not be on the Somme. Rawlinson did not advance this view to Haig, first because Birch, his previous artillery commander in the Fourth Army, had already done so, and secondly because the offensive had to go forward anyway. Another mistake was the failure to arrange adequate fire support for the subsidiary attacks that were made late in the day. In 7th Division and in 18th and 30th, the commanders ordered not only fire support for the second phase of the advance but more rapid movement of the attackers. How effective that could be was shown by the 4th Liverpool Pals attack against the Brickworks below Bernafay Wood and 7th Division's attack on Mametz.

The most remarkable error was the failure of Rawlinson to exploit the success of 13th and 15th Corps on the right. Rawlinson was disinclined to do so because Haig had not responded to his objections to the situation in the Maricourt salient, from which 30th Division attacked Montauban. There the French and British had to attack at right-angles to one another. The French intended to use their gains only as a defensive flank. Had the 4th Army advanced beyond Montauban without vigorous French support their right flank would have been exposed. Yet, it appears that the French were willing to advance, although subsequently British commanders complained that they were hanging back when the right flank took the initiative on 14 July. It needed only a change of plan by Rawlinson to commit the 9th, the 17th and the cavalry divisions on the British side. It is not at all certain that they might not have unhinged the German flank if the French had moved as well. Lieutenant-General Congreve commanding 13th Corps asked for permission to continue his attack beyond Montauban but had been turned down. Rawlinson preferred to continue his plan of deliberate limited attacks. That was a grave error.

It was tragic that so many young, enthusiastic volunteers, who could have fought intelligently later, instead of like machines, had been killed. In the months that followed the trained under-officers of the German army were also destroyed by the increasingly lethal British artillery. Whereas it had failed to flatten the trenches on 1 July, it did so in the next stage of the campaign. The casualties they suffered then forced the German infantry to thin out and conceal their positions, and hold them with fewer men. When the British reached the crest of the ridge and used tanks for the first time in September, the Germans decided to withdraw 10 miles behind a prepared line. It was ready for occupation by the spring.

What difference did artillery and tanks make to the style of fighting? It took until the final months of the war before accurate survey and more heavy howitzers enabled short bombardments, like that at Neuve Chapelle, to be accurate, to take the enemy by surprise and, thus, to allow the infantry, with tanks, to make better progress. But the casualties were still appalling. Successful battles were not necessarily cheaper in lives for either side. More accurate artillery and the increase in automatic weapons produced terrible casualties even though men ceased advancing in waves as they had on 1 July 1916.[24]

The 3rd battle of Ypres brought the end of long bombardments to destroy the enemy in his trenches. It had not only turned the ground into a morasse but made surprise impossible:

> The front line was not merely obliterated: it had been scorched and pulverized as if by an earthquake, stamped flat and heaved up again, caught as it fell and blown all ways ....There cannot have been a live man in it ... Before us yawned a deep muddy gulf, out of whose slimy sides obtruded fragments of splintered timber, broken slabs of concrete, and several human legs clothed in German half-boots ... The German trenches that we had studied on the map were blown to pieces and unrecognisable. One could see nothing anywhere, in fact, but a brown waste of mud blasted into ridges and hollows like a frozen sea, littered with debris, and melting on all hands into the prevailing haze.[25]

Although the war had lasted four years shells still exacted moments of terror and prayer as the soldier, from long experience, knew that it was going to be a close one. He still looked out for the nearest trench, like a child playing musical chairs and he was superstitious and looked out for tokens that would keep him safe one more time. In 3rd Ypres, shells, mud, cold and water were the enemies. He seldom saw his enemy.

I stood dazed by the din and didn't notice that our own barrage had lifted until somebody shouted, 'Come on!' ... nobody hesitated or looked back. I was simply a sheep and I went with the flock. We moved forward as if we were on the parade ground. But it didn't last long. With shell holes and impassable morasses we had to pick our way.... We fell into mud and writhed out again like wasps crawling out of plum jam.... We flopped into a shell-hole, lying around the lip, for there was about six feet of water in the middle. We had already seen what had happened to the first 'ripple'. They had all made for that spot of higher, drier ground, and the Germans, having retired over it, knew exactly what must happen, and the sky rained shells upon it.... The first 'ripple' was blotted out. The dead and wounded were piled on each others' backs, and the second wave, coming up behind and being compelled to cluster like a flock of sheep, were knocked over in their tracks and lay in heaving mounds.[26]

The battle of Cambrai, for which the infantry had been physically well prepared for long marches and continuous action, was so success-ful initially that the cavalry were caught completely napping by the opportunity to exploit.

And what was the cavalry doing? Why, carrying out the regular tactics for advancing by stages into enemy country! Troops halted in sunken road behind the village, two scouts sent forward to recon-noitre, one of them returns to report to the officer. No wonder they were late! I was furious with that young cavalry officer. It was really too absurd. Ribecourt had been captured at 7 a.m., the R.E. were loading up material from a German dump just outside the village at 9 a.m. and now, four hours later, the cavalry were advancing as cautiously as if Germans might be expected round every corner.[27]

Ten days later the Germans rolled up the Third Army front at Cambrai, taking everyone by surprise, as the tanks and infantry had taken them by surprise. But the Germans had no tanks. Clearly, the BEF was not ready for open warfare, which was made obvious on 21 March when the Germans struck the Fifth Army.

These latter attacks by the British with tanks gave the Germans no warning and their troops were caught in their dug-outs immediately the short, unregistered barrage lifted. The German attacks on the Somme, the Lys and then on the Aisne early on 27 May were pre-ceded by 'drum-fire', a stupefying torrent of high explosive shells mixed with gas which lasted for two hours and cut all telephone wires. Forward companies were overrun and battalions were fighting on all sides as soon as it stopped. Units split up and fought round single Lewis guns or troops of 18-pounders.

The officer and the corporal with two men went through the shrub-
bery. Looking through it I could see a big *route nationale*. There
were hundreds of our fellows running along it, like a football crowd
running for the trams. Jerry's machine-guns were going and they
were dropping, a score at a time and lying in heaps, khaki heaps.[28]

The impression during the fighting retreat that followed was that the
Germans had a machine gun each. And yet the tide turned in July and
it was the Germans who were retreating for the rest of the war.

Of course tanks played an important part in the victories that followed the attack on the Somme front on 8 August, named their Black
Day by the German army. But surprise was obtained by attacking
without preliminary bombardments. There were gaps in the German
front now and the infantry had been released from the dreary pattern
of wave attacks against an enemy in positions they could not see.

8 August. We were roused at 3 a.m. and ate a hot meal at the
cookers by the light of flickering candles. Cigarettes glowed in a few
brief puffs before the whistle went for fall in.... Low-flying planes
droned heavily in the distance; they were purposely disguising the
noise made by the tanks getting into position at the front line.
Darkness and ground-mist were hiding the movement into attack
positions of an array of 100,000 infantry and the gun-crews around
the battery positions, with guns loaded and run out, and ranges
checked, waited for their watches to crawl round to the fatal hour
4.20 a.m. At zero hour the bombardment fell in one mighty blast...
company after company, platoon after platoon, moved forward into
the bank of mist. Up in front the barrage sounded like strokes on a
mighty drum. We knew that at the first descent of this curtain of
shells the men of the 2nd and 3rd Australian Divisions, the
Tommies on our left and the Canadians on our right would, in their
battle formations, advance behind that moving wall of death, to
assault the front line of German trenches.[29]

Very early on the last morning Shadbolt was watching the men
dragging the heavy howitzers into a little clearing in the wood. The
day was grey and overcast and the raindrops from a recent shower
were dripping sadly off the trees. Above them a few pigeons, dis-
turbed by the movements and cries of the men, circled and wheeled.
A desptch rider rode up and handed him a message form. 'Hostilities
will cease at 11 a.m. today. A.A.A. No firing will take place after
this hour.'

This then was the end. Visions of the early days, their hopes and ambitions, swam before his eyes.

He saw again his pre-historic howitzer in the orchard at Festubert, and Alington's long legs moved towards him through the trees. He was back with the Australians in their dugout below Pozieres. He saw the long slope of the hill at Heninel, covered with guns, ammunition dumps, tents and dug-outs. Ypres, the Salient, Trois Tours, St Julien – the names made unforgettable pictures in his mind. Happy days at Beugny and Beaussart, they were gone and the bad ones with them. Hugh was gone, and Tyler and little Rawson; Sergeant Powell, that brave old man; Elliot and James and Johnson – the names of his dead gunners strung themselves before him. This was the very end. What good had it all been? To serve what purpose had they all died? For the moment he could find no answer. His brain was too numb with memories.

'Mr Straker.'

'Sir.'

'You can fall the men out for breakfast. The war is over.'

'Very good, sir.'[30]

5 Conclusion to Part I

The British army expected its French ally to play the main role on land in both wars. In the First World War it gradually gained in strength and ability until it was at least an equal partner. On the road to equality its weapons and methods improved steadily and, by the end, were the equal of the German and French in most departments and were superior in tanks and ground/air co-operation.

By the 1930s it was commonly believed that such a commitment to a continental war ought never to occur again. Indeed, it was widely believed that it should have been avoided in the First War by adopting what was called an 'Easterner' strategy; that is the Allies' main effort should have been directed against the 'props' of Germany, namely Austria–Hungary and Turkey. The huge casualties incurred on the Western Front would, thereby, have been avoided. This pervasive, but misguided idea, weakened Britain's political will to encourage and stand by the French in the face of the German threat after 1935. The political community convinced itself that, if war came again, the French could repeat their gallant performance of 1914 and 1915 and give the British Army time to gather strength to reinforce them.

Part II
The Mediterranean, 1941–2

6 The Desert Campaign 1941–2

I can recall wondering whether the decline of the country, absolute or relative, of which I was already aware in 1939, was reflected in the way the British Army fought in the first years of the war. Did the quality of our weapons, I asked, not indicate the decline of our industry? The morale of the country in 1939 seemed to me to be poor and it was not surprising that many who joined the army reflected its economic and social state. The regular army had been neglected and it was clear even to me, a nineteen-year-old with a short six months stint at the Royal Military Academy, Woolwich, that it was resigned to making bricks without straw. Dinner table conversation at home, as early as 1936, was about the dismal quality of our politicians and our unpreparedness for the inevitable war.

My initial experience of war was at Narvik, in May 1940, commanding a light anti-aircraft troop of four 40-mm Bofors guns and about 60 men. The Northwest Expeditionary Force did achieve its aim by capturing the town but we had to destroy our guns when we evacuated soon after. The returning convoy reached 74 degrees north latitude to avoid air attack but it failed, for the aircraft carrier, HMS *Glorious*, was sunk. Hurricanes that took off the deck to fight Luftwaffe bombers were unable to return and the pilots drowned.

I celebrated my twentieth birthday in Dover, where I started fighting my Battle of Britain. I had guns on the Western Heights, on the seafront, and on a mole in the harbour, where BBC reporters broadcast the moment when Sergeant Gallagher's gun shot off the propeller of a yellow-nosed Messerschmitt which crashed into the sea. When the air battle moved inland I had guns on various airfields in Kent and was then moved to Croydon, after questions were asked in the House of Commons when it was bombed. But my light guns could do nothing against planes flying above 5000 feet over London. It was all exciting enough. We were conscious of having our backs to the wall. Despite the favourable figures of casualties, announced like cricket scores by the BBC, it was quite clear that we were losing more fighters, if not fighter pilots, than the enemy. We were sure that the Germans would invade. There was little to oppose them. Only one infantry battalion was posted on my section of the coast near Lympne on 15 September. That seemed to suggest that the Germans only had to land to win. By one of those strange coincidences, it was the First Battalion of the Royal Ulster Rifles. The CO had been one of my father's company commanders, a favourite of mine when I was at school. Later in the war I learned more about the hazards of landing on alien shores, but Romney Marsh was not defended like Sword beach in Normandy.

From the army's point of view I did not regard the battle as a great victory, for we still had to meet the Germans on the ground where they were winning hands down. By October, bored with shooting un-successfully at hit and run Messerschmitts, I obtained a transfer to the Middle East. In January 1941 I was in a convoy round the Cape. In March I arrived in the Western Desert outside Tobruk. My experi-ences for the next year were to be there.

In the autumn of 1940, it was agreed that the Italian forces which had invaded Egypt from Cyrenaica in the summer should be attacked and thrown back to the frontier. The operation was to be named Compass and was to begin in early December. The invasion season in the English Channel had ended, releasing formations to reinforce Egypt, but not in time for them to participate even if they took the dangerous route through the Mediterranean (Map 5). Consequently, General Sir Archibald Wavell, Commander-in-Chief in the Middle East, had to carry out operation Compass with his own resources. His object was to secure his Egyptian base against an Italian advance on Alexandria and thus to enable him to transfer a division to help defeat the Italians in East Africa. Compass began on 9 December.

In November, the chiefs of staff in London warned him to be pre-pared to send help to Greece as well. In recounting what followed we must remember the context of 1940 and the spring of 1941. The Germans had not yet invaded Russia but Hitler was to issue a direc-tive on 18 December that preparations for Barbarossa must be com-plete by 15 May 1941.[1] When the Italians' adventure in Albania and Greece, which they invaded on 28 October, went wrong the Germans became concerned about their Balkan flank.[2] Following his instruc-tions about Greece, which had their origin in Chamberlain's promise to succour her if she were attacked by the Axis, Wavell went to Athens to see what could be done to help. The Royal Navy secured the fine Cretan harbour at Suda Bay and a battalion of infantry went to Crete from Egypt. Three bomber squadrons went to Greece, followed by engineers, signallers and supply services.[3] Naval convoys brought in

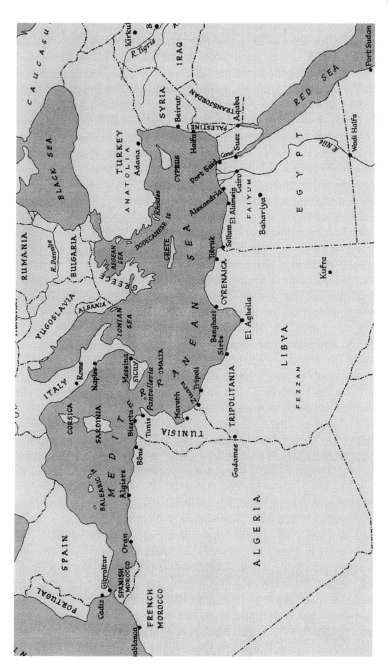

5   The Mediterranean

vehicles, boots, socks, blankets, clothing and whatever ammunition was suitable for the Greek Army. This assistance was in keeping with Wavell's conception that the security of the Middle East would be best assured by fighting well forward.[4]

The Greeks were grateful for supplies but still did not want the ground combat units that Wavell offered when he was in Athens again on 13 January 1941.[5] General John Metaxas, President of Greece, feared that they would provoke the Germans to invade and excuse the Yugoslavs from resisting if the Germans used their territory. He would not invite the British until the Germans invaded Bulgaria in preparation for an attack on Macedonia. Clearly, by that time it might be too late for an expeditionary force to be effective. This delay may have been fatal.[6]

By 31 January, Churchill's mind was ranging widely, and as usual well ahead of British capacity to act on his desires. Obviously he was concerned that the Germans would occupy Bulgaria and threaten Macedonia and Yugoslavia, hence his instigation of the Greek venture. Turkey was to be offered inducements to resist German threats, and part of that was British occupation of the Dodecanese islands, for based on them the Luftwaffe could cover the whole eastern Mediterranean. In the other direction, he wanted Benghazi to be opened as a port to reduce the calls on the Royal Navy for supplying the Desert Force. The Benghazi airfields were also to be used to support Malta, which was such an important element in keeping the Mediterranean open to British shipping.

On 22 February, the Greek government finally accepted with deep gratitude the offer of HM Government to send an expeditionary force from Egypt. The British mission to Athens had not grasped the exhaustion of the Greek Army, although they understood that it would be withdrawn promptly, as they had asked, from the Bulgarian border and from Albania to occupy the Aliakmon positions against a German drive. The Germans moved into Bulgaria on 1 March. The 1st Armoured Brigade and one New Zealand Brigade could not be in position until the third week in March: the rest of the 2nd New Zealand Division and one brigade of the 7th Australian Division not before the end of the month. Unless the weather delayed their move through Bulgaria, the Germans were expected to reach the Aliakmon position before them. Then it was learned that the Greeks had not withdrawn from Thrace and eastern Macedonia to the Aliakmon position after all.

It is to misread events to think that the political march to the Greek venture could have been halted in favour of an apparent opportunity that had opened in the desert in January. Winston Churchill gave Anthony Eden, Dill and Wavell the option of withdrawing from it in February, but only Eden was in a position to take the initiative. 'Do not consider yourselves obligated to a Greek enterprise if in your hearts you feel it will only be another Norwegian fiasco', Churchill wrote. 'If no good plan can be made, please say so. But of course you know how valuable success would be.'[7] Whether the political advantages of making the attempt to succour Greece, encouraging the Yugoslavs to fight, and putting heart into occupied Europe, would outweigh the probable military losses had yet to be seen. What was clear was that the military fate of the British and the Greeks was sealed before the former landed. On 6 April the Germans invaded Greece and Yugoslavia. The evacuation of the expeditionary force began on the 24th.

To turn back to events in the Desert in December: it was a surprise when Compass, which had opened as planned on 9 December, not only threw the Italians out of Egypt but chased them out of Cyrenaica and back to the borders of Tripolitania, about 600 miles away over rough tracks and only one metalled road on the coast. Furthermore, the 4th Indian Division, the only infantry division in the initial attack near Sidi Barrani, was immediately replaced by the 6th Australian Division before the advance into Libya began, and switched to Ethiopia, where, with the 5th Indian Division, a South African and two East African divisions, it proceeded to defeat the Italians in that vast country too. The victory over the Italian army in Cyrenaica did not change Wavell's plans. Rather, it gave him time to conquer East Africa and to send aid to Greece.

Indeed, there was no discord between Wavell and his political masters on strategy. He had not disagreed when, on 10 January, Churchill signalled: 'Nothing must hamper capture of Tobruk but thereafter all operations in Libya are subordinated to aiding Greece.'[8] A difference between Churchill and himself was that the former could never resist exploiting an opportunity even if it meant over-extending his resources. Indeed, the overwhelming success in the desert delighted policy-makers in London, but also deceived them about British potential. It did not change their minds about Greece, because Wavell remained firm and Sir Anthony Eden, Foreign Secretary, was determined to keep the Axis out of the Balkans and to encourage the Turks to support Britain. Nevertheless, it gave rise to the myth of the opportunity lost in the desert because of Churchill's emotional attachment to Greece.

General O'Connor and his Desert generals lent legitimacy to this myth. With a small, boldly led, desert-trained, professional force, they had destroyed a large Italian army. The Italian commanders had been shocked and demoralized by the mobility of the British force that had isolated and destroyed their defence positions, although they were mined and wired. Their marching infantry, without transport or adequate anti-tank defences, became prisoners in huge numbers. Only their artillery fought well. The Matilda tanks of the 7th Royal Tank Regiment, which were comparatively well armoured and mechanically reliable, had demoralized the Italian infantry. However, by the time Tobruk fell, few Matildas were runners. Nevertheless, after a bold advance across an appalling stretch of desert, a tiny force then intercepted and destroyed most of what remained of the Italian army at Beda Fomm on the road south from Benghazi, on 7 February.

No army had ever effected such an advance in such conditions in so short a time. Everyone was elated. It was the first British victory of the war. General O'Connor himself believed that they could march on to Tripoli although, by then, petrol, ammunition and spare parts were lacking and wheeled and tracked vehicles were on their last legs. All that Desert Force needed was reinforcement to finish the job: Greece pre-empted that, but there was another factor in the calculation; the Deutsches Afrika Korps.

Exploitation seemed the obvious policy to the field commanders. To the men in London and Cairo who had to weigh strategic and logistical considerations in the balance, at that moment it was out of the question. Had they fully grasped the parlous straits to which the victorious army had been reduced, they would have been in no doubt. Nor did they realize that the German corps injected into the fighting in February could extract such a price for the over-extension of the British in the Middle East. In fact it was to render the desert flank insecure for the next two years and bring the British desert army down to earth.

In this second phase the German army changed the tactical balance, temporarily in credit, into a debit. The state of the account was never fully accepted by Winston Churchill and his advisers, perhaps because there was not much that they could do about a tactical situation that centred on items like the quality of the cruiser tanks with which the army was mainly equipped. They were mechanically unreliable, deemed poorly armoured and mounted an inadequate two-pounder gun with an inferior sighting telescope. New arrivals in Egypt had to be modified for desert conditions and the workshops there were at first inadequate. Furthermore, the desert army had to grow from the small and well-adapted professional cadre that was familiar with the desert and had defeated the Italians into a larger force of Dominion divisions and 'white faces' from England. The amount of training and battle experience they needed before they could win the desert campaign was under-estimated.

The inadequacy of the new units became evident when the 3rd armoured brigade and the support group, of the inexperienced 2nd Armoured Division which arrived in Egypt from the UK in January 1941, replaced 7th Armoured Division of the desert force, and relieved two brigades of the newly arrived 9th Australian Infantry Division on the Tripolitanian border in early March. They were soon plunged into a running fight with the 5th Light Motorized Division that had disembarked in Tripoli on 12 February, and the 15th Panzer Division that followed in March. Veterans of the campaign in France, neither division was experienced in desert fighting but proved better than the British replacements. They were backed up by the Ariete Armoured Division and the Trento motorized Division that had arrived earlier to form an Italian armoured corps. In negotiations with Italian staffs in Rome the Germans refused to accept that the British could not be halted before they reached Tripoli, as the Italian asserted. They reinforced the Italians on condition that their ally agreed to a forward policy.[9]

A principal difference between the two forces from early 1941 until the autumn of 1942 was in their armoured units. In March, the British 3rd Armoured Brigade had one under-strength battalion of light tanks, one equipped with Italian M 13 tanks captured at Beda Fomm, and one battalion of cruisers, with engines requiring replacement and chassis maintenance and spares after a long approach march to the Agedabia area. The elements of the 2nd Support Group that was with them contained one motor battalion, one 25-pounder regiment, the Essex Yeomanry, which had been in Compass, an anti-tank battery and a machine gun company. The fitter parts of the division had been earmarked for Greece. The rest faced the Germans, who had 70 light and 80 medium Mark III tanks armed with short 50-mm guns, anti-tank units with the long 50-mm and some infantry mounted in armoured half-tracks.[10]

Wavell learned of the arrival of the Germans two weeks after Beda Fomm, but did not believe that they were capable of a major advance. He thought that the scanty British force could still resume offensive operations when it was eventually reinforced. When the Germans advanced on 24 March, feeding on British mistakes and mechanical break-downs, and gathering momentum under the impetuous and daring command of General Erwin Rommel, the survival of the desert force was soon in question. By the end of April, Tobruk was besieged and the Germans and Italians were on the Egypian frontier. On 6 March, the Germans had invaded Greece and Yugoslavia, and the British expeditionary force evacuated on the 24th.

General O'Connor, the victor of Compass brought up to sort out the muddle, although not given command, had been taken prisoner. When the crisis in the Desert coincided with the retreat from Greece, the latter adventure appeared to have been a poor military invest-ment. Thereafter, Wavell and his successor General Claude Auchinleck had to balance other demands against those of the desert. After Greece came the defence and loss of Crete in May, then the securing of Iraq and Iran and the clearance of Vichy forces from Syria. With the Japanese invasion of Burma and the Far East they had to release formations at the end of the year 1941. The relations of the comman-ders-in-chief with Churchill were coloured by these strains and by the latter's characteristic prejudices. Churchill would not accept that a superiority of three to two in tanks was required to fight the Germans on even terms. He would never accept the tonnage of supplies required by divisions fighting 200 miles, or more, in front of railhead, or the time that it took to build up supplies for an offensive. Logistics was one of Churchill's blind spots.

Indeed, logistics was eventually the undoing of the Afrika Korps, for their troops on the frontier had to be mainly supplied from Benghazi and Tripoli. Nor was Libya a German priority once the Barbarossa offensive into Russia began on 22 June 1941. Churchill never accepted that a unit that had trained in Britain for a year, and looked smart and pleased with itself, could be found not battle-worthy on arrival in Egypt. So he was sceptical when Wavell and Auchinleck reported that the tactical standard of British units was inadequate and that there had to be a pause in operations to put that right. How was it that the Germans were so much better than the British at fighting in the desert, he asked?

Churchill's interventions, not always through his Chiefs of the Imperial General Staff, Sir John Dill and then Sir Alan Brooke, were prompted by his experience in the First World War. He was convinced that he was a great strategist and understood how to handle comman-ders. At the Admiralty in 1914 and 1915 he had over-ridden his First Sea Lord, Admiral Jacky Fisher, and fallen out with him over the

Dardanelles. Naval operations are more easily centralized than land ones, but Churchill took the view that Sir Douglas Haig had been allowed too much liberty as the commander of British troops on the Western Front. So, in the Second World War, when he was both war minister and prime minister, Churchill harried his field commanders, sometimes accusing them of over-caution and even of an unreasonable fear of the enemy. Alan Brooke successfully frustrated Churchill's interference over details, advancing facts remorselessly. They took his staff hours to provide, but he simultaneously advised his commanders-in-chief to appease Churchill as much as possible.

The second phase of the desert campaign had begun, as we have seen, when General Erwin Rommel arrived in February 1941 and virtually took charge of Axis forces on the Tripolitanian border. On 24 March he seized his opportunity to brush weak opposition aside, invested but failed to take Tobruk, and advanced to the Egyptian frontier wire. After an abortive summer battle called Battleaxe, instigated by Churchill, for which the newly formed Eighth Army was not ready, combined British, New Zealand and South African forces attacked in November in operation Crusader, under Sir Alan Cunningham, the brother of the C-in-C Mediterranean Fleet. General Auchinleck had by now succeeded Wavell. Crusader was a fluid and amazingly confused battle fought in an 80-mile square between the frontier and Tobruk. It resulted in the relief of Tobruk and another advance to the Tripolitanian border. Once more Rommel, after a reinforcement of tanks, returned to the attack in January 1942, advanced eastward and, this time, paused facing the British Gazala position, west of Tobruk. In May he defeated Eighth Army at Gazala, captured Tobruk and drove a confused Eighth Army back to Alamein.

Thus ended the second phase and Rommel's last success. His subsequent attacks against the Alamein position were repulsed and in October 1942 the Eighth Army's successful battle there began the long advance that took it to Tunisia, junction with an Anglo-American force that landed in Algeria and Morocco in November, and ended with the defeat of the Germans at Tunis and Bizerta in May 1943.

My purpose here is to explain why a remarkable series of battles, successes and failures, fought over about 900 miles of desert from El Agheila in the west ended at Alamein in the east with an apparent reversal of fortune in October 1942. It is generally said that there began at Alamein a series of successes which lasted, with minor setbacks, until the end of the war. That is too smooth a description of the fighting, for even when we invaded Northern Europe we had not mastered the important art of combining infantry, tanks and artillery, although our technique had improved. For we had to undergo a long learning process. To explain it we must go back into pre-war policy, pass through the years of learning in 1940, 1941 and 1942 and look at the army's performance by 1944. Even then we had not acquired equipment that was the equal of our opponent's.

7 The Armour Problem

The official historian, General Playfair, made the inferiority of British tanks a central factor in his account of the Desert battles. He interrogated technologists and combatants about the details of British and German tanks and wrote a concise appendix on the subject in volume III of his *History of the Second World War*. Surprisingly, few British commanders or regimental officers could tell him precisely how and when the Germans modified their tanks, nor were they informative about the performance of German anti-tank guns or their ammunition. Indeed, British Technical Intelligence in the Desert was months, years in some cases, behind events in the field. Nevertheless, commanders were aware of the shortcomings of their own weaponry in general terms. General Auchinleck frequently reported to London that the Crusader was mechanically unreliable and that its armour was easily penetrated by the German 50-mm anti-tank gun as well as the less effective (short) 50-mm tank gun. The slower Valentine infantry tank also suffered heavy casualties, although better armoured than the Crusader. Both mounted the 2-pounder whose performance was obviously inferior to the 50-mm, and neither had the equivalent of the Mark IV's 75-mm high explosive shell(HE).

Playfair wrote that their technical shortcomings did not explain satisfactorily British tactical failures in the Crusader battles (November 1941) or, in particular, Gazala (May–June 1942). Auchinleck, himself, was aware of this, although tactics and armaments were obviously closely related. In both battles, the aim of British commanders, 'the destruction of the enemy armour', was unexceptionable, but to achieve it their battle tactics had to suit their equipment. Both sides tried to destroy their enemy's armour to enable his static troops to be destroyed at leisure. The conception was the Mahanist idea of destroying the enemy's battle fleet. Indeed, desert and sea battles were similar. In parts of the desert the terrain allowed vehicles to move fast in any direction, making it possible to surprise or to be surprised by the enemy. Information from air and ground reconnaissance and radio interception played a large part in telling a commander the enemy's strength, location and movement, so that he could surprise him. The tactics of enticing opposing armour on to anti-tank screens or minefields, into positions where they might be taken in flank or be enveloped by a superior force, had naval parallels. The Germans used their superiority in anti-tank gun range and accuracy, and in tank armour, to apply these tactics more effectively than the British. Their tank ammunition included a round with an explosive charge which burned the opponent and made recovery useless. In combining infantry, field and anti-tank artillery with tanks, they were unrivalled. Although both sides avoided engaging in battle with half-filled petrol tanks, and preferred to place themselves between the enemy and their own supplies, the Germans took greater logistical risks than the British and sometimes paid a penalty. Indeed, the British depended on maintaining their tank strength by resupply and on outlasting the Germans' logistically. They would lose many tactical battles but remain in the field when their enemy had withdrawn exhausted. In essence, Crusader was decided by logistics.[1]

Their contemporary comments indicate that General Auchinleck himself, Lieutenant-General Willoughby Norrie who commanded XXX Corps in Crusader and at Gazala, and other senior officers understood the tactical problems their armour was set by panzer units only at the general level of a staff college directing staff 'pink ' brief. They understood, quite clearly, that unless they could win tactical battles the Desert campaign would continue to swing backwards and forwards and each phase would be determined by a combination of logistics and attrition. However, tactical successes required techniques, suitable for the equipments available, to be mastered at lower levels. The details of these techniques had accumulated in many experienced and fertile minds in the combatant units, for instance in that of Jock Campbell the gunner commander of 7th Armoured Division Support Group. But no one had collected the technical and tactical wisdom of individual units and applied them as rules of thumb for the whole army. Nor were the facts assembled in one place at one time. Above all the divisional and corps commanders had not yet managed to employ their formations to best advantage, given their shortcomings and assets. There never seemed to be time to fit the pieces of the puzzle together.

More time was certainly needed, as always in war, and the pressure from London to relieve Malta, and to take Tripoli denied General Auchinleck that luxury. But there were other obstacles in the way of a mature Eighth Army. Divided regimental provenance of armoured units, the Cavalry versus the Royal Tank regimental traditions, delayed the practice of a unified doctrine about the proper employment of tanks. The army's regimental system in general, with all its advantages, obstructed the co-operation of infantry, tanks and artillery. Not the least important of the obstacles it created, although not an insuperable one, was that anti-tank guns were handled by the artillery and latterly also by the infantry, rather than by the tanks.

All this, added to technical weaknesses, was taken for granted by commanders. But it was unspoken and hence commanders never stated clearly, in their plans, that they intended to exploit their strengths and avoid paying for their weaknesses. That required conceding their relative weaknesses and analysing them. The most obvious application of this concession was to exploit the strength of the artillery and to handle the tanks defensively. Instead, they emphasized tank combat and decentralized their field artillery, negating their advantage. Anti-tank guns were also decentralized, seldom operated with tanks, and were not used offensively.

Except for the arrival of the Grant tank in April and May 1942, and the issue of some 6-pounder anti-tank guns to the artillery, which allowed 2-pounder guns to be handed down to the infantry, not much changed between Crusader in November–December 1941 and Gazala in May 1942. In telegrams to London, General Auchinleck explained the lack of success of the Eighth Army at Gazala in June 1942. He admitted that they were amateurs fighting professionals and that they had to learn on the job. He asked for time, the one precious commodity never willingly given by one commander to his opponent. Auchinleck's despatch on the subject on 24 June 1942, after Tobruk had fallen, tried to answer Churchill's criticisms:

> As to accepting decisions brought about by enemy action, we will do all we can by improving our tactics and leadership to prevent their recurrence; but as you know we are trying to train an army and use it on the battlefield at the same time. We are catching up but have not caught up yet.[2]

In a signal to General Archibald Wavell on 23 June 1942 Auchinleck wrote:

> inferiority of material probably primary cause of defeat of our armour but inferiority of training and leadership also likely to have been responsible. We never get TIME to catch up and our leaders are mostly untrained by German standards and most of them have yet to grasp fully the principles of cooperation of all arms on the battlefield and of concentration of forces though we have done all we can to impress these on them. They have fought magnificently

but RAC have again lost confidence in Crusaders and one can NOT blame them....[3]

Indeed, Auchinleck's Eighth Army had arrived late at the post, its technical and tactical deficiencies having a common pre-war root. Not only was it then decided that the British Army would not again fight a great continental campaign against 'the big battalions' of the top military league, but that it would take third place to the Royal Navy and the Royal Air Force in modernization. Only in the last year before the war began was the Army warned for Continental-style warfare.

By 1939, it was late in the day to convert an army's theory about the shape of a future war into detail about how to arm and equip it. Ideally, as did the Germans in 1914 and again in 1939, you plan a war and you equip an army to fight it. In general the Royal Navy, the master-arm of a maritime power, had managed to do that. Even it made mistakes over its anti-submarine tactics and technology, over gunnery and armour, and over torpedoes and its air arm. At Jutland, the tactical battle was won by the Germans. The Royal Air Force was confused over the application of its bomber policy, failing to work out the detail of navigation to its targets, bomb design, and aircraft defence. The army began by ignoring the lesson of the final months of the First World War, and like the rest of the country maundered on about the horrors of trench warfare. The popular conclusion was that war should be avoided but if it came it would be defensive and static.

Some professionals saw the future differently. For them, the final year of the war from Cambrai, in November 1917, pointed the way to the future. The future lay in accurate, rapid artillery fire depending on survey, radio communications and air support, with tanks and infantry in armoured vehicles. Together, they would penetrate the enemy's front and cut the communications between his headquarters and his fighting formations. Thus far, the concept was excellent. But when it came to its application, the imaginative J.F.C. Fuller shirked the hard work of mastering the details of reconciling equipment and tactics. One of the problems of the Tank Corps in 1916–18 had been particularly obdurate. The infantry had been the master-arm and the tanks had to conform. A joint doctrine in which infantry, tanks, artillery, engineers and signals co-operated as equal partners never emerged. In the infantry, the idea of a tank as an armoured machine gun to support infantry going about its normal business died hard. In the cavalry, the idea of it as an armoured horse dashing through a gap in the front to pursue a broken enemy prevailed, even until late 1944.

There were some, particularly those like General C.M. Broad, who transferred from the artillery, who visualized tanks carrying field guns and machine guns to destroy opponents in a dogfight in or behind his defended zone. Overall, there was a divide between a naval concept, in which tank fought tank using guns which fired armour-piercing shot, and tanks as infantry support.

By 1939 the gun on the battle tanks was the 2-pounder, primarily designed to destroy other tanks. The naval, armoured horse concept was dominant. But as a static, defensive war seemed likely, an infantry tank carrying machine guns and a 2-pounder with heavy front armour was built. For infantry support a high explosive shell would have been more suitable than the 2-pound steel divot, but time, resources and ideas were against it . The 'battle' tank was called a cruiser and was comparatively fast. Cruiser models were given the prefix A and reached the A 15, or 'Crusader II', in 1941. The infantry or I Tank, represented by the Matilda in 1940, was obsolescent in 1941 and was being superceded by the slightly faster Valentine. In 1939 a Vickers light tank was also in service both in Europe and the Middle East.

Despite confusion about the employment of their tanks the British situation in May 1940 was comparatively promising. The 2-pounder could penetrate the front armour of German tanks, and the front armour of the Matilda could resist any German anti-tank gun except the 8.8-cm Flak, which was not yet deployed as an anti-tank weapon. After the fall of France in June 1940, the Germans tested their standard 37-mm anti-tank gun against the Matilda and found it wanting. Sensibly their main battle tanks, the Mark III and the Mark IV, were designed so that they could mount progressively more powerful guns in their turrets. The Mark III received a 50-mm gun firing a $4^1/2$-pound shell. An anti-tank version of this gun had a longer barrel and higher muzzle velocity. This gun was mounted in the Mark III (Special) which appeared in the Desert in May 1942. The Mark IV already carried a short 75-mm firing high explosive, and in 1941 it received a longer 75-mm 'special' capable of firing anti-tank or general purpose high explosive shells. It appeared in the Desert in June 1942.[4] The flexibility of German organizations as well as design allowed them to build a series of self-propelled assault guns on the same chassis as their tanks. These were not universally successful when they reached outlandish size but their use signified the way artillery, infantry and panzers worked together as a matter of course. German infantry guns were also a development that demonstrated a joint approach to tactics as well as a practical use for field guns. They were used informally by the British and Australians in Tobruk, but never became official.

Unhappily, the British lost nearly 700 tanks and 850 anti-tank guns in France and Belgium in 1940. It is true to say that technically, they never recovered.

> The cry was now to rearm rapidly for home defence, for which purpose cruiser tanks, whose speed and mobility had been so well exploited by the Germans, were wanted in preference to I tanks. But production cannot be switched about at a moment's notice, and the choice was not between a good tank and a better one, but between a fairly good tank and no tank at all. The result was that some of the armoured divisions had to be rearmed with I tanks. Similarly it was decided to persist in the manufacture of the 2-pdr tank and anti-tank gun, even though this meant delaying the production of the 6-pdr [which was ready to go into production in April 1940].[5]

The mechanical weakness of the cruiser series, and the Crusader in particular, was the subject of a special enquiry under Mr C.R. Atlee in the spring of 1942.

> The finding was that the Crusader had been pressed into production before the pilot model had been adequately tested. The situation had called for haste, and speedy production was essential; it had been obtained at the cost of mechanical reliability and fighting efficiency.[6]

British tank deficiencies were the result of pre-war neglect followed by wartime haste. The tank is a complex production. A reliable engine, a hard-wearing chassis which is easy to maintain, and a convenient fighting chamber go a long way towards making it dependable. The American Sherman, which became the allies' main battle tank from late 1942 onwards, satisfied in those respects. But there was much more to creating a very good fighting vehicle. The quality of the armour and its positioning, the capability of its gun and sighting telescope, and the versatility of the ammunition are other major considerations. In these respects the Germans led throughout the war. In the Desert, British commanders were not only informed tardily about German developments but were unable to counter them in Cairo workshops when they learned of them. They received no practical assistance from the UK, where tank programmes were not altered to suit Desert experience, perhaps because production figures would have suffered.

Among other considerations, the design of a tank must achieve a good compromise between adequate engine power, armour, speed across country, range, gun-power, bridge category (size and weight), silhouette and the vision of the crew when closed down. Effective armour cannot be as light as is desired. A particular round of ammunition cannot suit all purposes. In short, it is impossible to design a perfect, all-round tank. A comparison of the much-feared Tiger Mark VI panzer with the Sherman illustrates this point. Almost invulnerable and carrying a dauntingly effective 88-mm gun, the Tiger was slow, difficult to maintain and could never have accomplish advances of up to 100 miles in a day, which the Sherman could achieve on its tracks, and be ready to fight. But the latter was termed 'The Tommy Cooker' because it burned easily, did not have an effective gun by the final standards of 1944, and suffered disproportionately at the hands of Panther Mark Vs, Mark IV and Mark III Specials. In fact, the balance of armoured power between the Germans and the Allies did not shift markedly between 1941 and 1944. In 1944, as in 1941 and 1942, the Allies depended on numbers and replacing enormous tank casualties. In other words on attrition.

The armour of tanks in the Second World War was measured by its hardness and its toughness. The Brinell scale indicated its hardness, which was its capacity to resist deformation. Toughness is armour's capacity to absorb energy before fracturing. The thickness of armour was a rough indication of its capacity to resist penetration at the normal, so sloping armour obviously gave better protection. Face-hardening was designed to shatter an anti-tank projectile, but if the projectile had an armour piercing cap (APC) it was better able to withstand shattering and to shatter face-hardened armour. The energy of an anti-tank round at impact is represented by mass times velocity squared, and a ballistic cap will help to maintain the velocity over a longer distance. The struggle between armour and anti-tank guns was continuous from 1940. Yet it was a surprise, the implications of which were only tardily realized in the Desert in March 1942, when the Germans attached face-hardened plates at vulnerable points of their tanks in late 1940. These plates shattered the 2-pounder solid shot that had no cap (APC). Later, 30mm of face hardening was incorporated with the homogeneous section of the armour, bringing the thickness to 50mm. The plates were then dispensed with. This second modification reached the Desert late in 1941. Tests in 1942, when the American Grant had come into service, showed that the Mark III H (additional plates) broke up the 2-pounder at all ranges and gave protection from the 6-pounder and the Grant's 75-mm at anything over 500 yards. After a second hit, the bolts on the plates began to shear. However, the Mark III J, with its integrated 50-mm armour, obviously did not suffer in this way.[7] Spaced armour, in the form of a separate 20-mm plate began to appear on Mark III J Specials in July 1942.

A depressing fact about the Crusader II [A 15] of which there were 278 at the start of the Winter Battle, in November 1941, was that its 50-mm homogeneous (tough but not face-hardened) armour could be easily penetrated by 50-mm projectiles.

> The Middle East was very worried about the time taken to match the improvements made by the Germans, let alone get ahead of them. They urged that the 6-pr should be provided with the best possible ammunition, but were told that although this was in hand, neither (A) piercing (Capped) nor ballistic capped shot would be available for the 2-pr and 6-pr until 1943.[8]

At the start of Crusader, in November 1941, neither the generals nor the men in units were as clear about the details of German superiority as appears here. However, from the results of previous battles they knew that their anti-tank artillery and the armour of their tanks were inferior and that a 2:1 or at worst only a 3:2 advantage in numbers of tanks was required to give them an even chance of success in an attrition. Excluding light tanks, with guns less than 37mm, and early cruisers, the British started with 445 tanks in XXX Corps, which contained the armoured brigades. The Germans and Italians had 320.[9] In addition there were 132 Valentines and Matildas in XIII Corps and about 100 cruisers and Matildas besieged in Tobruk. For the intended tank battle XXX Corps had a 4:3 superiority but overall it was 2:1.

The object of the 'Winter Battle' (Crusader) in November 1941, was to relieve Tobruk, and then advance into Tripolitania. The method was to destroy the German 15th and 21st Panzer Divisions and the Italian Ariete armoured division. The force besieging Tobruk would then be destroyed followed by the static defenders of the frontier positions in the area of Sollum. The armoured battle would be fought by General Norrie's[10] XXX Corps consisting of the 4th, 7th and 22nd armoured brigades and the two brigades of the 1st South African division. The rear of the corps would be protected by the 22nd Guards Brigade. The 22nd Armoured Brigade had arrived in Egypt from the UK on 1 October and had just received all their A 15 tanks from the ships and the workshops, where modifications were made, on the 23rd.

It was generally agreed that no less than three months was required to train formations for desert battle. Lieutenant-General A.R. Godwin-Austen's XIII Corps, with the 2nd New Zealand and 4th Indian Infantry Divisions supported by the 1st Army Tank Brigade would mask the Axis frontier defences and then advance up the Trigh Capuzzo to relieve Tobruk. A break-out force from Tobruk would come from the 70th Infantry and the 32nd Army Tank Brigade. A tar-macadam coast road carried most of Rommel's supplies but the Tobruk garrison had forced him to build a by-pass round the town, climbing the first escarpment at El Duda (Map 6), passing below Sidi Resegh and the aerodrome at El Adem before returning northwest to the coast road west of Tobruk. Rommel had deployed his panzer divisions east of Tobruk roughly between Gambut and Sidi Azeiz preparatory to taking Tobruk from the south-east in order to relieve his supply problems and clear his rear for an advance into Egypt. The Ariete was at Bir Gubi south of El Adem.

Brigadier Howard Kippenberger, who fought with 2nd New Zealand Division until he lost a leg when temporarily in command at Cassino in 1944, believed that British failures were tactical rather than technical. As editor of the New Zealand official histories he told General Playfair that errors in presenting corps to battle led to expos-ing British technical weaknesses. Put another way, the battle plans did not assume these weaknesses and take the necessary precautions. This was the case in Crusader. Lieutenant-General Sir Alan Cunningham, Eighth Army Commander, planned to advance XXX Corps to Gabr Saleh to entice the Panzer divisions lying between Bardia and Tobruk into a fight. XXX Corps was also to protect the left flank of XIII Corps as it advanced up the Trigh Capuzzo towards Tobruk, a task allotted to 4th Armoured Brigade, equipped with the light General Stuart tank, called the Honey. It had a 37-mm gun firing a capped AP round. In Norrie's opinion these two roles conflicted. He was correct.[11] Nor did he believe that a 'winner take all' armoured battle would result from his establishing his armour at Gabr Saleh. He con-sidered it essential to force the enemy to attack by seizing ground vital to him. Gabr Saleh did not fit that description. The obvious ground was the triangle of features on the escarpments south-east of Tobruk, namely Sidi Resegh, El Duda and Belhamed, from which the by-pass could be dominated. He planned to have his three brigades within supporting distance of each other in that area. This idea was agreed, but then the engagement of the 4th Armoured Brigade on the right and a task given to the 22nd Armoured Brigade, to attack the Ariete

86

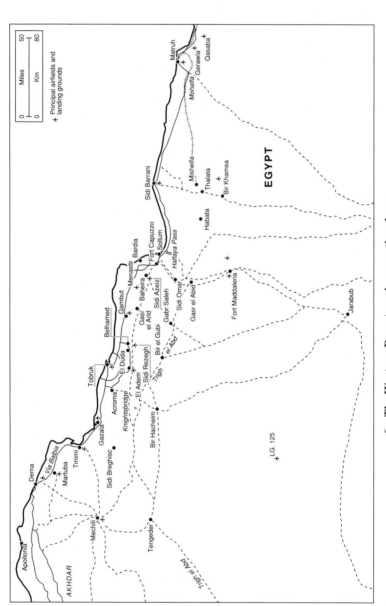

6 The Western Desert: main operational area

Division at Bir Gubi on the left, split the corps. The result was that initially only the 7th Armoured Brigade in the centre would be available to attack Sidi Resegh.

A confused series of engagements took place between 19 November and 10 December, by which time the centre of gravity of the fighting had moved west of Acroma before the enemy withdrew to Agheila. In remaining in control of the extended battlefield, which was about the size of East Anglia, the British had won, albeit not decisively. The enemy withdrew in his own time and the British did not dictate the course of the battle at any stage. Willoughby Norrie had this to say about it:

> There has been no spectacular tank battle with the whole of the armoured forces of both sides engaged at once. Nevertheless, the enemy's armour has been reduced to a mere skeleton of its former proportions. This has been achieved not by superior weapons or superior armour, for the enemy had better of both. It was the man in the tank and the man behind the weapon that won a succession of smaller combats. Bit by bit with wonderful gallantry and dogged determination, he wore down and destroyed the enemy forces.[12]

In other words, it had been a battle of attrition. Its course was confused and there were times when it seemed to be lost. Its centre was undoubtedly the Sidi Resegh triangle to which 7th Armoured Division tanks and support group returned after being ousted from parts of it several times. The charge that British armour fought in penny packets, turning to the assistance of isolated infantry brigades, such as the 5th South African and 6th New Zealand Brigades, instead of concentrating on German armour, is not sustainable. The senior commanders maintained the aim of winning the vital ground and breaking the siege of Tobruk, although when the battle was virtually won, they failed to exploit their advantage. On the other hand, when General Cruwell, commanding the DAK, could have won the battle of the triangle decisively, he was turned aside by Rommel who – thinking he had finished with the threat to Tobruk – embarked on a wide sweeping raid to the frontier region. Rommel hoped to panic the British into withdrawal and to relieve his own garrisons cut off there. It was a badly organized mission, and although it certainly created a stir, to the extent that General Cunningham considered the withdrawal of XXX Corps behind the frontier wire, it lost him the battle. While he was absent, XIII Corps' advance up the Trigh Capuzzo brought the New Zealanders and the 70th Division into the triangle and gave the battered armoured brigades time to recover tanks and reform their squadrons. Finally, the DAK and Ariete had to re-take their positions at considerable cost in order to fight their way out of the loosely confined box between Bardia, Sollum and Tobruk, leaving the battlefield and their own Axis frontier garrison to the Eighth Army.

In saying that the aim of winning the vital ground was maintained, I have skipped over a conference called to consider continuing the battle on 23 November, when Rommel started his raid to the frontier. Brigadier Galloway, BGS 8th Army (Later Lieutenant-General Sir Alexander Galloway) described the scene.

> There was a beaten feel about 8th Army and 30 Corps had been 'shot up like a covey of partridges' – although the individual birds i.e. 7 Armd Div were in very good form.... The Crusader battle was eventually largely won by 13 Corps action aided certainly by the efforts of 7AD .... Although the relief of Tobruk was incidental to the original conception, it became the necessary condition for any further success. Godwin Austin had to plan it. He became the opposite number to Rommel. His was the plan to relieve Tobruk and eventually his was the corps that did the trick.... Pretty soon [describing Cunningham's performance] the Army Commander gradually ceased to control the battle. He was, I regret to say, the opposite of Rommel. He retired to his caravan and eventually, quite rightly, to Alexandria, I am sorry to say, but not in time. The conference was one of the efforts to convince the Army Commander that all was not lost.[13]

On 25 November, when Rommel's raid was still creating a crisis of confidence, Auchinleck removed Cunningham and appointed his own Deputy Chief of Staff, Neil Ritchie, to command the Eighth Army. Ritchie was in Auchinleck's hands and was unfamiliar with the capacities of his new subordinates. He was not a desert warrior and found himself at odds with those who had firm ideas about how to handle the DAK. Crusader was anything but a set-piece battle from D + 1 onwards, and its day-to-day conduct was really in the hands of Godwin Austin, Gott, Jock Campbell and a handful of experienced lower commanders in 7th Armoured, 2nd New Zealand and 4th Indian Divisions.

It remained to be seen how future battles would be conducted with the uncertain hand of Ritchie at the helm, Auchinleck leaning over his shoulder and a rather insubordinate group of generals questioning their orders.

The casualties on each side reflect the attritional nature of the battle. Of 65 000 Germans, 10 100 were missing, 1100 killed and 3400 wounded. Of 54 000 Italians, 19 800 were missing, 1200 killed and 2700 wounded. Of 118 000 British and Commonwealth, 7500 were missing, 2900 were killed and 7300 were wounded. Thus the totals were 38 300 Axis and 17 700 British and Commonwealth casualties. As for tanks, there were about 500 British battle casualties and breakdowns by 12 December and 340 Axis. Of these figures, probably half were recovered and repaired.[14]

8 The Gazala Battle

In Crusader, the British commanders maintained their aim of taking the vital escarpments on which lay the features Sidi Resegh, El Duda and Belhamed. They were the key to victory because they dominated the Axis road around Tobruk. General Cruwell drove XXX Corps off them and might have won the battles for them finally had Rommel not drawn his panzers away to the frontier, where he achieved nothing and lost many tanks. XIII Corps re-occupied the escarpment. After the relief of Tobruk it appeared that the British had an opportunity to destroy what remained of the DAK and the Italian force between Bir Gubi and Gazala. But their technical and tactical inferiority in the battle had cost them dear and they were unable to exploit their success. Only one armoured brigade, the 22nd, was fit to accompany Godwin Austen's XIII Corps in the advance to Agedabia. It attacked the DAK right flank in the last week of December, was mauled in two actions, in which it ran on to anti-tank guns and was counter-attacked by tanks and infantry, and had to be withdrawn to refit. Apparently it had learned nothing from a headstrong attack it made against the Ariete at Bir Gubi on the second day of Crusader. Indeed, in the middle phase of the desert war, from Crusader to Gazala in May and June 1942 (Map 7), the commanders failed to concentrate their three armoured brigades and to co-ordinate the work of the field and anti-tank artillery, the motor infantry and the tanks.[1]

22nd Armoured Brigade was replaced by the 2nd Armoured Brigade of the 1st Armoured Division and the support group. Like 22nd Armoured Brigade, the other brigade in the division, which arrived in Egypt in October 1941 and was immediately committed to Crusader, 2nd was rushed up to the desert before it was acclimatized. It was intended that it and the 4th Indian Division should attack Rommel's position at Agheila in early February. However, in January, Rommel's tank strength was doubled when two convoys containing tanks arrived at Tripoli and he seized his opportunity to attack first.

At Agheila, the 1st Armoured Division received Major General F.W. Messervy, formerly commander of 4th Indian Division, as locum for Herbert Lumsden, who had been wounded in an air attack on 22nd Armoured Brigade. Not to make his name as an armoured leader, Messervy was, nevertheless, an experienced soldier with plenty

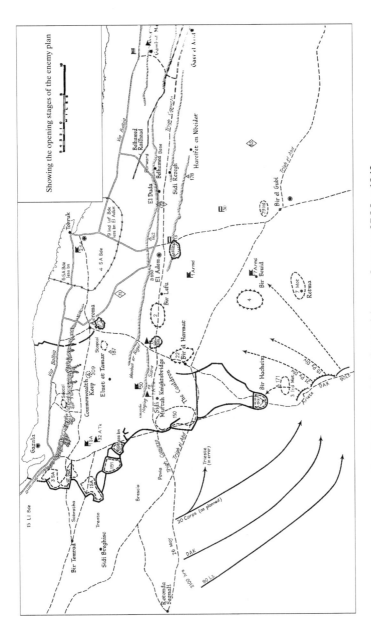

7   The Battle of Gazala: positions at dawn on 27 May 1942

of guts. He, Brigadier C.M. Vallentin commanding the support group, and Godwin Austen, commander XIII Corps, recorded the events that caused the second retreat from Mersa Brega to start on 21 January and end at Gazala in early February.[2]

On their arrival in Egypt in December, the newcomers were treated to a few alarmist stories about the desert fighting but also to the un-varnished truth about Crusader. They were soon disabused of the idea, current in the UK, that it had been a great victory. Brigadier G.M.O. Davy, commander 7th Armoured Brigade, told Vallentin that his tanks had been outgunned and most of them had been destroyed around Sidi Resegh. He roundly condemned the 2-pounder gun on his tanks. Herbert Lumsden, who had flown out ahead of his division, told Vallentin that co-operation between the armoured regiments and their supporting arms 'was not all it should be', and that the perform-ance of the armoured regiments was disappointing, particularly in gunnery. But Vallentin noted that although Lumsden expressed himself as 'keen on co-operation', to him 'the Division' meant the armoured brigades. Lumsden sent 2nd Brigade up to the desert to train alone, leaving Vallentin's Support Group to follow when it was ready. There was already a general view, strengthened after the next battle at Gazala, that the infantry was a liability, and that armour was failing because it was made to move hither and thither to protect it, instead of being committed to its main job of destroying enemy tanks. The truth had not yet penetrated that, whichever side attacked in the recent battle, the defenders inflicted disproportionate casualties when their artillery and infantry were properly co-ordinated with tanks.

GHQ's administrative staffs handled the arrival of 1st Armoured Division in the Middle East disgracefully.[3] The division needed to assemble equipment and vehicles and start desert training urgently, but an apparently disinterested Movement Control staff saw no reason to give anyone priority in 'the system'. It required a determined search to find the ships carrying their equipment; their existence sometimes denied by the staff, although ship's names and serial numbers were quoted to them. After 10 days of battling against obstruction, Alastair Beattie, commander of the Support Group Signal Squadron, discovered the ship containing the headquarters' essential armoured command vehicle and all the headquarters signals vehicles. He had, himself, to track down a suitable crane to unload it. The ordnance staff intended to deliver the division's own vehicles and equipment from the UK to depots and to replace them with others from store, which they alleged had been modified for the desert. Much of this transport proved to be on its last legs, the vehicles having been stripped of every tool and spare. Calibrated and lovingly maintained gun sights and other technical equipment had to be protected from acquisitive ordnance officers. The Second Battalion, the 60th Rifles, being alerted to this danger, intervened in the unloading of 50 trucks containing all their wirelesses just in time to save them from being consigned to an ordnance pool.

The work to be done before a UK division moved up to the desert may be likened to preparing for a major expedition. It might be months before anyone had a roof over their head again and most personal kit had to be left behind in store under the guard of soldiers who had been medically down-graded. A great sorting-out of the essential from the merely desirable took place. Practice vehicle-loading parades weeded out anything that might overload vehicles and cause them to break down or get bogged in soft sand. Wheeled vehicles had to be 'desertized' by fitting radiator condensers, sand mats or tracks, brackets for spare petrol and water cans, and by cutting holes in cab roofs for aircraft look-outs. For the long journey to the Tripolitanian border at Agheila, each unit loaded one day's vehicle, three days' reserve and three days' hard rations in hand. The basis of the ration was bully-beef, stew, cheese, biscuits, jam, tea, sugar and powdered milk. Grey, dusty and slightly mouldy loaves of bread were sometimes included. Water amounted to three days' reserve plus three days' in hand at half a gallon per day for all purposes including radiators. Petrol tanks were full and 100 miles' reserve and another 100 miles' in hand were in cans. Supplies were to be turned over at depots on the route so that the above amounts were in reserve or in hand on their arrival at the Tripolitanian frontier.

Desert navigation was practised before departure. Navigation was done by compass bearing and distance and checked against the occasional natural feature and barrels marked with eight-figure map references. So odometers on vehicles and compass variations were tested and drivers drilled to check tyre pressures frequently. Like a sea convoy, units moved in extended desert formation with about 150 yards between vehicles – this used less space fore and aft than a column and facilitated control. On moving into closer night laager, vehicles were driven into the same relative positions, as in Roman camps, in order that they could be found in the dark or in a sand storm. Listening posts were placed outside the laager with a few weapons and a telephone. There was a drill for breaking laager in an emergency. Radio batteries were charged at night and the noisy charging engines, or 'chaw horses', were usually banished to the adjacent desert.

An irritating extra chore was absorbing a new radio telephony (R/T) procedure and a map reference code, neither of which had been used in the UK. Complicated lists of frequencies and call signs were changed, each on different days, and a useless, from the point of view of security, Eighth Army code for items such as petrol – described as dairy – and commanding officers – big, little and super melons – had to be learned. All of this, and the vehicle modifications, should have been effected in the UK. That they were not illustrated the lack of liaison between Home commands and the Middle East.

The Support Group moved off on their long march on 26 December bound for Matruh, the Egyptian frontier and then the Libyan Desert. After a pause for vehicle maintenance and fresh orders, on what was to be the battlefield of Gazala at Bir Harmat, west of Tobruk, they found bad going east of Bir Tengeder on 5 January en route for Antelat. There were varieties of bad going and each had to be treated differently. Ridges of soft sand were tackled in low gear at high speed, or avoided by a diversion. Hummocks, common and difficult for wheels, were steered around and sometimes tackled in column. Rocky ridges were often impassable unless a tenuous track snaked round the boulders. Sudden winter and early spring rains reduced low-lying salt pans to glue-traps, or simply created mud. Learning to avoid getting bogged and having to dig out were acquired arts passed on from driver to driver. It could often make the difference between life and death, or at least between being taken prisoner or escaping from a pursuing eight-wheeled armoured car. Lack of experience in desert movement showed up the UK pale-faces when compared to the dusty, brown-faced 'desert types' that 1st Armoured Division met on arrival at Mersa Brega.

A slewed grid between map sheets was a hazard of desert navigation, and desert gunnery as well. Near Tengeder there was a difference of five degrees between adjacent sheets of the 1/500 000 map. The normal method of ordering a march bearing was to measure it off the grid and convert the angle to magnetic, adjusting it for compass error and magnetic variation before issuing a compass bearing for every vehicle. On this occasion, care had to be taken not to put the grid slew on the wrong way. To avoid that hazard you could give out the magnetic bearing instead of leaving the conversion to the unit navigators.

In the march up to the desert, 2nd Armoured Brigade's tanks were carried by rail 180 miles to Matruh. Then they motored 500 miles on their tracks from Matruh to Antelat. As can be imagined, they arrived in a sorry state, with many left to be recovered along the route. Only 80 miles' of petrol remained in the brigade at Antelat. At this time petrol containers were 4-gallon flimsies and as much as 40 per cent of their contents leaked or evaporated before they were delivered. Later, robust $4\frac{1}{2}$-gallon 'Jerrycans' were copied from the DAK. The brigade strength was about 78 cruisers and 54 Stuarts. It was as well, then, that it remained in reserve to train and to reconnoitre the German defences, rather than closing up to the Mersa Brega line between Agedabia and Agheila. The 1st Support Group took over there from 7th Support Group, commanded by the famous Jock Cambell. Campbell was about to receive a Victoria Cross for his exploits at Sidi Resegh.

Like the 7th Support Group, the 1st Support Group was formed into four Jock columns whose role was to harrass the enemy but not to stand and fight, for the Group had only a composite squadron of 24 Stuart tanks, apart from field and anti-tank guns and two infantry battalions. The 200th Guards Brigade on their right, near the sea marshes, also deployed four columns, but it had only two battalions in the brigade, one of which was divided between the columns.

Soft sand and large and closely spaced camel thorn humps made the German position at Agheila difficult to approach on wheels. Anti-tank and field guns, towed by wheeled vehicles, could not easily be brought in and out of action, and certainly not under fire. 1st Support Group had 170 Fordsons, which had a weakness in the transmission and lacked spare assemblies. Their tyres were largely Firestone, which generally burst before they had completed 1000 miles; spares were unobtainable. The Humber armoured cars and carriers of the 12th Lancers and the King's Dragoon Guards were, in any case, on their last legs, but the former's had, perforce, been fuelled at one time with high octane petrol which had virtually destroyed their engines.

The armoured car observers did not expect the enemy to attack and consequently were less alert than they ought to have been about German activity indicating reliefs, withdrawals, reinforcements, or a major attack. Before that attack came, Messervy withdrew all but a squadron of the cars to re-organize and repair their vehicles. That certainly increased the likelihood that the Support Group and the Guards would be surprised if the DAK attacked. GHQ should have warned the Eighth Army that Intelligence, actually received from Sigint sources, Y Service and Enigma decrypts, told them that the Axis convoys that reached Tripoli in December were known to have carried tanks and that two more in January brought vehicles, ammunition and material 'of great importance to the DAK'. In fact Axis tank strength had risen from 90 to 173 by 17 January. Like the armoured car observers, the minds of the Deputy Director of Intelligence's (DDMI's) staff in Cairo were not open to the idea that Rommel might attack. They over-estimated the effects of Crusader on the DAK and the ability of inexperienced Eighth Army troops to maintain the initiative. They were insufficiently concerned with the problem of supplying the Eighth Army so far from its base, and they did not grasp that its numerical strength did not equate to its fighting value. Indeed, they were about to attack what they wrongly believed to be a greatly weakened enemy.[4]

With that in mind, Messervy's address to some of Vallentin's troops on 16 January, five days before Rommel attacked, is not so surprising. 1st Support Group War Diary records that he told them: 'Future operations will be rather like a practice camp; there will be little action and it will be boring. Enemy is short of transport and the object is to destroy one or two vehicles every day and to keep his tail down!' 'Future operations' meant the next two or three weeks after 16 January. In February the Eighth Army would attack down the road with 4th Indian Division and effect a left hook with the armoured division. An insane plan to land the New Zealanders from the sea in the rear of the Agheila position had been dropped.

The DAK operation that started on 21 January was a pre-emptive strike designed to catch the British before they had built up their supplies and reinforced. Major F.W. von Mellenthin, Rommel's senior intelligence officer, calculated that for two weeks from 12 January, the Axis would be stronger than the British and intercepts told him that they were short of supplies. DAK would also be stronger in the air. The Italians agreed only to a spoiling attack but when the attack was successful, Rommel determined to press on for as long as he was able. On the 23rd Rommel's command was renamed *Panzerarmee Afrika*.[5]

Rommel recaptured Benghazi and swept 1st Armoured Division and 200 Guards Brigade back to Gazala but the withdrawal did not become quite the débâcle of March 1941. Churchill was angry at the loss of Benghazi and its airfields because it endangered Malta again. The operation was badly managed by General Ritchie. Although he had not been told about Rommel's intention and capability because of DDMI's mistake over relative tank strengths, he was unwarrantably optimistic about the outcome of his own offensive. He had been unwise to keep a comparatively large force forward because it consumed supplies at a time when his own plans depended on building them up. When the Axis advance split his force between the 4th Indian Division in the Benghazi–Jebel area and the units withdrawing from the Mersa Brega line across the desert towards Mechili, he countermanded Godwin Austen's order for the former to retire from Benghazi and instead ordered them to counter-attack, on the grounds that Rommel had divided his forces and that his northern thrust was weak. He was wrong because Benghazi was Rommel's main objective. Brigadier H.R. Brigg's 7th Indian Infantry Brigade suffered casualties attempting to obey Ritchie's order, but they were fewer than they might have been because Briggs broke out southward and escaped through the desert back to Mechili. Godwin Austen objected to being overruled, asked to be relieved of his command and, when XIII Corps reached the Gazala line, was replaced by Strafer Gott, recently the commander of 7th Armoured Division. The Eighth Army could ill-afford to lose one of its seasoned leaders.

From believing that his enemy was weak, Ritchie now doubted whether he could hold Gazala or Tobruk. He planned to make the frontier his base for the next offensive. If that was the plan, then the supplies being built up in Tobruk had to be evacuated lest they fall into the hands of the Axis. This was begun. Godwin Austen wrote:

> The Army Commander informed me that it had been decided that a strong position should be prepared by 30 Corps on the general line Bardia-Maddalena ... and that I must at all costs, hold the Gazala position for at least one month. I replied that I hoped it might be found possible to regard the Gazala position as supremely important and to decide not to relinquish it unless compelled as it denied Tobruk to the enemy. But he said it was doubtful whether resources would permit it.[6]

On the day 4th Indian Division occupied the Gazala position, 4 February, Ritchie reassessed the position because the commanders-in-chief ordered him to hold the Gazala position as a base for a counter-stroke to retake the Cyrenaica airfields. Auchinleck was being pressured from London to attack as soon as possible but he insisted that he must have a 3:2 advantage in tanks. Whether that meant battle tanks actually in armoured divisions or included I tanks, tanks in workshops and in reserve, or even in convoys on the way, was argued tediously between Cairo and London almost until Rommel settled the matter by attacking on 26 May. Auchinleck was also distracted by German threats to his northern front on the Turkish and Iraqi border and in Syria, and Japanese advances which caused him to send the 70th Division and the 7th Armoured Brigade to Burma. But Churchill considered the relief of Malta to be the central issue and kept nagging Auchinleck to attack even if the latter was not satisfied that the conditions for success existed.

The status of Tobruk, the fall of which in June was to cause so much pain to Churchill, presented Ritchie and Auchinleck with a problem that neither solved. Tobruk lay at the edge of the battlefield of Gazala, as it had in Crusader when Rommel was in danger of being struck in rear by a division with tanks debouching from there. This time Rommel was determined to eliminate it before moving to the frontier. Admiral Cunningham told Auchinleck that the Navy could not support a siege again; the Air Force could not provide it with air cover and Auchinleck was not prepared to lock up at least a division in its defence if it were invested. Hence his equivocal order to Ritchie on the subject in early February:

> It is not my intention to continue to hold it once the enemy is in a position to invest it effectively. Should this appear inevitable, the place will be evacuated, and the maximum amount of destruction carried out in it, so as to make it useless to the enemy as a supply base. In this eventuality the enemy's advance will be stopped on the general line Sollum–Fort Maddalena–Jarabub.[7]

Auchinleck made it appear that Tobruk was to be held if possible, but not necessarily. That only made sense to the commanders if Gazala were to be held temporarily, as Ritchie had first intended. But when it was decided to fight at Gazala and mount a counter-stroke, Tobruk had to be fully stocked. According to Auchinleck's instruction, if Rommel won the battle at Gazala, Tobruk's supplies and its harbour were to be destroyed to deny him their use. In practice, there would be no time to do that before Rommel invested the town. Nevertheless, supplies stopped flowing out of Tobruk and began to pour in again on a big scale. A railhead and supply depots were built near Belhamed. As Tobruk was vulnerable to an enemy movement around the south flank of the Gazala position, it had to be garrisoned. 2nd South African Division, a division not deemed ready for mobile desert operations, was put into it. Auchinleck did not admit to Churchill that the fate of Tobruk depended on the outcome of the battle at Gazala until it actually fell on 21 June. With the booty of Tobruk Rommel was able to reach the gates of Alexandria.[8]

What was the general plan for meeting Rommel's offensive? Postwar letters to General Playfair do not make it clear what individual commanders thought was Rommel's plan. They did agree that he would swing round the southern desert flank, possibly attacking Bir Hacheim on the way, or crash through the centre on the line of the Trigh el Abd, where the 150th Brigade of 50th Tees and Tyne Infantry Division, held an isolated defensive 'box'. It was less likely that he would attack along the coast road. A map exercise at HQ XIII Corps, at which Ritchie was present, decided to cover the first two options. The armoured divisions should be placed within supporting distance of each other, the 1st on the Trigh el Abd to counter the centre thrust, the 7th south of it to counter the outflanking option. The recently arrived 3rd Indian Motor Brigade was located south of Bir Hacheim, in Rommel's probable path. The 7th Motor Brigade (ex-7th Support Group) operated freely as Jock columns to watch and report on enemy movement round the southern flank and to harass his supplies. It was based on the Retma Box, a half-completed defence position about midway between Bir Hacheim and Bir Gubi. Gott's XIII Corps held the fixed defences from Gazala to the Trigh el Abd and the area including El Adem and the railhead outside Tobruk, for which a separate brigade was allotted. Norrie would fight his armoured divisions as a corps with the object of destroying the enemy armour which consisted of the 15th and 21st Panzers, the Ariete and the 90th Light (ex-5th Light) Division.

Gazala was a battle that ought to have been won when Rommel placed himself in a potentially losing position after 48 hours. The DAK and Ariete swung round the south end of the Gazala line, surprised and overran 7th Armoured Division, threatened Tobruk with the 90th Light Division but was loosely surrounded in the rear of the line in what came to be called 'The Cauldron', where his supply echelons had to run the gauntlet of Jock columns and armoured units as they tried to follow him. At that stage he was short of supplies and 15th Panzer Division was out of petrol. An ill-co-ordinated and unsuccessful attack was mounted against him after a delay on 5 and 6 June. He then broke the 150th Infantry Brigade in their isolated, but well-mined defensive 'box' of XIII Corps, and was able to resupply the DAK through the gap created. After that he had interior lines and was able to destroy the armoured elements of the Eighth Army piecemeal. Hacheim fell on 11 June. When Rommel divided his forces to attack El Adem while containing the armoured brigades around Knightsbridge on 11 June, XXX Corps made a final attempt to destroy the panzers in the Cauldron. Rommel concentrated in time and destroyed 105 tanks, about half of the armoured brigades' total. The fall of Tobruk and the retreat to Alamein was then inevitable.

The British commanders who fought the battle were not impressive. Ritchie had not commanded in battle until he was elevated to replace Cunningham during Crusader. He was then under Auchinleck's thumb, but influenced by a syndicate of forceful subordinates. His recent management of the retreat from Mersa Brega had been faltering. Willoughby Norrie, the large, jolly cavalryman commanding XXX Corps, had delegated the important decisions in his first battle, Crusader, to Strafer Gott, then commanding 7th Armoured Division. Gott was a strong personality and the only experienced desert warrior in the top command after Godwin Austen had been sacked. At Gazala he commanded XIII Corps. Gott thought little of Norrie and had a firm hold on Ritchie. During the battle he tried to get Ritchie to sack Norrie for not co-ordinating the actions of XXX Corps and for allowing it to fight dispersed. Yet Gott himself was not ruthless and single-minded, like Jock Campbell. He was too kind, treating his soldiers with affection and care. At Gazala he allowed the South Africans and the 50th Tees and Tyne Division under his command to be defensive when he ought to have insisted on their acting offensively. Agar Hamilton, the South African official historian, knew Gott and was familiar with the South Africans in Gott's corps:

> Gott's personality was so powerful that it dominated everyone he met – and yet he was totally incapable of handling an operation. He exercised an overpowering influence over Ritchie and it would not be too strong to describe him as intriguing against other commanders. Ritchie's ADC during the Gazala battles remembers Gott coming back to his car, with Ritchie, and the latter agreeing that 'Norrie will have to go.' I feel that Norrie's inertness during the Cauldron affair was due to the fact that he felt he was being continuously by-passed. This draft (Playfair's Volume 3) makes it abundantly clear that the Eighth Army had no commander.[9]

When Auchinleck was fighting on the Alamein line in July, Hamilton wrote of Gott and Ramsden:

> In those later attempts by Auchinleck to counter attack, the chief impression I get is the nervelessness of Gott, and when Ramsden replaced Norrie, the two corps commanders made a sorry pair. My mind vaccilates between the belief that Gott really grasped his own incompetence but felt it his duty to go on, and the conviction that he was perfectly happy with the way things were going.[10]

Alan Brooke, the CIGS, noted in August, when he was with Churchill in Cairo to appoint new commanders in the Middle East, that Gott's wife said that he was exhausted, as he may well have been by then. 'Gott, though, had the confidence of very many people'.[11]

Ritchie wanted Gott to use his two infantry divisions and the army tank brigade to attack the Italians opposite him. But Gott was unwilling to do so or to persuade the commander of 1st South African Division, the cautious Major-General D.H. Pienaar, to act. He did not keep Ritchie informed of this and Ritchie misled Auchinleck when he signalled:

> 50 Div and 1 SA Div are already operating against his line of communication and this is being intensified by using Valentines as well. Over the last two days these divisions have got some 350 pw ... I believe a thrust by 1 SA Div due west is the right action and this is to start tonight.[12]

Major-General W.H.C. Ramsden, then commanding 50th Division, disliked Pienaar because he refused to take over more line when Ramsden had to extend his southward to support the Free French at Bir Hacheim under Brigadier-General M-P Koenig. He blamed Pienaar for the defeat of his 150th Brigade, which was isolated. Indeed, Gott allowed that to happen without, apparently, being aware of the German attacks. Koenig was another awkward commander who refused re-supply by 7th Motor Brigade under Brigadier Renton, when he had decided and demanded that he be allowed to withdraw from Bir Hacheim, although holding it a little longer would have greatly increased Rommel's supply difficulties.

The two armoured division commanders performed poorly. Messervy, recently appointed to command 7th Armoured Division, had handled a mixed force of infantry and tanks in Battleaxe, in June 1941. As commander of 4th Indian Division he was an experienced desert fighter but he was unused to the pace of armoured warfare. Jock Campbell had just taken command of 7th Armoured Division when he was killed in a car accident. Most people agree that had he been alive the battle might have had a different outcome. Although Messervy had warning of Rommel's advance round the left flank he was surprised by it and taken prisoner temporarily and his 4th Armoured Brigade was overrun and dislocated. He blamed Norrie for not allowing him to move to his battle position because Norrie did not believe Rommel's main thrust was heading his way. The isolated 3rd Motor Brigade was a hostage to fortune, but it could have avoided trouble by moving deeper into the desert until Rommel's force had passed and then closing in behind him to hunt down his supply columns. When 7th Motor Brigade was dispersed as a group of Jock columns, 7th Armoured Division was denied its support group, although its columns warned the Eighth Army in plenty of time what was coming. A fabian policy of denying Rommel the opportunity of engaging isolated regiments and brigades and then fighting XXX Corps as a unit when Rommel ran short of supplies, seemed to be implicit in conclusions of the XIII Corps conference. Norrie did not have the personality to impose his will on his commanders and fight a corps battle along those lines.

Herbert Lumsden was in his first battle with 1st Armoured Division. He had not trained the division and had been absent, wounded, in their retreat from Antelat. He was inclined to question his orders and was not a good team man. When 4th Armoured Brigade was overrun in the first hours Norrie told him to send 22nd Armoured Brigade to help them. Lumsden's Commander Royal Artillery, Frizz Fowler, was scandalized when Lumsden ordered his GSO1 to impose maximum delay in obeying the order. Lumsden felt that Messervy had got into a mess and he was not going to send good money after bad by rescuing him. Later, he fell out with Montgomery during Alamein because he would not accept that armoured divisions were designed to fight for ground with all their arms combined, and not simply to break through a gap like First World War cavalry.

Perhaps it is not surprising that opinions varied about the abilities of the commanders. Gott, particularly, had his strong supporters. The commanders certainly failed their units by employing them in penny packets. And yet it may be justifiable to argue that the battle was lost because of poor unit tactics and gunnery. Tactical mistakes made at that level added up, and across the front led to the Eighth Army's defeat. We shall examine this thesis in the next chapter. Here we shall be concerned with operational mistakes made by the commanders.

The principal error, as in Crusader, was fighting the tanks as though they alone were the decisive arm. This error had not been eliminated when the Second Army fought in Normandy. At Gazala the field artillery generally fought in single batteries, often in Jock columns. Its slugging power as divisional artillery was not exploited. Armour advanced or withdrew without using the 2-pounders with which most motor battalions were by then equipped, or the newly arrived artillery 6-pounders – most of them dispersed among the field artillery. Motor battalion officers came out of the battle angry and frustrated by the inability of armoured commanders to learn from their past mistakes. One motor battalion officer remarked that he was never allowed to put his anti-tank gun trails on the ground and fight. Put baldly, the lesson was that, with inferior tanks, XXX Corps had to place reliance on the guns and the infantry that defended the guns. Casualties to 25-pounders performing as anti-tank guns were high, usually because the tanks were elsewhere. Field guns were overrun by mixed forces of panzers, among which were Mark IVs firing high explosive from hull-down positions, and infantry carried forward in half-tracks. The guns should not have been fighting for their lives without support from the other arms. Field artillery was seldom concentrated to fire high explosive at the enemy's anti-tank guns, which should have been carefully located, his panzer grenadiers and the runners that moved from tank to tank with orders. The present writer recalls the 2nd Armoured Brigade watching 50 odd panzers and supporting troops for most of two days without firing a shot at them. He was reprimanded and then laughed at for firing 50 rounds of gunfire from his battery (400 25-pounder shells) at them in sheer frustration. We shall never know what damage they did, but they forced the enemy to withdraw.

The 6-pounder anti-tank gun was a new factor on the British side since the winter, but when the battle started XXX Corps had only 40 per cent of its establishment of guns and had had insufficient time to train with them. The Grant tank with its sponson-mounted 75-mm gun firing HE and solid shot was a considerable addition to the armoured regiments' fire-power. 4th Armoured Brigade had two Grant squadrons out of three in its regiments and the other armoured brigades had one in theirs. They did considerable damage in the first two days but the regiments had only been equipped in the month before the battle started on 26 May, and the crews were learning as they fought. Their high explosive ought to have placed Axis anti-tank guns in difficulties and been useful for supporting the motor battalions. Their range certainly surprised the Mark III crews who, nevertheless, still knocked them out in large numbers with the long 50-mm anti-tank gun and 88-mm guns.

Eighth Army Intelligence developed in June and July but it was not of great service in the Gazala Battle. The Enigma source, except Chaffinch, the German Army's Enigma key, was too general and sometimes too late to help in the tactical battle. It gave reports of German tank states but that was more expeditiously provided by the Army's Y service, which gained in reputation as its information proved correct. Y gave a fairly clear report on the location of Rommels divisions just before 26 May, whereas other sources led the Eighth Army to think that the attack would come in the centre, or even in the north. Unfortunately, the inability of the armoured divisions to win their battles even when informed of *Panzerarmee* intentions nullified the tactical value of Sigint. Intelligence staffs seemed uninterested in the number of Mk III and Mk IV Specials that were arriving. On 7 June Cairo was informed that the ratio of Mark III and IV standard tanks to their Special versions was 4:1, but the Eighth Army did not pick it up until 10 June and then it only stated that 'Mk III and Mk IV specials' had been established as being present in Libya with reasonable certainty. On 31 July an Enigma return reported that the ratio of new to old-style tanks was 1 to 1.[13]

This account makes it clear that the Eighth Army was still a poorly trained and equipped force. The idea of an armoured division of one armoured brigade and one motor brigade had been introduced after Crusader but not put into practice. Regiments were not familiar with their new tanks. The distribution of the new anti-tank guns was incomplete and those in action were not used closely with armour unless the field guns were so employed. And, as we have seen, command relationships were upset by Ritchie's uncertain grip on his subordinates and his pupilage to Auchinleck.

All these uncertainties may explain the conclusions of the Middle East Defence Committee about the military situation just before Rommel attacked. By 29 April, decrypts indicating that Rommel would attack Tobruk 'from May onwards' had been confirmed by Enigma.[14] On 9 May, under renewed pressure to attack Rommel in order to relieve Malta, which had been neutralised by air bombardment and was threatened by invasion, they stated that 'Malta was not vital to the security of Egypt, and while the recovery of Cyrenaica could not guarantee the early revival of Malta's offensive capacity, a premature offensive against Rommel would entail risks in Egypt more serious than the loss of Malta'. In fact, the Defence Committee stated, if the enemy could be induced to attack them, 'it might very well be the best thing that could happen'.[15] Their assumption, one only warranted if the Eighth Army were defending prepared positions and using appropriate tactics, was that the attacker would lose more than the defender. In view of the *Panzerarmee* strength of 637 tanks against the Eighth Army figure of 718 in the armoured divisions (including 1st Armoured Brigade) and another 276 Infantry tanks, a defensive battle was essential until the *Panzerarmee*'s strength had been reduced. Unfortunately, Ritchie did not follow Auchinleck's advice to him on 20 May:

> I consider it to be of the highest importance that you should not break up the organization of either of the armoured divisions. They have been trained to fight as divisions, I hope, and fight as divisions they should. Norrie must handle them as a Corps Commander, and thus be able to take advantage of the flexibility which the fact of having two formations gives him.[16]

However, the divisional artillery had been broken up into a regiment for each brigade group and the motor brigades were not fighting with their relevant armoured brigades. 7th Armoured Division had no motor brigade. Furthermore, there were four armoured brigades, if 1st armoured Brigade is included, rather than the two which satisfied the new organization to which Auchinleck referred; that is, one armoured and one motor brigade in an armoured division. It seems that Auchinleck did not know that only the worst elements in his reform (the brigade group unit) had been adopted, and that the armoured divisions were not trained to fight as divisions.[17]

9 Fighting

> One of the perpetual optical illusions of historical study is the impression that all would have been well if men had only done 'the other thing'. (A remark of Herbert Butterfield quoted by Major-General Playfair in his correspondence on Volume III of his *History of the Second World War: The Mediterranean and Middle East*)

The memory of combatants is a shaky foundation on which to reconstruct the course of battles, particularly ones as confused as Crusader in November and December 1941 and Gazala in May and June 1942. Playfair's staff, armed with a mountain of written and oral information from participants, admitted that they could not record unit engagements even if they had the space. They summarized the reasons for British failures in battle as command mistakes and inferior equipment. At the strategic and operational level from whicb they wrote they were correct. Had they been able to attend to battle tactics, criticized by Generals Wavell and Auchinleck in their despatches, they could have clarified their conclusions.[1]

In this chapter I shall first describe the ambience of the campaign, then describe three engagements through the eyes of some of the participants in order to make specific connections between the tactical and operational levels of the fighting. The examples I have chosen are the German attack on Tobruk in April 1941, a fragment of the battles at Sidi Resegh the following November, and the disaster in the Cauldron at Gazala in June 1942.

Playfair's reading committee said of his first draft that he had not brought the colour and drama of the battlefield alive. They wanted his readers to sense the smells, sounds, sights and fears, the personalities and, above all, the comradeship which were the common backdrop to all our memories of combat. Poetry would have been a better medium than prose to kindle the imaginations of readers who have never been in the desert, let alone a battle.

There is a hierarchy of memories of the desert. Those associated with the senses are the most poignant, for they bind together all who served there, friend and foe alike. On spring mornings, even in the midst of a battle, we awoke to hear birdsong from the peace of a nearby wadi and the smell of burning sage-brush cooking fires. In battle there was the stink of cordite from opened breeches in gun pit and tank, and on the move the hot, acrid dust sucked into the back of 3-ton trucks filled our nostrils. We recall the grit between our teeth and the heat and claustrophobia as we waited for a yellow dust storm to blow away out to sea. And the taste of Maconichie's stew, as we stood by a fire at the end of the day eating from an aluminium mess tin, so hot that it burned our lips. An enamel mug of hot, sweet tea, brewed with salty, chlorinated water, accompanied it. The clank and squeak of tank tracks in the night and the hollow stomach when we thought that they might be approaching panzers; and the shivery feeling after 24 hours of battle without sleep.

In summer mid-afternoon, the heat-haze made observation impossible and both sides slept. It was also a time for talk and friendship, although one ear and eye remained alert. I recall lying heat-exhausted under a truck in the curiously angular country at the edge of the Quattara Depression during the retreat from Gazala: We had found a *bir* from which the column drank unwisely well after weeks on short commons. It was impossible to plumb the depths of thirst. The common incidents, even the most dramatic in our lives seldom passed from the handwritten lines of a letter in a historian's file describing it to the printed page of the campaign history.

For most of us a campaign history is remote. Reality was sitting up an observation pole in Tobruk when an 88 mm airburst sent us down the ladder helter-skelter, lest a second more accurate shell obliterate us. We survived, later to crouch in a derelict Mark III tank or to stand on the turret of our Honey tank, hull-down behind a ridge, directing a round of gunfire that might have ended someone else's life.

Social memories concerning comrades, leaves, food, home and family are commonest. In Territorial units men had known each other in peacetime, all their lives perhaps, and confidences about the home-town were exchanged after listening to the BBC evening news on a No. 11 wireless set.

Christmas in Tobruk

There were six of us that Christmas
(and a war was on in the desert),
A wireless set, six Englishmen the crew;
By the truck two aerial masts,
Gaunt fingers, pointing skywards,
Strained eager at the guy-ropes,
Quivering ....
Within

An atmosphere of home, warmth and light;
The pipes glowing,
Cans of beer (good honest English brew),
Carefully hoarded, ready for the day,
Eked out with captured cognac.
There was food too –
No turkeys or plum-puddings,
But a biscuit potage
Bubbling on the Primus
Flavoured with apricot jam;
And the sandwiches – sardines from sunny Portugal,
Inevitable bully, persistent, omnipresent,
With cheddar from Australian grasslands
Thick spread on wholemeal biscuits;
And the nuts, too –
Valencia almonds,
Ripe, russet hazels insistently recalling
Rich autumn hedgerows at home.[2]

Unless they directly concerned events on the larger stage, Playfair had to pass by many minor incidents that would have added colour to his story. Cyril Joly's classic study of tanks in the desert, although fiction, describes fighting in a tank regiment better than any straight history. Every detail of daily life in his book, besides the battles, could contribute to the *History*. A seer, sitting under a tree in India, explained this to his pupil. Asked how the tree was created he took a fig and handed it to him. 'Open it,' he said. The pupil did so. 'What do you see?' 'Many tiny seeds.' 'Take a seed and cut it open.' The pupil did so. 'And what do you see now?' 'Nothing!' 'My son, that subtle essence you cannot see is the reality from which the fig tree sprang.'[3]

Moving up the scale, and nearer to featuring in the *History*, are particular, immediate, life-threatening situations. Those recorded later in this chapter are pointed, burned into the mind and never to be forgotten. The moment after the tank had been struck and before its inside became an inferno. The scramble to bale out and the moment of indecision whether to run or shelter from machine gun bullets behind the tank. Such a dramatic incident, when repeated 50 times in an afternoon, shorn of its personal tragedy, shock and terror, appears only in summary in the *History* to explain a battle lost. 'I was brewed up by a Mark III on the airfield at Sidi Resegh. Poor Trooper Dawson never got out,' Captain James recorded sadly. 'My brigade was destroyed at Sidi Resegh',

Brigadier Davy told Colonel Vallentin of 1st Armoured Division Support Group in Cairo, as he described the inadequacy of his tank guns and armour. When James' experience had been repeated several hundred times, it became a theme of the History of the campaign.

> As we came on
> that day, he hit my tank with one
> like the entry of a demon.[4]

Again, picture the total absorption of a gun detachment engaging advancing tanks. In a split second, a shell strikes the gun-shield and the crew are wrapped around the trail or thrown like bloody, rag dolls on to the green, ammunition boxes.

> Look. Here in the gunpit spoil
> the dishonoured picture of his girl
> who has put: *Steffi Vergissmeinicht*
> in a copybook gothic script.[5]

In a similar scene the British Number One of a gun survived to recall the event, and never to forget it. His was the last of the eight guns in his battery to be destroyed in the battle of the Cauldron. Earlier, in dawn silence, dew on the ground, men had walked past the guns to a battalion objective. There was the moment when the guns opened fire behind them, their shells humming close overhead, to fall on the objective ahead. How reassuring! Then the enemy woke up and their shells fell among the advancing infantry. Bodies slumped; mounds were left on the ground to mark the advance. Suddenly, machine guns opened up on them, not from the objective but from beyond it. The enemy was not where he was supposed to be. Looking round, a rifle-man noted that fewer men were walking forward beside him. Earlier, there was security in numbers; now, no friends were visible. That meant trouble, he thought.

In each of these episodes the soldier's awareness of others closed in a few notches. He was no longer concerned with the orders of battalion and company commanders let alone generals. He was one of a small group fighting the enemy personally. His training told him what to do, and how to avoid contributing to a statistic in the History books by becoming a casualty. It had taught him not to die for his country but to make the other poor sod die for his. It was a shock to find that the enemy had been taught the same lesson.

In the split second when he becomes a casualty his status changes again. He is no longer an active member of a team cut off from its neighbours; no longer sharing the action with his friends. He is alone. He is aware that he has not been here before; that he cannot share this new experience. It is his alone, even if others lie wounded round him. The shock of separateness, he feels, is a kind of death.

In the mythology of battle 'the soldier' is an abstraction, quite a different species from a civilian. That is wrong. A soldier, like a civilian, wants his military life to be familiar. A difference between the twentieth-century soldier and his predecessors is that he is a civilian trained to do things that no one in their right mind would do, were it not for a war. Training seeks to reinforce the better attributes of a civilian. That includes familial loyalty. His primary group, an infantry section or squad, a tank crew, a gun detachment perhaps, is his family. As long as its integrity holds, it protects him against outrageous fortune. His officer, in the soldier's judgement, should ensure that his group is committed to battle advantageously; that it will survive and win. He will protect it from unfair treatment by the sergeant-major, and from stupid orders from anyone. He will keep it informed so that it is not taken by surprise. He will deal with malingerers, so that the other soldiers' honest efforts are acknowledged. When there is a crisis he will cushion the shock by calmly doing what is necessary to restore the situation to normality. Montgomery was understood and liked by the rank and file because he fulfilled these functions in the army as a whole. As an admired figure whose team always won, he became a role model. Rommel was admired by the British and the Germans equally. The mistakes he made were unknown to the rank and file before History revealed them.

Were I to write only from the point of view of individuals, I would contribute to a myth by omission. A collection of memoirs from the Battle of the Somme may recapture the horror of a particular day and place, and even give a fair impression of the experience of an infantryman on any day between 1 July and 1 December 1916. But not the soldier in the ranks, the platoon commander nor the company commander was competent to describe the course of the battle, let alone contribute much towards its History. They could not connect their experiences with those in the many levels above them in the command hierarchy. In reverse, it may be said that in the Second World War commanders were more sensitive to the effect of their orders on their subordinates than were their First World War predecessors. But many division, corps and army commanders were looking through a glass darkly at the tactical anatomy of their battles in both wars. Ideally, historians should resect an event, to use a surveying word, from the various standpoints from which they and their subjects view it. A triangle of error between those views would still remain, nevertheless.

Combatants in units were not much concerned with doctrine or theory but with comfort, survival and overcoming their immediate opponents. In analysing their engagements, they were competent to account for the successes and failures of their primary group in terms of the compatibility of its equipment and tactics to its task, and with reference to the performance of the enemy. Such analyses are more trustworthy, when they exist, than manuals or post-battle summaries which are seldom written at the sub-unit level and are often influenced by hindsight. Unfortunately, low-level, after-action analyses are rare. Those intruders, death, wounds and time, usually prevent their being written. When found, they provide a valuable link between the operational and tactical levels of command.

Tactical lessons were learned as rules of thumb for the survivors who passed them on by word of mouth. A tank backs out of a firing position rather than turning its vulnerable flank or rear to the enemy, for example. Lives depend on many such drills every minute of the day. In contrast, operational mistakes, such as dividing forces in face of a superior enemy, were covered at staff and command schools, but continued to be made because a loud, rude voice on 'the blower' seldom belaboured brigadiers, let alone major-generals and above, when they made them. Furthermore, the tactical result of operational mistakes was not often immediately attributable. The advance of three regiments of tanks into the face of strong anti-tank defences in the cauldron battle on 6th June, 1942, was ordered by a senior officer. He was not immediately removed from command nor did his subordinates refuse to obey his orders, although at least one remonstrated. There is an account of the result in this chapter, but we do not know why such a foolish attack was ordered.

> The colonel in a casual voice
> spoke into the microphone a joke
> which through a hundred earphones broke
> into the ears of a doomed race.[6]

A mistake of the Afrika Korps provides our first tactical case. 5th Panzer Regiment under-estimated the capacity of the troops holding Tobruk in April and early May 1941. It had swept aside the inexperienced and poorly equipped elements of the 2nd Armoured Division at Mersa Brega and assumed that a frontal assault down the El Adem road on 13 April would be successful. When the Australian infantry lay low and let the tanks through, concentrated artillery and infantry fire stopped the German infantry from following them. Ahead, the tanks ran into field guns which stood their ground and cruiser tanks caught them in flank.

Their part in the German operations, which were divided into a reconnaissance in force on 11 April and a full attack on 13 and 14 April, was recorded by artillerymen of the South Notts Hussars (SNH) and 1st Regiment Royal Horse Artillery (RHA), and by Captain Rea Leakey of 1st Royal Tank Regiment. The South Notts Hussars had been rushed up to Tobruk (Map 8) just before it was invested on the 11th. Driving without lights, but in brilliant moonlight, they crossed the anti-tank ditch on the El Adem road by a mined causeway. Passing the fork roads at 'Charing Cross' they ran down over the escarpment into a monumental traffic jam caused by troops moving up towards them from the western, Derna road entry into Tobruk. They turned round and went into action between A/E and B/O batteries of 1 RHA in a regimental line of guns prepared to withstand an immediate tank attack. Nothing came of it, although firing was heard to the west.

The two batteries of the SNH redeployed on a wider front under command of the veteran 1 RHA with its desert-famous officers and men. Robert Loder Simonds, Peter Hemans and John Goschen 'a young star, brave and resourceful as a troop commander', and BSM Jean Batten of E Troop, among them. The German reconnaissance on the 11th was repulsed by the guns. By 13 April, two squadrons of 1st Tank Regiment, part of a mixed force of two regiments of cruisers and light tanks and a troop of Valentines, were in position behind them. The 1 RTR tanks had just arrived by ship from Egypt. The officers were largely strangers to one another. Rea Leakey recorded:[7]

> Noel and I drove our battered old truck down to the harbour and there we found the Regiment busy disembarking and still working like beavers on the tanks. When they had collected them from workshops in Cairo they found no wireless sets were fitted. Guns were still in crates and covered in grease, and many other items were lying in the bottom of the turrets. Whilst the ship was at sea the crews had gone down to the hold and started on the task of getting the tanks fit for action. There was no time to lose: as each tank was hoisted off the ship the crew seized upon it and the work went on.

The Germans had left six destroyed tanks behind after their attack on 11 April. On the night of 13 April a larger force of tanks broke

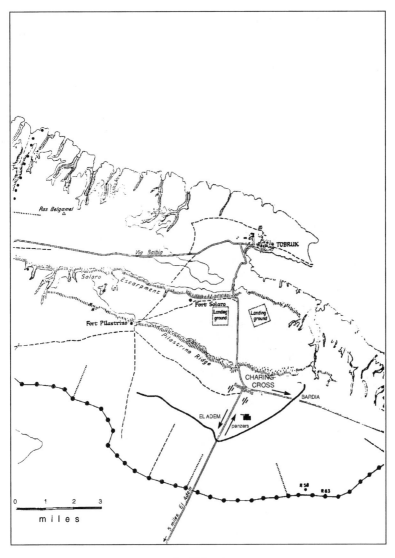

8 Tobruk

through the perimeter and lay up in a hollow about three quarters of a mile inside the wire until first light. The delay allowed the anti-tank guns of M Battery in 3 RHA and the 3rd Australian Anti-Tank Regiment to take up a position from which they could enfilade the Germans when they advanced towards the field guns at first light. 1st RTR were positioned to counter-attack. From the gun positions straddling the El Adem road the attack came in across the front and then turned towards them down the road. All the guns fired under the control of their sergeant Numbers One. That was usual, for the gun position officer seldom took charge once the firing started unless he saw tanks creeping up on the guns from a flank. A subaltern of the Chestnut Troop recorded the experience of his battery.

I spent the night at an Australian company headquarters and when the Gun Position Officer – Chilver Stainer – came to relieve me one hour before dawn it was clear that the enemy were up to no good; the anti-tank ditch on the perimeter seemed to be full of men and we could hear the noise of tanks. Chilver [Guy] clambered up into the OP, a wooden structure some 20 feet high on rising ground close behind the perimeter.

I made my way back to the guns, and had barely arrived there when he rang up. He said that about 20 or 30 tanks had broken through the infantry and had passed close to the OP. They were heading for our battery position. He had taken cover in a nearby well while they passed.

Peter Hemans, commanding A/E Battery, ordered 'Tank Alert', but although we could hear the rumbling of tanks it seemed an age before anything happened. At last six black objects huddled together in groups of three appeared to the right front of the Troop. It was still very dark and difficult to judge the range, but we set our sights at 400 and opened fire.

The first shot from No 1 gun set the leading tank on fire. No 2's first round lifted the turret clean off another tank – a good start, but we had stirred up a hornets' nest. Soon there were 15 or more tanks firing at us with 75-mm and machine guns. We scored hit after hit, but I fancy we put a number of shells into tanks that were already dead. During this period two officers – the only officers with the guns – and four other ranks were hit. The tanks were now working round our right towards E Troop. Just as our No 1 gun swung round to engage them, a 75 mm shell landed on the trail, killing all the detachment and setting fire to a box of cartridges. At the same time

1. Field Marshal Montgomery (then Lieutenant-Colonel Montgomery and Commander of the 17th Battalion of Royal Fusiliers), 1918.

2. Field Marshal Sir Douglas Haig with the Army Commanders, Generals Plumer (2nd), Byng (3rd), Birdwood (5th), Rawlinson (4th) and Horne (1st). Behind them are Generals Sir John Davidson, A. A. Montgomery-Massingberd, Sir Louis Vaughan and others. Cambrai, November 1918.

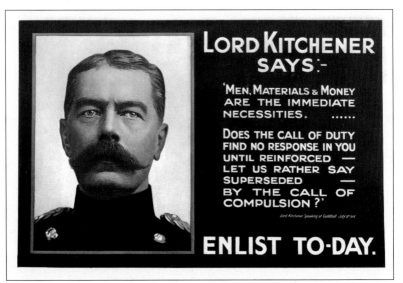

3. Kitchener of Khartoum – propaganda poster.

4. British artillery seen firing into the enemy's positions, December 1941.

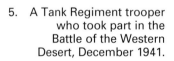

5. A Tank Regiment trooper who took part in the Battle of the Western Desert, December 1941.

6. A British artillery officer examining a German helmet which he found after the battle near El Gubi, December 1941.

7. Lieutenant-General Willoughby Norrie sending a message over the radio to his forward Commanders, 29 December 1941.

8. Major-General W. H. E. Gott, Commander 7th Armoured Division, being driven around Benghazi by Brigadier Jock Campbell, OC Support Troops, 29 December 1941.

9. General Montgomery speaking to Allied correspondents, June 1944.

10. A British Sherman Firefly of the 27th Armoured Brigade in action against enemy troops attempting to capture the Orne bridge near Ranville.

11. Royal Tiger.

12. British Generals' Conference, 10 June 1944. Group photograph after the Conference – General J. T. Crocker, Lieutenant-General M. E. Dempsey and Lieutenant-General G. C. Bucknall.

a gun of E Troop received a direct hit on the shield, disabling the whole detachment. The BSM ('Jean' Batten) although wounded, manned the gun himself and continued to fire. Nos 2, 3 and 4 guns were in great heart, and every time a tank was hit a cheer went up. For perhaps half an hour the battle continued thus; then gradually the firing slackened till all was quiet. The surviving German tanks had pulled back.[8]

Turning eastward, the tanks ran into the anti-tank screen and as they withdrew 1st RTR counter-attacked. When the German attack on 13 April started, Leakey had moved his five tanks forward on the left of the field guns, and found himself on the flank of German tanks that were held frontally by the solid shot and high explosive of the 32 25-pounders. Fortunately his own crew was experienced. Milligan, who was allowed to smoke in action, the cigarette stuck to his lower lip, was the gunner. He was a dead shot so long as he could smoke. Adams was the signaller and ammunition number.

'Loaded', yelled Adams, and away went another solid shot tearing at the thick enemy armour. The fumes of burning cordite made us cough, and our eyes watered and soon the turret was so thick with smoke that I could only just make out the figure of Adams as he loaded shell after shell into the breach. We were firing faster than ever before and so were my other four cruiser tanks.

It must have been a minute before the Germans spotted us and by then their tanks had received many hits from our shells. They appeared to panic because they started to turn in all directions, many of them turned about and started to return the way they had come. But then they were on to us and we could clearly see the flash of their guns. The tank to my left was hit several times and brewed up. I saw some of the crew bale out. Then another of my valuable cruisers went up in flames and there were three of us left. I noticed one man of the crew dragging himself along the ground, badly wounded, and machine gun bullets were hitting all around him. I felt I had to give him cover. It was a stupid move because when broadside on we were hit. Milligan was killed and we brewed up. With fire licking round our feet and the few remaining shells exploding we baled out. The front machine gunner died. A neat hole through the armour. The other was lying by the tank his right leg off just below the knee. I got the big lad on my back and with bullets flying got him back to a truck. They cut off the leg attached by a bit of skin. An ambulance took him back to the Tobruk hospital and he lived.[9]

Lacking their support weapons, because the German infantry had been almost wiped out by the Australians who surfaced and attacked them with the bayonet on the perimeter, the tanks retreated. The Stukas had been active during the attack but the guns continued to fire. Fortunately, many of the aircraft, which originated from El Adem airfield and could be seen taking off, bombed the harbour by mistake.

This engagement was the first serious defeat the Germans had suffered in the desert. The two engagements cost them 22 tanks out of 44 and the 8th Machine-Gun Battalion more than three-quarters of its strength. It ought to have taught the British the useful lesson that it was problematic for tanks to attack guns and tanks in defended positions without support from their own guns and infantry. But they made that mistake many times in the future with dire results.

* * *

Men emerged from their sleeping bags and blankets. Cooks lit fires and the smell of burning camel thorn mingled with petrol fumes as the first tank engines coughed and started. Chaw horses were switched off. Water in cut-down 4 gallon flimsies was put on fires to boil for tea. Bacon was unrolled from the oily paper in which it had been packed in brass-coloured tins, bread fried in the fat and beans poured into the mixture. A breakfast with beans and bread was a luxury that would not be enjoyed again in the next few weeks. But this was the first day of battle action. A circle of enamel mugs and mess-tins waited round the fire. Teeth were cleaned and half a mug of water used to wash hands and faces. Squadron leaders walked over to the CO's tank for orders while crews loaded bedding on tanks. Drivers checked their tracks. Three ton trucks off-loaded cans of petrol by each tank. Radios were switched on to listen-out for messages but wireless silence was in force. Morse, snatches of conversation and mush came from headsets dangling over the side of tanks. It was 19 November 1941 and the second day of Crusader was about to begin.

Squadron leaders returned and gathered their troop and tank commanders round them. 7th Armoured Brigade, commanded by George Davy, was to advance on Sidi Resegh, take the airfield and with 7th Support Group defend the area between the airfield and the escarpment to the north of it. That was to be the preliminary to lifting the siege of Tobruk from which the garrison was to break out to meet them. 15th and 21st Panzer Divisions were still to the east between Gambut and Sidi Azeiz on the Trigh Capuzzo. 4th Armoured Brigade had engaged elements of the panzers advancing towards Gabr Saleh the previous evening. 22nd Armoured Brigade was to take Bir Gubi occupied, it was believed, by the Italian Ariete Division. The three brigades, it appeared, were to fight separate battles. To experienced soldiers that seemed an obvious error. A cautious attempt to cover all the bases meant being strong nowhere. The initiative would be surrendered. Desert battles were won by concentrating against weaker targets and taking them by surprise. Confidence in the commanders was shaken. The old hands were apprehensive.

This was different from the spirit of Compass in December 1940, when risks were taken to keep the enemy on the run. But General Cunningham had no experience of the desert or of tank warfare. Willoughby Norrie had replaced Pope, an experienced officer who had been killed in an air crash, as commander of XXX Corps. This would be his first battle. Godwin Austin, commanding XIII Corps, had fought in East Africa with Cunningham, but he was to make good use of his brigadier general staff, John Harding, who was an experienced desert warrior.

7th Armoured Brigade Group had under command 2nd and 6th Royal Tank Regiment, and the 7th Hussars, Davy's own regiment, although he had started his career as a Gunner. He had about 130 tanks, being under-strength. In support were F Battery RHA and a company of the Rifle Brigade. They took the airfield that night and Davy placed 2 RTR and the 7H on the escarpment south of it and 6 RTR with F Battery and the Rifle Brigade company on the airfield. Jock Campbell, who commanded the support group, was put under Davy's command by Strafer Gott when the three men met on the captured airfield at about 9 p.m. on 19 November. Campbell's support group was not expected to arrive until the next afternoon, an avoidable delay which, once more, shook Davy's confidence – this time in Strafer Gott who commanded 7th Armoured Division. It meant that Davy would be short of the two motor infantry battalions, the anti-tank battery and the field regiment in Campbell's group in the meanwhile. Their absence was felt immediately.[10]

A regiment of the 90th Light Division advanced in section blobs directed by an officer riding on a white horse next morning. F Battery engaged them, but with no infantry Davy decided not to use his tanks, which was just as well as the Germans had pulled anti-tank guns up the re-entrants of the northern escarpment above the Trigh Capuzzo from which they could enfilade the airfield. F Battery's fire was so effective that the attack faltered and the leading companies fell back. The horse was not hit. Soon after this engagement the support group arrived, led by Jock Campbell in his famous staff car with its roof cut off. It was recognized everywhere. Gott was with him and ordered Davy to capture the northern escarpment and to join the 70th Division, which had broken out from Tobruk with El Duda, about two miles to the north of Sidi Resegh, as its objective.

At 11 p.m. on 20 November Davy gave out his orders to the COs. The two armoured regiments on the escarpment, with about eighty tanks, would remain to watch towards the south-east while 6th Tanks, the 60th Rifles and the Rifle Brigade attacked towards El Duda. The attack was to be at 8.30 a.m. next morning. This plan went wrong almost at once. At 8.00 a.m. 200 tanks were reported advancing from the south-east. The Germans did nothing by halves. The attack towards El Duda was to continue, for the Tobruk garrison was presumed, wrongly, to be just reaching it. 2 RTR and 7 H, with one field battery and J Battery of 2-pounder anti-tank guns, would have to hold off the two panzer divisions. Davy took command of this operation leaving Jock Campbell to command the northern one.

Both operations were disasters. 70th Division, delayed by hard fighting, did not put in an appearance but 6 RTR ran into a superior force and lost all but six tanks. It had been much the same story with the other tank regiments when Jock Campbell joined Davy on the southern escarpment. Davy recorded:

> About 4 p.m. however, I was with my three surviving tanks alongside F Battery's position when there appeared from behind me and half a mile to my left, a cut down car with Jock standing up and waving a blue flag, followed by the four or five remaining tanks of the 6th RTR. Jock behaved exactly like an umpire in the Kadir Cup, following a flushed pig until he was sure it was a boar of respectable size, followed himself by three competing spears, then dropping his flag and shouting 'Ride!'.

7th Armoured Brigade had been reduced to about squadron strength. The force that had started so full of hope was trying to deceive the enemy by bustling activity. In fact it needed time to gather up its crocks, take in reinforcements, join up with the other armoured brigades, and consider how it could do better next time. But it was just the situation in which Jock Campbell excelled in fighting a hopeless battle around the airfield, on which he was to win the Victoria

Cross, keeping up morale by small acts of aggression whenever and wherever he could collect miscellaneous guns, motor companies and troops of tanks. Davy recorded his impressions of his friend at this time.

> We concocted together the situation report we would send to the division headquarters. There was a simple code for telling them of our casualties, which was reasonably secure for short periods. The rest was done in clear over the radio. We had to put a brave face on things because of the enemy who could not help but overhear … . We could not show any signs of weakness … The message was the usual confident desert report: 'Situation well in hand.' The alternative would have been 'Situation in hand' which was actually understood to be rather more optimistic than with the 'well' inserted. But we did not feel all that confident. I had only nine, out of my original hundred and twenty-nine tanks fit for action, and all of these had been hit at least once. Both the Greenjacket battalions had had severe casualties. And we had seven hundred tough German prisoners to look after.[11]

As they moved south, a 'magnificent and closely packed German column, headed by a score or two of tanks, passed as it were under our tail,' wrote Davy. This gave Jock his opportunity. The support group was not far away and he saw the 7th Hussars, now cut off by the German column from Davy, engaging the enemy from the north. He sent over an officer to order the 7th Hussars to join him. Next, a battery of South African guns, ordered to join Davy, were seen to alter course 90 degrees to join Jock instead. 'Of course', remarked Strafer Gott, 'the character of the desert battles changes when Jock is not there.' 'Whenever he saw the enemy he threw everything at him, shells, bullets, tanks, trucks, men and he would have thrown the cookhouse utensils and his own boots as a last resort,' wrote Davy. He expected others to do the same.

> There are many different make-ups in people who earn a Victoria Cross. There are those who simply lose their temper and go wild; Jock was not one of those. There are those who do not experience fear; I think Freyberg was one of those, but I am not so sure about Jock. There are those whose self-control is such that even for long periods of exposure to fire they show no personal reaction to danger; I think Jock was one of them. In such conditions he was a shining example to everyone. If he had a fault it was impatience … when he could not wait if he had something to throw at the enemy.

When shells were falling round him and an officer of the 3rd Hussars, during one of Colonel Maletti's occasional excursions into the desert in the Italian period, Jock sniffed happily and said 'smells just like France in the last war.' The word 'happily' does not imply a smile. He did not smile much, although when being shot at he could look happy.[12]

*   *   *

The decisive engagement in the Gazala battle took place during the long days of 5 and 6 June 1942. The British aim was to crush Rommel's force in the Cauldron. The 30th Corps was to advance west from south of Knightsbridge using infantry to drive a wedge through the enemy's anti-tank screen in darkness. The armour would then advance through the corridor they had made into the rear of the enemy and close his escape route. XIII Corps would seize the Sidra ridge on the north side of the Cauldron and later advance westward to Tmimi. The attack went wrong. The enemy was further west than had been surmised, so that a very heavy bombardment and barrage fell on empty desert. The infantry was then counter-attacked and driven off their objective. The 22nd Armoured Brigade, believing that the protection of the infantry was not their business, did not intervene. When the armour advanced in the second stage it ran into the German anti-tank screen and suffered disastrous casualties. No single commander or headquarters was appointed by Norrie to control the battle. The airforce lacked a bomb-line and appeared to be unwilling to respond to calls for support as a result. Rommel, detecting the muddle in the Eighth Army, counter-attacked, captured Knightsbridge and, on 10 June, destroyed most of the rest of the British armour in the open desert to the east of it.

Before the battle, remembers Sergeant Raymond Ellis, a 22-year-old veteran in 107 RHA, South Notts Hussars, they had just fought off a tank attack in which guns were firing all round the 360-degree arc. There was a day's respite and then they were told to prepare for an advance to Derna. They were to discard all surplus kit, including drag-ropes, extra water and rations. He took no notice of the order remarking that only a lunatic would have complied. 'We'd got beyond worrying about the overall battle and took no notice of what people said was happening in the outside world; nor did you question orders unless they directly affected you. You concentrated strictly on your own job, on your detachment's survival.'[13]

There was to be a barrage for this battle which would start at 3 a.m. The worst parts were waiting for the battle to start and after it was over, Ellis recalled. The gun pits only had a few rocks around them because digging was difficult and tank attacks were expected, so deep pits were out of the question. No one had heard of 'the Cauldron' or 'Knightsbridge' at that time. This was just another battle. Ellis was physically tired and also tired of battles and the desert. He had been in the siege of Tobruk. His gun detachment were new to battle. 'They were obviously frightened. They were all so home-sick – seemed so young.' But he had passed that, although they were, most of them, older than himself. He was just war-weary.

You collected your firing programme. You had your lamp ready and your watch and then it was time to take-post. Everything was very quiet. Zero five, four, three, two, one fire! And the battle started. It was a barrage with lifts after every few rounds. Later he heard that the enemy had withdrawn so it all fell on empty ground.
  Cease Firing! Limber Up! Advance. It was very dark. Then we arrived at a crest and everything opened up on us. We had come up over the rim of the crater. The Numbers One are standing on the seats of their Quads, head out to watch out for holes and trenches. It is carnage. Fire everywhere. Dawn, and we continued to advance. The enemy shortened his range. It was like the Light Brigade at Balaclava. No one in the detachment was hit. But where else could you go but forward? In the end the GPO waved his hand pointing a flag to a flank, indicating 'guns into action.' It was a drill. We dropped into action and that was the last place that the South Notts Hussars fought. The Quad went back to the wagon lines.[14]

They fired all that day. There was a curved circle of ridge in front. They saw that they were in a saucer. You could see the tanks that had gone through the gun position with lorried infantry earlier, moving around on the ridge three-quarters of a mile away. Some of the infantry were Scottish, Ellis thought. He could see that a tank battle was going on up there. Solid shot buzzed past and high explosive overs landed close to them. Indirect fire support was given by the battery directed by orders from their OPs on the ridge. They were not told what they were firing at. They were under counter-battery fire from time to time. Nor did they know that they were in a dangerous position if the Germans occupied the ridge. Tanks came back to refuel occasionally, and then went forward again.

In the evening they heard the sound of approaching tanks but as the ridge was held they did not worry. Then they saw that they were withdrawing British armour carrying infantry. It appeared that they were deserting the guns. Someone called out: 'Where are you going?' 'Don't leave us here!' More infantry followed, some were in trucks and others marching. This went on most of the evening and into the night. It looked like a retreat. Then came the order that no one was to undress or leave the guns. It was very ominous. Raymond Ellis took his boots off and lay down.

At dawn on the second day, Captain Slinn and Lieutenant Geoffrey Timbs came round the guns. They said that the battery was to fight a rearguard. 'One of those last round sort of things. It was going to be hellish. There would be very few alive at the end of the day. Both officers were killed.' How did the youngsters on the gun take it? They were nervous but they did their job. The sun came up and nothing happened.

> Then panzers came forward slowly to discover where our tanks had gone. They edged towards us. Soon they made for us in attack formation. We had some armour piercing, 20 pound shot but kept them until the tanks were so close we could not miss. Otherwise we fired high explosive fuse 119 cap on and then 117, the more sensitive fuse used against infantry. The gap between each of the four guns of the troop was 30 yards. The guns actually opened fire together at about 600 yards, although each was under the control of its Number One. It was not an officer's battle until guns were knocked out and one of them replaced the wounded. There was no protection for the guns. Just a few shallow trenches for the crew.[15]

That first attack broke down about 440 yards in front of the guns. The panzers weaved as they withdrew because they were presenting their most vulnerable parts to the guns. Ellis still had 20 AP shot left. There had been no casualties on his C Sub but the troop had had some, mainly from the 75-mm of the Mark IV tanks. Cartridge cases were cleared away and shells were capped and placed ready for loading. A few more stones were piled in front of the guns and the trenches excavated a few more inches.

The next attack was similarly beaten off, the panzers suffering more casualties. In the lull the Germans brought up their artillery. Shells came down on the guns, particularly 88-mm airbursts. The detachments took cover in their 12" holes. There was the throb of aircraft and Stukas could be seen making for them. The aircraft banked and dived almost vertically overhead. A few trucks were hit and burned. The noise was terrifying. It seemed a miracle that anyone was left alive.

At about 9 a.m. the tanks came in again. This time they got very close and the gunners had to take post under shell fire. It took all their will to concentrate on one thing at a time. They hit a Mark IV in front and it caught fire. Ellis was watching it when suddenly he found himself in the air, spinning. He fell in a heap by the trail. The breath was knocked out of him. Immediately it happened again and this time he was stunned. He came-to kneeling by the gun which was upside down. It had taken two direct hits. He realised that the tanks had been pushed out again and more of them were burning in front of the position. The Cuneo painting depicts the scene accurately. He was covered in blood. All the crew were obviously severely wounded at the least. Then he saw that he was the only one alive. He got behind the gun and lay in a hole.

The 88-mm shelling began again. Slinn and Timbs were killed at this stage. He saw A subsection under a black airburst. It appeared that only numbers two and four guns were still in action. He went over to number one gun, and found it operable but the crew were all dead. Then other men started to appear to help him man the gun. They were command post staff and drivers. With their help Ellis went on shooting.

In the next stage the panzers were hull down and using their 75-mm to snipe at the guns. Stukas came in several times. The Germans marked their forward positions with purple smoke. Then the tanks got near enough to use their machine guns. By midday there were tanks behind them. One of these bracketed his gun. Crew members were hit but others kept coming to replace the wounded. A Royal Signals man appeared and was wounded; a Gurkha appeared and was killed. Ellis elevated the gun to fire at charge 1 at a tank hull down behind a ridge. Apparently he eventually hit it but his shells landed among the wounded where Harry Day, the medical orderly, was treating them.

That was his last shot. With the remaining crew member splattered against the shield from the machine gun of a tank 30 yards away, silence suddenly fell on the battlefield. It was all over. Ellis felt terribly thirsty. Looking around he saw his C Sub gun still upside down. The crew lying dead where he had left them. Then he burst into tears. A Mark IV tank commander, a sergeant, called him over from his turret. They looked at each other for a long moment and then both shrugged, eyes up to heaven; mute and mutual reaction to the carnage around them.

All of this was the outcome of the failure of the attack on the Afrika Korps which, after earlier disposing of the 150 Brigade Box, had prepared for the inevitable counter-blow from XXX Corps. But poor reconnaisance, lack of co-operation between infantry and tanks and the usual German anti-tank screen had disposed of the Corps' attack decisively.

Rea Leakey, had come up to the desert against orders, and joined the crew of one of his regiment's new General Grant tanks as a gunner. He recorded his experience in the disastrous tank attack that had gone in up ahead of the gun positions:[16]

A major tank thrust was to be launched against the enemy in the Cauldron, and never before or since have I known armour to be handled so badly. It shook my faith in the senior Armoured Corps commanders. Those responsible had been trained to handle horses, and in a few cases it took a year of war to convince these gentlemen that the day of the horse in battle was over. But, of course, I was only a gunner in a tank in this battle, and my knowledge of the larger picture was very limited. However, on this fateful day there were few who did not realise that we were being launched into an attack that was doomed to fail from the start. But ours was not to reason why.

Regiment after regiment of tanks moved up on either side of us and halted. Almost as far as the eye could see stretched this long line of tanks. We had artillery support but very little; as far as I can remember, our allotment was four guns and there was certainly no preliminary bombardment. Some two miles ahead of us the ground rose slightly, and then it fell away. It was here that the enemy awaited us, not tanks but many carefully concealed anti-tank guns. At least the plan was simple; this great line of tanks that stretched across the desert was to roll forward, crash through the enemy and on to the undefended spaces beyond. I remember my commanding officer protesting bitterly at the madness of this attack. He knew so well what lay beyond that ridge, but all he got for an answer was the sack.

At ten o'clock the long line of tanks moved forward and the roar of hundreds of powerful engines filled the air and warned the waiting Germans that we were coming. As I sat with my eye glued to the gunner's periscope I thought of my old gunner, Milligan, and silently prayed that I might shoot as accurately as he. Sergeant Adams was commanding the tank immediately on my right, and I wondered what jokes he was telling to keep his crew amused. The subaltern in command of my tank was nervous, and tried to conceal it by singing lustily. I checked the firing gear for the last time, and all was in order. The guns were loaded.

As we approached the crest of the rise, the order was given to speed up and the tanks on either side of us followed suit. But we were the first to reach the sky line, at least of those in our immediate vicinity, and as we came into full view of the enemy so the shells arrived. Clouds of dust and smoke soon blinded my vision and I never saw any of the anti-tank guns that now started to take their toll. In the first second we must have received at least four direct hits from armour piercing shells. The engine was knocked out, a track was broken and one shell hit the barrel of the 75-mm gun and broke it. Then quite a heavy high explosive shell dropped on the mantlet of my 37-mm gun and pushed it back against the recoil springs. That shell landed inches above my head but the armour plating held firm, and I suffered nothing more than a singing in the ears. But a splinter hit the subaltern in the head, and he fell to the floor of the turret dead. I found that my gun would not fire.

Almost every tank in that battle met with the same treatment, and the whole line was halted on the crest of that small ridge. I half climbed out of the gunner's seat so that I could see over the top of the turret, and the sight that met my eyes was terrifying. These Grant tanks carried a large supply of ammunition for the 75-mm gun stowed underneath the main turret. If an armour piercing shell happened to penetrate the armour and hit the ammunition, the result had to be seen to be believed.

Sergeant Adams' tank was halted less than ten yards from me, and as I looked across I saw him and his crew start to bale out. He had one leg out of the cupola when suddenly his tank just disintegrated; the turret, which weighed about eight tons, went sailing into the air and landed with a dull thud in front of my tank; the side of the tank split open with the force of the explosion and exposed what remained of the inside – a blazing jumble of twisted metal. Not a member of the crew had a chance of survival.

In the shocked lull that followed, Leakey was able to call up the Adjutant on his radio and report his situation. He arranged for a recovery tank to pull him out and for smoke to be dropped in front of his tank when he called for it. The German anti-tank gunners, reckoning that the battle was over, started to dance around their guns in glee.

It was as he was sitting in the wrecked tank smoking with his crew, and waiting to be rescued, that Leakey noticed that his 37-mm gun recuperator spring had re-exerted itself and the gun appeared to be firable. He ordered the driver and the 75-mm men to bale out. Then he slowly traversed on to the nearest anti-tank gun and disposed of it and its crew with a few shots. Three German tanks had driven up and halted broadside on. He brewed up all three. Then all hell descended on them and the radio operator baled out. Leakey followed 'faster than a champagne cork leaving the neck of a bottle' just before the high grade aero petrol ignited, turning the inside of the tank into an inferno as the tank blew up.

XXX Corps never recovered from this defeat and yet the senior commanders did not learn the lesson of it. One of the functions of divisional and corps commanders of artillery is to concentrate the fire of guns. That had been done in the abortive infantry advance. For the second battle the screen of anti-tank guns had not been brought under concentrated fire. Instead they reverted to the old tactics of a cavalry charge against firepower. The infantry should have been pitted against the anti-tank guns. When the guns thoroughly engaged looking after themselves and the panzers had moved forward to help them, the Grants and the anti-tank guns would have been well-placed to pick them off. It sounds easy but, of course, it is not. The drill for such an operation had not been developed let alone perfected, and so it was not attempted.

It is interesting to note that Rommel's panzers suffered the same fate at the hands of British anti-tank guns at Medenine in 1943.

Part III
North-West Europe

10 The Second Army in Normandy

Here I must recall some events in the Desert that affected me directly. My regiment, 104th Royal Horse Artillery (Essex Yeomanry), was withdrawn to Palestine after the battles around El Duda, Belhamed and Sidi Resegh in November and December 1941. One battery was sent to Burma with 7th Armoured Brigade and a replacement for it was formed. In April a new 6-pounder anti-tank battery became part of the regiment to protect the field guns from tanks. We joined 1st Armoured Brigade at Mena camp outside Cairo and trained hard with them for two months as their artillery regiment. The main units in the brigade were the 4th Hussars, the 1st and 6th Royal Tank Regiments and the 1st Sherwood Foresters.

When the battle of Gazala started on 27 May 1942 we were on our way back to the Desert. To our anger and frustration, the 1st Armoured Brigade was broken up and we never fought with the units with whom we had trained. We ourselves joined 2nd Armoured Brigade, an outfit that struck us, during our short stay with them, as windy, cautious and ineffective. It had not adopted the concept of combined arms action that we had practised in 1st Armoured Brigade. Generally, cavalry armoured corps commanders mishandled the artillery and infantry under their command. That was a feature of the Gazala battle. While we were with them 2nd Armoured Brigade's tanks watched a formation of panzers passively. For a junior officer such inactivity was frustrating. I did not know that the panzers were holding us off while their other units liquidated 150 Brigade's Box in the Gazala Line. I lost patience one morning and stalked a block of tanks and soft-skinned vehicles about 2000 yards in front of us in my Honey light tank. This was the occasion on which I shelled them with 50 rounds of gunfire from the eight guns of the battery. It certainly stirred them up and made them move but unless you were lucky enough to cause a brew-up you could not tell what casualties you had inflicted on personnel.

After the disastrous tank battles around Knightsbridge, in which we took no part, the battery joined June Column in 7th Motor Brigade and harried the rear of the Afrika Korps facing Tobruk. At the frontier wire near Madalena we shelled panzer grenadiers riding in their half-tracks, but they were not impressed enough to halt and we retreated. Taking a southern route along the edge of the Quattara Depression the same panzer grenadiers followed us at a distance. Junecol was as unadventurous as the 2nd Armoured Brigade had been, and on several occasions we allowed supply columns to slip by without firing more than a few rounds at them. My memory of those days was of depression that we were so poorly led.

On 29 June, when most of the army had reached Alamein, we were ordered to delay the enemy on the road between Fuka and Daba. As my Stuart tank's gearbox had broken down, my battery commander told me to take his Marmon Harrington armoured car and his crew instead of my faithful Morris eight-hundredweight, with its shattered windscreen and gasping autovac. Although the Morris was reliable and my own crew and I knew each other, I unwisely agreed. Up on the road I registered a point 800 yards ahead and waited for the enemy. After an hour a column of infantry in half-tracks appeared with a tank as escort. I ordered a few rounds of gunfire, but there was no reply from the guns; apparently, they had ceased firing without informing me. With nothing to deter them, the enemy advanced up the road towards me and I told the driver to clear out. We were 50 yards from the road and as he made towards it he remarked that on rough terrain the wheel had been known to fall off. Even as he spoke the armoured car swerved to the left and came to a halt. The left front wheel had come off. We were at once under heavy fire from short range and had to bale out hastily and beat a retreat. There was no time to grab water or weapons which, improvidently, we were not wearing. Bombardier Styles, my signaller, was an asthmatic and we only just managed to help him over a nearby ridge between the road and the sea.

Out of sight of the German column, which lost interest in us, we set out along the shore to walk 30 miles to Daba airfield, the next place that might be held by the Eighth Army. The roar of traffic on the road to our right indicated that the enemy were still advancing. We walked all the first night, at one time passing through a German medical unit where we hoped to steal a vehicle, but could not find one unattended. We lay up in the dunes the next day suffering from thirst although we found an open bottle of lemonade which gave us some relief. We reached Daba airfield during the following night where we filled some officers' mess bottles at the well. Then we lay up under the cliffs on the shore as it was growing light.

We slept all morning. In the evening we intended to refill our bottles and head for Alamein. We had reckoned without the Luftwaffe, which arrived with a squadron of Messerschmitt 109Gs in the afternoon. A look-out took post immediately above us on the cliff. He kept us pinned down behind rocks. In the evening we decided to make a break and crept along the shore and into the dunes. There we were spotted by a standing patrol which arrested us. We were taken back to the airfield where an amiable station commander interviewed us and gave us cold coffee while he conversed in a friendly manner. He apologized for having to surrender us to the Italians, but those were the rules. Soon we were in the back of a truck on our way to Mersa Matruh.

A year later, after three attempts to escape from camps in Italy and periods of solitary confinement as a punishment, the Italian armistice brought my imprisonment to an end in early September 1943. By then I was in Camp 49 near Parma in northern Italy. With two hours to spare before a German column rolled up to take us off to Germany, we were released into the countryside. The local people generously brought us clothing and gave shelter to those who wanted it. Three of us, Michael Gilbert, Tony Davies and I, anticipating a German sweep of the area, moved away from the vicinity of the camp and started walking south into the mountains.

For seven weeks we hiked down the spine of the Apennines towards the fighting zone north of Salerno. The *Contadini* sheltered us in barns at night and fed us mainly on potatoes, polenta, vegetable soup, and bread and cheese. Occasionally we were reduced to bread, olive oil and salt, which we found to be a delicious and ancient meal. On 31 October, Michael Gilbert and I, the two survivors, met a Canadian armoured car patrol in the village of Lucito north of Campo Basso. Tony Davies and a South African, Hal Becker, who had recently joined us, had been shot at while we were walking through the Sangro line that was being prepared for occupation. They had had to run for it. Tony was captured with a broken ankle, having fallen over the edge of a quarry into the arms of a German working party. Poor Hal had been shot and killed. We learned of these mishaps only after the war, for we were ahead at the time and could see nothing of the drama behind.

After passing through Intelligence debriefing at XIII Corps, where we refused an invitation to return through the lines and retrieve some generals sheltering in a monastery, we were evacuated through Taranto. There we caught an LST (Landing Ship Tank) to Bizerta. I next met her Royal Canadian Navy commander at a convoy conference as we started off for Normandy in June 1944. The ship behind us struck a mine outside Taranto. At Bizerta we had the choice of flying to Algiers or taking a train. In Italy we had suffered at the hands of administrators and had learned to be entirely sceptical about any outside agent. Salvation depended on our own efforts, we believed. So we chose the train as the safer option. But the brakes were faulty and we were derailed when we ran into the back of a stationary train at Constantine. None the worse for that we arrived in a camp on the Algiers race course and were installed in a bell tent. A storm on the first night flattened the camp. In the morning we positively insisted on being sent to a holiday camp, where we spent the next two weeks in great comfort. A trip to the Atlas mountains for a few days skiing was on the menu. Then Mike returned to his unit, the 12th HAC, in Italy. The Essex Yeomanry were in the Canal Zone so I took ship for England. On 12 December the Franconia reached Liverpool and I had Christmas at home.

In the meanwhile my CO in the Essex Yeomanry, Hammer Matthew, had been appointed the commander of the artillery of VIII Corps. It was to be the armoured corps of Second Army bound for the invasion of Europe. Hearing of my return, he invited my father and me to lunch in Penrith, where he offered me a battery in the West Somerset Yeomanry, the towed 25-pounder regiment in the Guards Armoured Division. The condition was that I join at once. I was able to insist on a course at the School of Artillery in January and in February took over my battery at Slingsby in the North Riding of Yorkshire.

I had learned my field-gunnery in the siege of Tobruk at the hands of William Quinn, my troop commander. He had been RSM of the Royal Military Academy, Woolwich, where I was a cadet when war started. I could not have had a wiser teacher. The course at Larkhill brought me up to date, for much had changed since 1942. Two escaping friends were on the same course and I was to see much of them during the coming campaign, when they were in XXX Corps.

The switch from the irregular life of a prisoner of war to serving in an army vastly different from the Eighth, one that had formed its personality through years of training in the UK, was a jolt. The Eighth Army had been scruffy, informal, practical and battle-hardened: the Second was formal, serious, smart and went by the book. Except for my battery sergeant-major Sydney Pond, who had been signal sergeant in 414 Battery, I was among people who had been together for years but never in action. That included my commanding officer, potentially not a happy situation. It took me almost until we landed in Normandy to adjust. Fortunately, Willy Newall, a veteran from 1 RHA, took command before we crossed the Channel.

Training in England consisted mainly of movement and wireless exercises and practice camp, which was tactically artificial. At practice camp we worked briefly with the officers of the 5th Battalion the Coldstream Guards whom I was to support in 32nd Guards Brigade. We did no exercises with the armoured regiments, who were supported by the self-propelled 25-pounder regiment, the Leicestershire Yeomanry in the 5th Armoured Brigade. I never saw infantry and armour working together in England. The infantry brigade and the armoured brigade were expected to operate separately. The general idea was that the infantry made the gap and then the armour flooded through it like the cavalry of old. Or the infantry formed a firm base from which the armour operated. This was the mistaken tactical view long held in the UK. I was quite confident in my regiment's ability to support 'our infantry', but none in the ability of the three arms to fight together.

My task was to provide the commanding officer of the 5th Coldstream with the artillery support that his battalion needed. The support I could offer had increased greatly since 1942. We had concentrated the fire of several regiments, using land lines, in Tobruk. This had been developed further just before Alamein, and was now the pivot on which the tactics of the infantry and the armour turned. Winston Churchill remarked in October 1941, as he cast a critical eye over events in the Desert, that 'Renown awaits the Commander who first, in this war, restores the artillery to its prime importance upon the battlefield.' By June 1944 it was commonplace to concentrate the fire of the 72 field guns of an infantry division, using wireless, in less than four minutes from the time the target details were given after registration. This was called an Uncle Target. The fire of a corps, or even of all the guns of the army that were within range, could be brought down in a fairly short time simply by prefixing the fire order with the words Victor, William or Yoke Target repeated three times. By giving a time on target order the shells could arrive almost simultaneously – a truly terrifying experience for the enemy. The field gun was still the 25-pounder, rather light for the task. D-day assault regiments had the self-propelled 105-mm, which had more punch. Corps artillery with 4.5-inch and 5.5-inch medium guns, the latter with a 100-pound shell, was available to support divisional attacks. The heavy gun was a 7.2-inch, but its work was mainly in counter-battery and destructive work behind the forward defences.

Very soon after we started fighting in Normandy, I learned that every battle hinged on what the artillery could do to help the other arms. The prominence of the artillery was a change from the desert. Artillery wireless communications, on which fire support depended, had improved greatly but was still an anxiety, particularly in the evening when mush and interference were perpetual. Good signallers at the observation posts and on 'Control' were worth their weight in gold. An officer was expected to be able to take over a set, keep it on net and get the best out of it. He was useless if he could not deliver fire orders to his guns. The infantry was less well served. Number 18 sets, used between companies and battalion headquarters, were unreliable. The signaller carrying the set on his back in action was often picked off by a sniper. The tanks had the same 19 sets as ourselves and their wireless discipline, insecure in the Desert, had been tightened up. They seldom used the absurdly transparent codewords popular in the Desert. It was still difficult for an infantryman on foot to communicate with a tank commander in his turret, his headset firmly over his ears, his eyes glazed over as he listened to voices on his own radio net. More than once I saw a jeep or a carrier flattened by a reversing tank, the passengers having to leap clear. I cannot forget the sight of Major Willoughby of the Leicestershire Yeomanry having his legs crushed by a tank in the bocage of Normandy.

An infantry division's strength was about 18 000 men, of which 8482 were infantry, 6289 other combat arms and 3576 employed in headquarters and services. It consisted of three brigades of three battalions, three field artillery regiments, an anti tank regiment with 17-pounders, the replacement for the 6-pounder which had been handed to the infantry battalions, a light anti-aircraft regiment with 40 mm Bofors guns, an armoured reconnaissance regiment, a machine gun battalion with 4.2-inch mortars as well as the Vickers machine gun, an engineer regiment, a signals regiment and service corps, ordnance and electrical and mechanical engineers.

Since 1940, the fire-power of the battalion had increased. However, the humble Lee-Enfield rifle No. 4 had not been replaced by an automatic or semi-automatic rifle as the personal weapon. The cheap and not entirely reliable Sten machine carbine had appeared as the short-range automatic weapon. The Bren, with its slow rate of fire of 600 rounds a minute, was still the light machine gun. The 6-pounder anti-tank gun had replaced the 1939 anti-tank rifle and the 2-pounder, and a Projector Infantry Anti-Tank (PIAT) was now used by brave infantrymen in platoons against tanks, buildings and bunkers at short range. The lightly armoured, tracked carrier still provided for reconnaissance, and for carrying fire-power about the battlefield, including the 3-inch mortar platoon. Artillery FOOs in infantry divisions used carriers as well. Normally, an army tank brigade, or an armoured brigade with its own artillery and motor battalion, was allotted to the division for specific operations. It provided a regiment of three squadrons for each brigade.

In general the fire-power of the infantry battalion was inferior to that of its opponent. In particular the Germans had two MG 42 machine guns, with a rate of fire of 1200 rpm, in each infantry section. It gave the section four times the fire-power of its British opposite number.

The cutting edge of this big division was the rifle company of about 120 men. In action only two platoons in each company, two companies in each battalion and four battalions in the division, would be in the first wave of an attack, so that less than half the 4300 infantry in the rifle companies walked forward in the first line of an attack. Furthermore, it was not unusual for company strengths to be down to 70 men and battalions to three companies. A shortage of infantry was already looming before D-day. There was nothing to spare in the national manpower supply although, as the campaign developed, transfers of men to the infantry from arms in which casualties were lighter, antiaircraft for instance, was effected. Retraining of these men was necessary, naturally.

On being called up, every recruit was given six weeks' basic training as an infantryman, so every soldier had a rudimentary knowledge of infantry work. After basic training he was selected for a particular Arm. Unfortunately, except for volunteers, the infantry tended to be assigned men who, while physically fit, were in the lower IQ categories. The infantry spent only 10 weeks in special-to-Arm training, the shortest of all. The Royal Signals were given 30 weeks, the longest. Next the soldier began elementary training as a member of a team, section or tank crew. He spent this five or six weeks in one of the three reserve divisions. Then he joined a holding unit where he was supposed to continue training until there was a vacancy in a field unit. This was the weakest link in the chain, for the soldier went 'off the boil' and many COs complained that soldiers arrived in action who had not thrown a grenade or fired a bren gun recently. If individuals were not confident about handling their weapons, their mates could not trust them in the stress of action. Small tactical units depended on personal relationships which casualties severed so that the bedrock of the team was a man's ability to handle all weapons. The Germans included a small training sub-unit in the battalion which, in theory, every arrival attended for a day or two on his arrival.

The Guards Armoured, the 7th, 11th and Canadian 4th Armoured divisions each had two brigades, one of lorried infantry and the other of tanks. The former had three infantry battalions, the latter three tank battalions using Shermans or Cromwells. The Cromwell was a development of the Crusader armed with a 75-mm gun. In addition there was a motor battalion, an armoured reconnaissance battalion and an armoured car regiment. In the artillery there were two field regiments, one of which was self-propelled. A self-propelled anti-tank regiment was armed with the American M 10 with a 3-inch gun. There was an anti-aircraft regiment of Bofors. At the time of Operation Bluecoat in late July, when tactical cooperation between tanks and infantry was at last developing, armoured divisions worked in four combat teams each of an infantry battalion and an armoured regiment or battalion. The motor battalion and the armoured reconnaissance regiment made up the fourth group. The infantry were carried forward in 3 ton lorries but walked into battle. The motor battalion could mount all its men. The British armoured division lacked the armoured assault vehicles which carried a percentage of the German and American panzergrenadiers or armoured infantry across fire-swept areas in battle. Not until Lieutenant-General Guy Simonds mounted some of his 2nd Canadian Corps infantry in self-propelled Priest 105-mm gun-howitzers, from which the guns had been removed, 'defrocked Priests', did 21st Army Group armoured divisions have the same advantage. Eventually called Kangaroos, they were not standard equipment in armoured divisions.

I and XXX were the Second Army's assault corps. The 7th Armoured, 49th West Riding and 51st Highland divisions, and the 4th and 33rd Armoured Brigade were 'Follow Up' formations of these corps, to come ashore as soon as possible after the original assault landings of the infantry and supporting armoured brigades (3rd British, 3rd Canadian, 50th Tees and Tyne infantry and the 4th, 8th and 2nd Canadian armoured brigades). Next came two 'Build-Up' corps which would land as soon as there was space for them. VIII Corps, the armoured corps, was commanded by Lieutenant-General O'Connor, himself an escaper from Italy: XII Corps, largely infantry, was commanded by Neil Ritchie, ex commander of the Eighth Army. These completed the British contingent except for Major-General Hobart's remarkable 79th Armoured Division which contained 'The

Funnies', assault engineers with explosive-throwing tanks, flame throwers, mine-clearing flail tanks, tanks carrying fascine bundles for fillng ditches, and tanks which carried bridges to span ditches on their backs. The 3rd Canadian Infantry Division, part of 1st Corps in the assault, later joined the 2nd Canadian Corps, commanded by Lieutenant-General Guy Simonds, with 2nd Canadian Infantry and 4th Armoured Division. It joined the battle in July.

Vehicles were waterproofed in order that they could wade ashore. The DD tanks with canvas sides performed like motor boats but they were easily swamped in the rough conditions of D-day. In the Guards Division, the Sherman tanks with which battery commanders and their Forward Observation Officers (FOO troop commanders) were to be equipped were not issued until just before we moved into the concentration area. Consequently, at the last minute, we had to rehearse the use of the Walky Talky number 38 set, and such refinements as rebroadcasting a fire order from a hole in the ground through the number 19 set on the tank, which could remain under cover. Our drivers had to learn a new tank and the signallers to aim and fire the 75-mm gun.

The Sherman had been satisfactory in the Western Desert when it had been a huge improvement on its predecessors. At the regimental level I heard nothing before D-day about its weaknesses when facing the Mark V Panther and the Mk VI Tiger. Its relatively soft armour, its tendency to burn and the penetrative deficiency of its 75-mm gun were not discussed. The gun was accurate, more accurate than British guns, but if the shell could not penetrate at the first strike the gunner might not be given a second shot. A 17-pounder was mounted on one tank in four. Called a Firefly, its flash and smoke were very visible. It could penetrate the front armour of the Panther but not the Tiger. As this Firefly was only issued just before D-day there had not been time to work out the tactics of its use. For the sake of security, presumably, units were not prepared for the relatively long fields of fire south of Caen or the bocage west and south of Bayeux, where short fields obtained.

The landings went ahead on 6 June and rapidly secured a lodgement. Penetration inland to take Caen and make room for the Build-Up divisions was not effected. A great storm between 18 and 21 June delayed the crossing of Build-Up divisions and their ammunition. 32 Guards Brigade landed ahead of the armour of the Guards Division and we moved into a position on the western edge of Carpiquet airfield still held by the 12th SS Panzer Division. 5th Coldstream suffered several bombardments from Nebelwerfers – a new experience for most of us. The guns supported operation Epsom to the south of us and the advance of 59th Division and the Canadians towards Carpiquet from the north. The Division as a whole was not engaged until Operation Goodwood on 18 July.

11 The Conduct of the Normandy Campaign

Two armies, each of two corps, landed between D-day and D+2 on the American beaches Utah and Omaha, and the British Gold, Juno and Sword. Montgomery planned to expand the British beachhead at once to include the road, rail, river and canal centre of Caen (Map 9). By D+2 armoured units were to intrude to disrupt German efforts to cordon off the invaders. On the American sector, the Cotentin peninsula would be cut and Cherbourg, at its northern tip, taken to provide a major port as soon as possible. The bridgehead would be expanded to allow space for the Build-Up corps responsible for the break-out. By that time two American armies, the First and the Third, and the Second British and First Canadian – the latter representing only one extra corps – would be in the line.

The timing of the plan's three phases – landings and junction of the beach-heads, expansion of bridgehead and break-out – was approximate, for it depended on the enemy's actions. As the Germans built up their strength, Montgomery anticipated that the front might 'glue up' about D+14 if the British had not reached the vicinity of Falaise south of Caen and the Americans were still fighting in the bocage around St Lô. Preventing that situation arising by penetrating the comparatively open country south of Caen on the British front was an essential part of Montgomery's plan.[1]

The plan was based on the fundamental facts of geography. The Germans would have to hold their right flank firmly, first as an anchor for their front and then as a pivot for the orderly withdrawal of their western flank to the Seine. A defeat on their eastern flank would probably doom their forces further west. Unless that occurred, the allied break-out would begin on the American front in the west, at the handle of the door not the hinge. Its direction would be designed to seize the Atlantic ports on the right and to reach the Seine on the left. In a document issued on 8 May this part of the outline plan read:

> Once through the difficult bocage country, greater possibilities for manoeuvre and for the use of armour begin to appear. Our aim during this period should be to contain the maximum enemy forces facing the Eastern flank of the bridgehead, and to thrust rapidly

140

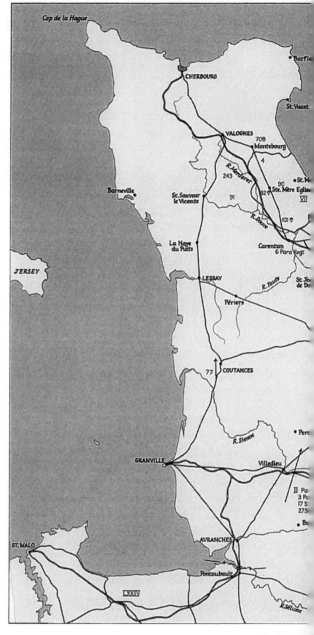

9 Norm

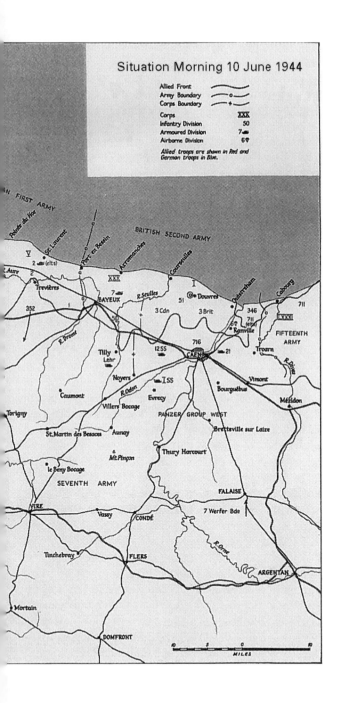

Situation Morning 10 June 1944

towards Rennes (80 miles east of Quiberon Bay) [on the west flank].

On reaching Rennes our main thrust should be towards Vannes (near Quiberon Bay) but diversionary thrusts with the maximum use of deception should be employed to persuade the enemy that our objective is Nantes.

If, at this time, the enemy weakens his eastern force to oppose us North of Redon (40 miles southwest of Rennes) a strong attack should be launched towards the Seine.[2]

Montgomery's assessment of the possible course of events was accurate. The Americans were stuck in bocage, the British did not penetrate to Falaise, the front did 'glue up', the British contained 75 per cent of German armoured units until the break-out on the American flank. In general terms, then, the campaign followed Montgomery's plan. Its final stages yielded more than anyone expected, for the Germans could not stand on the Seine. On the other hand, the tactics of the campaign confounded Montgomery, Eisenhower, Bradley and other pundits forcing Montgomery to modify what he insisted were details in his plan. Herein lay a controversy over its execution.[3]

The central set-back was that the British did not take Caen in the first few days. That part of the city south of the Orne remained in German hands until the last 10 days of July. Consequently, movement in the British sector north and east of the Orne was severely restricted for lack of space. Neither army reached its objectives by D+15, with the predicted result. The Americans who were to have reached the line St Lô–Periers by D+5 did not do so until 18 July (D+43). After Caen had fallen, the Germans continued to resist British attempts to expand the bridgehead towards Falaise, the German pivot. So, although the campaign ended with a resounding victory, earlier than planned by D+90, and its shape was much as Montgomery envisaged, tactically it went off the rails at the start.

Montgomery's critics usually fail to distinguish the tactical from the strategic story, let alone to identify the political motives of those responsible for the various levels at which the campaign was fought. An example is the demand of the air forces that Montgomery expand the bridgehead quickly to allow for airfield construction. Airfields south and south-east of Caen were necessary for fighter aircraft to cover the crossings over the Seine. In that respect Montgomery's ground plan, to advance towards Falaise and there resist German counter-attacks to prevent the British breaking out south-eastward towards the Seine, suited the air forces. Nevertheless, when the ground fighting fell behind schedule, the RAF reacted as though Montgomery's plans were for their benefit alone, although he was perfectly satisfied with the tactical air support he was receiving. This became an issue in Operation Goodwood, which was intended to make a significant advance towards Falaise on 18 and 19 July with the help of a major effort by the strategic air forces. When the results disappointed them senior RAF officers, led by Eisenhower's deputy Supreme Allied Commander, Air Chief Marshal Sir Arthur Tedder and the commander of 2nd TAF, Air Marshal Sir Arthur Coningham, condemned Montgomery for making a half-hearted effort. With some justification, they claimed that in requesting strategic air support, Montgomery had led them to believe that he intended a decisive break-out to the south-east. Indeed, in the first hours he claimed as much. When that proved to be untrue, he told them that his main intention had been to attract the majority of German armoured formations on the Caen sector, and hold them away from the Americans in front of St Lô. The RAF complained that Montgomery had deceived them. His campaign plan was failing, they asserted, for was not his master plan to break out towards the south-east? This idea of holding on the left in order to break out on the right was new, they asserted. The Second Army was not pulling its weight. Montgomery ought to be replaced. Tedder sold this idea to Eisenhower who, while he had no intention of sacking Montgomery, did not agree with what he understood was his strategy.

Eisenhower spoke to Winston Churchil on 26 July and the following day to 'a few responsible persons' to argue that there were complaints in the American press that the British were not doing their share of the fighting. He wanted the whole front to be aflame. When it was pointed out that the British had 650 panzers on their front while the American faced 200 where their break-out had already started and was progressing well, and that Montgomery had explained his strategy to Eisenhower at St Paul's School in April, there was not much that Eisenhower could say in reply. Indeed, it appeared that Eisenhower and Tedder confused the tactics of the campaign with its strategy. Nevertheless, Tedder's criticism was widely accepted and taken up by the American news media.[4]

Montgomery certainly gave Eisenhower and the RAF the impression that Goodwood would be 'decisive', but cautious commander that he was, his orders to Sir Miles Dempsey, commanding Second Army, were equivocal. Afterwards, he dismissed criticism by saying that he had reinforced the German impression that he intended to smash their pivot and advance towards Paris. Later, Dempsey argued that as the RAF had been consistently sticky about providing strategic support he had to convince them that Goodwood was intended to be a decisive break-through. He was, indeed, prepared to exploit a success as far as Falaise but it was not his main concern.[5]

Their efforts to seize Caen and the high ground to its south-east, west and south-west absorbed the British in June and July. But as they were not successful in gaining much territory Eisenhower's disquiet was, to that extent, understandable. Instead of reaching Falaise, as he had planned, and forcing the Germans to attack him there and suffer heavily from his dominant artillery and tactical air force, Montgomery himself had to mount a series of expensive, offensive operations for small advances well short of Falaise, while the Germans defended. Nevertheless, the effect was that the Germans had to use most of their elite divisions sitting on the lid of a box from which the British were continually attempting to escape. Were their British front to collapse the Germans would have lost control of the front. The price they paid for stabilizing it was losing the ability to reinforce their other wing until it was too late to halt the break-out of the American First Army at St Lô on 25 July. This result was close to Montgomery's intention in April and May 1944, although the manner of achieving it was not according to plan.[6]

The ending of the campaign was a surprise in that, instead of swinging back against the Seine, the Germans moved every division they could spare west to block the American's penetration. But they were too late. The Third Army was pouring out of Normandy into Brittany and south-east towards Paris, while parts of the First Army was moving round the German southern flank in a smaller envelopment. Their counter-stroke prevented the Germans from swinging their front back to the Seine in an orderly fashion. They put themselves into a pocket between Americans on the south side and the 21st Army Group on the north. While the German right-wing pivot retained some cohesion the rest of their front disintegrated and their armies in Normandy were virtually destroyed in the so-called Falaise pocket.

Thus the American break-out at St Lô set the scene for a battle of annihilation. By D+90, the planning date for reaching the Seine, the Allied Expeditionary Force had destroyed the German armies in Normandy, crossed the Seine and taken Brussels and Antwerp. Montgomery's calmness when the front appeared to be stalemated had been justified.

If we accept Tedder's conception of what was occurring on the ground at the time of Goodwood as ill-informed and even perverse, what remains of his criticism? An answer is Tedder's point that the Second Army's tactical performance in the operations around Caen in June, July and August was unimpressive.[7] Its divisions certainly did not achieve as much as Montgomery and Dempsey expected, despite their dominant artillery and air support. How much of this was owing to the shortcomings of units, how much to the misdirection of commanders and to what extent Montgomery's subordinates took into account those shortcomings is difficult to assess. What is certain is that commanders and units had grossly underestimated German infantry and armoured firepower.

At the beginning came the failure to take Caen on D-day. An attempt to exploit a gap in the German front between the American 5th Corps and the British XXX Corps and to outflank Caen from the west by taking Villers Bocage failed between 12 and 15 June. (D+6 to D+9. See 3: 'Fighting Experiences'.) On 18 June, Montgomery wrote to his two army commanders:

> It is now time to move on to other things. Enemy can still milk divisions in Brittany and southern France, but he lacks good infantry to release his panzer divisions. The old policy of 'stretch' which beat him in Sicily then begins to emerge when we can snap his roping-off policy. When we are all facing the same direction after Cherbourg and Caen have fallen we must defeat the German Army between the Seine and the Loire. Caen is the key to Cherbourg. By Wednesday 21 June we shall have fresh reserves ready.

Unfortunately the great storm intervened from 18 to 21 June. It interrupted supply, delayed the arrival of the build-up divisions over the beaches for three days, and set back operations for longer.[8]

A second attempt to envelop Caen from the west by a drive through Aunay-sur-Odon and Evrecy to the bridges over the Orne between Thury Harcourt and Amay-sur-Orne, and from the east towards Bourguebus, Vimont and Bretteville-sur-Laize was still-born because there was insufficient room in the eastern bridgehead and the storm delayed the arrival of build-up divisions and ammunition for the western operation. A strike of the US XV Corps on the right of XXX Corps was cancelled because the storm delayed its landing. Epsom, the third attempt to outflank Caen by taking Hill 112 south of the Odon between 25 and 29 June, was succeeding when Dempsey ordered O'Connor to withdrew a squadron of the 23rd Hussars and a company of the 8th Rifle Brigade. He was concerned about panzer counter-attacks against the flank of the salient and crossings of the Odon leading up to it. Hill 112 was a crucial position overlooking the ground south of Caen. Its recapture later was expensive. Refighting Epsom would be inconclusive, but the dominance of British defensive artillery suggests that it could have been held.

On 30 June, Montgomery wrote to both Army Commanders:

> My broad policy ... has always been to draw the main enemy forces into battle on our eastern flank and to fight them there so that our affairs on the western flank could proceed the easier. It is on the western flank that territorial gains are essential at this stage. For this, forcing the enemy to place the bulk of his strength in front of Second Army makes it easier.

At this stage 2 and 21 Panzer and 1, 2, 9, 10 and 12 SS Panzer and Panzer Lehr opposed the British.[9]

The American First Army attacked southwards on 3 July between Caumont and St Lô. Pivoting on Caumont its intention was to swing south and south-east to the general line Caumont–Vire–Mortain–Fougeres. When Avranches had fallen, 8th Corps of Patton's Third Army would enter Brittany. A strong right wing would sweep south of the bocage towards Laval–Mayenne and Le Mans–Alencon. This was a modification of a pre-D-day plan for the right wing. But Bradley's attack bogged down short of St Lô. Afterwards Montgomery called a meeting at which, according to Dempsey,'Bradley arrived rather dejected and remarked to the C-in-C that he had failed.' Dempsey suggested that Bradley attacked on too wide a front but Montgomery told him not to worry at all, but to regroup, take his time and try again on a somewhat narrower front when he was fully ready. Dempsey was ordered to continue attacking around Caen, to make the enemy believe that the main Allied breakout effort was to take place in that sector and so continue to attract the enemy armoured strength towards it.[10]

Operation Charnwood resulted on 10 July, in which strategic bombers, used for the first time in Normandy, enabled a frontal attack to clear Caen north of the Orne. Goodwood, in which the RAF interest has been explained, and Atlantic, followed. Caen south of the river was taken and outflanked to the east and south-east. Goodwood, on 18 July, differed from former battles in being fought mainly by three armoured divisions in the centre while the infantry, Canadians on the right and British on the left, fought on the flanks. A large proportion of German armour was held on the Caen front as a result of the Germans expecting a continuation of these battles.

Their estimate appeared to be correct when 2nd Canadian Corps, under Lieutenant-General Guy Simonds, attacked in the open country beside the Falaise road over the Verrieres ridge on 25 July. It was a bloody struggle to provide a base for a drive on Falaise but its secondary purpose was the thankless one of holding German armour away from the Americans. Tactically it was an expensive failure. Meanwhile, St Lô had fallen to the Americans on 19 July which provided a base for their break-out, Operation Cobra, which was to have heavy air support. Clear weather was necessary for that. Poor visibility caused its postponement on 24 July, but unfortunately as the order did not reach all air force units, American ground troops which had not withdrawn to pre-battle positions were bombed. The delay of one day actually caused the Germans to shift more troops east of the Orne to face Simonds, because they expected a British drive towards Falaise with heavy air support.

Instead of a heavy air strike on the road to Falaise, a powerful blow was struck in fine weather on 25 July, on a rectangle 6000 yards wide and 2400 yards deep west of St Lô. Cobra launched Lieutenant-General Joe Collins' VII Corps with three infantry divisions. Two armoured and one motorised division were ready to follow when a break in the relatively thin front had been established. The air bombardment had been more carefully worked out than those on the British front and, although once more it caused American casualties, 700 killed and wounded, it reduced the opposition to impotence where it was accurate. Nevertheless, Collins' men had to fight determinedly for a gain of a mile on the first day. But that was enough for Collins to release the armour at first light on 26 July. From then onwards the break-through became a torrent and then a flood. Cobra decided the outcome of the battle of Normandy. But there was still stern fighting to be done further east and at Mortain when the Germans unwisely shifted divisions to the breach on the American front.

A directive from Montgomery on 21 July which initiated Simonds' operation on the road to Falaise warned XXX Corps to take over from the 5th US Corps in the Caumont area. On 27 July Montgomery reported that the Americans were succeeding and that 21st Army Group attacks south of Caen towards Falaise were to cease. VIII Corps would be switched across the front to the right of XXX Corps.

The main blow of the whole Allied plan has now been struck on the western flank; that blow is the foundation of all our ops, and it has been well and truly struck. The armies on the eastern flank must now keep up the pressure ... [Second Army] must hurl itself into the fight in the Caumont area so as to make easier the task of the American armies fighting hard on the western flank.[11]

This was to be Operation Bluecoat, which continued until Mt Pincon was taken and the front on the British right became fluid. The VIII and XXX Corps were the piston that drove the Germans into the Falaise pocket from the west while First US Army swung in from the south. Totalize and Tractable, battles conducted by the First Canadian Army on the road to Falaise, followed in August to form the north side of the trap into which the Germans were being driven. They were innovative battles, certainly, but it can be justifiably argued that the Canadian and Polish armoured divisions, which were fighting their first battle, did not adapt quickly to novel conditions. They made tactical mistakes. On the other hand there were glaring command errors. Bradley failed to close the trap from the south. There was confusion between Montgomery, Bradley and Eisenhower over whether the trap lay in the Falaise–Chambois–Trun area or in a wider pocket bordered by the Seine. This occurred when responsibility for the direction of operations was passing from Montgomery to Eisenhower with Montgomery and Bradley as his equal subordinates.

After the war, a partisan controversy arose over the closing of the Falaise–Argentan–Chambois–Trun pocket (Map 10, pp. 150–1), in which a large part of the German forces in Normandy were surrounded and destroyed. Great though the victory was, some writers argued that it ought to have enabled the allies to finish the war 'by Christmas'. The evidence for 'this missed opportunity' is weak and only the case against the First Canadian Army for being slow to close the pocket from the north, is convincing. Exaggerating the number of survivors from the pocket helped both to explain the recovery of the German armies on their frontier and the failure of the allies to finish them off there in the autumn. Thereby, blame for the conduct of the autumn battles could be shifted to the managers of the last stage of the battle in Normandy and to those who planned the advance beyond the Seine. The fact that, in Normandy, there was little if any dispute between Bradley and Montgomery over the campaign there suggests that post-Normandy rows were the product of hindsight about the plan for and the conduct of the frontier battles after Falaise.

Perhaps the most rigorous analysis of the Falaise affair is still Carlo D'Este's chapter, 'The Falaise Controversy'. He concluded, unexceptionably, that Bradley and Montgomery, between them, did not ensure that Patton's forces on the south side of the pocket were effectively employed. Bradley halted his divisions short of Argentan, for he was afraid that they would clash with 21st Army Group head on. Afterwards Bradley acknowledged this as an error which had nothing to do with their northward movement taking them over the 21st Army Group boundary, as some critics asserted, for Montgomery had verbally overruled written orders on its location. With more reason, he thought that they would be taken in flank by German divisions breaking out from the west. But that should have been taken as the rub of the green. It should also have been accepted that the whole operation could be only loosely controlled, because the location even of friendly troops was known only approximately and tactical moves had to be spontaneous.

The 'error' was that neither Bradley nor Montgomery decided firmly and early enough that the original pocket, the larger one against the Seine, which had been Montgomery's original conception but had been replaced by Bradley's short envelopment in the Falaise pocket with Eisenhower's agreement, should be restored while, at the same time, closing the smaller one. That the shape of the latter was changing as some Germans escaped and others fought to assist them from outside, was not attended to soon enough. The reaction of the Canadian, Lieutenant-General Crerar, to this change after being told by Montgomery to shift his thrust further east towards Trun, was too slow. The Polish armoured division had become isolated at Mount Ormel between escaping Germans and troops of 1 SS Panzer Corps on the outside trying to break in. The Poles were the cork in the bottle fighting desperately and in need of help. On the American side Bradley had reverted to the 'long envelopment' by sending two divisions of Patton's 15th Corps on that mission. He did not reinforce the short envelopment south of the Poles with the rest of 15th Corps troops until 5th Corps arrived to relieve them. Thus a delay occurred on both the Trun and Chambois flanks.

About 40 000 German prisoners were taken in the pocket. Army Group B calculated that 40 to 50 per cent of those that attempted to break out reached I SS Panzer Corps. Another calculation has 40 000 Germans escaping across the Seine in a disorganized state and incapable of halting the subsequent advance of the allies east of the river. The absence of the air forces over the Seine ferry sites, and the failure to knock out the Putange bridge allowed 1st SS Panzer Corps to evacuate some vehicles. But General Hans Speidel said there were

150

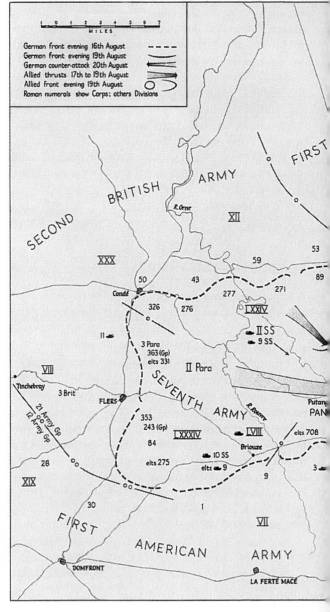

10 The Falaise P◀
16 to 20 August 1

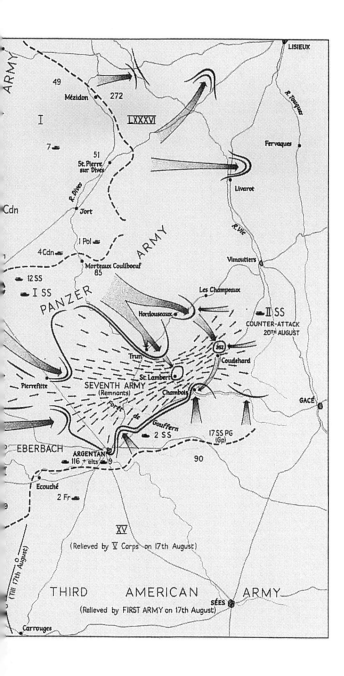

barely 100 tanks left out of six panzer divisions. General Model said only five decimated divisions returned to Germany. 21st Panzer Division, that had gone into action on D-day, had 300 men left. It is otiose to complain that a few more might have been snared had different decisions been made.[12]

12 Fighting Experiences: Tilly-sur-Seulles, Villers Bocage and Operation Goodwood

Before the landings Montgomery said that he wanted two armoured brigades to advance inland to disrupt the enemy's build-up beyond Caen and Villers Bocage. They were not to seize ground but to enable the assault divisions to stake out a deep bridgehead. He described them as 'cracking about'. That was not what the first armour ashore did. The 8th brigade in XXX Corps came ashore on D-day. On D+1 it made for Villers Bocage but ran into Panzer Lehr holding Tilly-sur-Seulles. Thereafter it supported 50th Division's slow advance in that sector. 27th, delayed by traffic congestion and fighting behind Sword beach in the I Corps sector, never started to fulfil Montgomery's idea. It supported the 3rd Division, which was responsible for taking Caen. But 3rd landed on a narrow, one-brigade front west of Ouistreham and the congestion that delayed 27th Brigade prevented an armoured and infantry attack on Caen developing. 3rd Divisional commander was over-sensitive about his flanks and never drove his brigades forward. In fact, neither armoured brigade was trained to 'crack about' in the enemy rear, but to support infantry. In the circumstances that was the role to which both brigades were committed.

Nevertheless, in previous landings, Sicily, Salerno and Anzio for instance, Montgomery and his corps commanders learned that immediate exploitation was vital while the invaders still had the initiative. So Montgomery's idea was right. Yet the assault divisions had been allowed to believe that getting ashore was the main hurdle. Having survived the ordeal on the beaches, they were not psychologically prepared to fight their way inland quickly, to take risks and to tolerate open flanks. When the front started to congeal, they were getting tired and were mentally ill-prepared for the small, grinding, daily attacks necessary to improve their positions against obstinate and skilful opponents, and to keep the front open.

A gap between Montgomery's rhetoric about bold action and what his divisions achieved may be explained, in part at least, by his knowledge that Second Army's infantry strength could not be sustained for long after the build-up divisions had been committed. Infantry lives had to be saved to delay the cannibalizing of divisions. Set-piece attacks behind heavy artillery and air force bombardments were the best tactics in the circumstances, it was believed. Their disadvantage was that they restricted the opportunity of units to use aggressive, infiltration tactics and, therefore, discouraged improvised, opportunist actions to get inland quickly.

Before he left Italy to take over Second Army, Dempsey understood that he was going to be short of infantry in Normandy. In England, Montgomery passed him his letter of 19 March 1944 to Sir Ronald Adam (Adjutant General) in which he informed Adam, *inter alia*, that: 'We have got to try and do this business with the smallest possible casualties. If we play our cards properly, I believe we could do it fairly cheaply...'. In Sicily and Italy, he and Dempsey favoured deliberate attacks with careful fire plans which, they believed, almost invariably saved lives. That was to be their method in Normandy as well.[1]

Dempsey also followed Montgomery's policy on co-operation with the RAF. The two headquarters were to be side by side, their location chosen to suit both services. That had been Montgomery's policy ever since Tedder, Coningham and he teamed up before Alamein. The arrangement had not always been smoothly effected. In the long advance across Tripolitania, for instance, 2nd TAF HQ chose to be near its airfields rather than with Eighth Army headquarters. In Normandy 'integration must be carried down to regimental level', Montgomery said. Dempsey's divisions used control cars and army/air liaison officers to direct air support. The system was efficient, but like that for artillery fire plans, it slowed up attack operations when troops relied too much on it.

The dependence of infantry and tanks on external fire-support excused them from using their own weapons to full effect. As well, artillery and air tasks were usually designated as area targets which tended to inhibit army units from accurately locating enemy positions by patrol and observation. Until that was done infiltration was difficult, some of the effect of bombardment was lost, the expenditure of explosives was increased and the enemy[2] was not proportionately harmed. All of this was compounded by the Germans' ability to conceal themselves.

Montgomery's dependence on Alamein-like tactics in Normandy was the keystone of this symbiosis, for they were designed to occupy positions on the map assumed to be held by the enemy, rather than to destroy his units by fire and movement. Casualties were expected to be inflicted on the enemy when he counter-attacked the features that the Second Army seized. This First World War notion worked well provided the enemy believed the feature to be worth retaking, that it was immediately organized for defence, and if lost that the enemy were thrown out by a counter-attack by fresh troops. However, continuous offensive action to destabilize the enemy had not been stressed in England since Montgomery introduced the idea there before he left to take over Eighth Army in 1942. Furthermore, the Second Army did not have the manpower to practise those tactics. When units reached the objective they were often weakened by casualties and disorganized by the absence of stragglers. The position was then lost to a counter-attack. Another formal attack was mounted, after a pause of hours, by a unit that did not know the ground. This stop-go style led to over-orderly and rigid tactics which the enemy found easy to predict and which slowed the tempo of operations.

With reason, many corps and divisional commanders were unsure whether their infantry and tanks could cope with fluid operations which they, themselves, were unused to controlling. Open flanks unsettled them. Consequently, Dempsey's clearly expressed intention to keep the front fluid for as long as possible, preferably until the build-up divisions of VIII and XII Corps were ready to attack into gaps in the German front, was obstructed from the start by the poor preparation of commanders and units alike for fluid operations. Whether or not it was too late in the final preparatory period between January and June of 1944 for the Mediterranean commanders, Montgomery himself, Dempsey, and his corps commanders, even the respected O'Connor, to develop greater initiative at the lower levels, the task they would have faced was evident from previous training exercises in the UK. Exercise directors and their umpires were discomforted if units outsmarted the exercise enemy by avoiding him, and did not reward them when they did so. They found it impossible to assess the result of the sort of loose engagement in which the Germans excelled. Exercise results could be more conveniently assessed by counting the guns, shells and companies committed, by planning from a map, assuring smooth staff-work to assemble troops, and by applying technology generously. 21st Army Group's tactics in Normandy flowed from this construct of the battlefield.

Corps ran operations. They were commonly over-ambitious. Consequent failures did not lead to fundamental changes in method. Perhaps it was too late for that. There was tactical ability within divisions but top-heavy corps planning and the set-piece format gave it no scope. Corps commanders too often let small successes go begging because they sought major corps victories and called off an operation to repeat the formula in another attack. They seldom recognized an opportunity to exert tactical leverage to obtain an operational effect. This major British fault showed itself in the inability of divisions to exploit success after a promising start, not only in the days following the landings but subsequently.

Before the landings, Dempsey remarked that unless he seized Caen in the first two days it would take him until July to clear it. He reasoned that if the enemy retained control of the city and its communications he could deny Second Army the space it needed east of the Orne to mount a strong attack round its flank. The plan on Second Army's right was to thrust south to Villers Bocage and Caumont so as to provide a firm base for the Americans to swing south-west to outflank the defences of St Lô. When Caen was not taken immediately, the thrust by the British right flank to Villers was seen as a means to loosen the German grip on the city. When 50th (Tees and Tyne) Infantry Division, supported by 8th Armoured Brigade, which had taken Bayeux on D+1 and headed for Tilly-sur-Seulles and Villers Bocage, was stopped by the Panzer Lehr division outside Tilly, the task of exploiting gaps in the enemy cordon, as in the Montgomery concept, and also of outflanking Caen from the west, fell to 7th Armoured Division, the only armoured division in the follow-up. It came ashore on D+2.

With these two aims competing in his mind, Dempsey told Lieutenant-General G.C. Bucknall, who commanded XXX Corps, that he would commit 7th Armoured Division on 10 June (D+4) to take Villers and then attack Caen from the west. Its task was more ambitious than the armoured brigades which had been intended merely to disrupt the enemy's build-up. While XXX Corps was directed on the axis Tilly–Noyers with the newly captured position at Villers for flank protection, I Corps would move round Caen from the east.

231st Brigade of the 50th Division, had made contact with 5th US Corps on the coast. The latter defeated the 352nd German Infantry and after a day's rest and reorganization on 11 June, its three divisions, from right to left the 29th, 2nd and 1st, would be ready to advance next day. Intelligence deduced that there was a gap in the German front between the remains of the German 352nd facing the 29th and 2nd US Infantry and the Panzer Lehr division holding Tilly. Only on the evening of 12 June was it learned that 2nd Panzer, which had been delayed by air attacks and broken bridges in its march to the front, had reached an assembly area south of Falaise, and was about 35 miles from the front on the previous night. As usually happened on a road march, its tracks were behind its infantry component. In 21st Army Group's Intelligence projection it was believed to have replaced 1st SS Panzer in the German build-up and to be a fitter division. 21st Army Group expected it to be assigned to the Caen front so it was to be a surprise when the Americans met its reconnaissance battalion holding Caumont on the afternoon of 12 June.[3] To the west 3rd Parachute Division was reported coming up behind 352nd, and 17th SS Panzer Grenadier Division was expected to arrive on the west flank also. Clearly, there was no time to be lost if the allies were to exploit the gap.

The American advance that began on 12 June had been instigated by Dempsey, although it was part of the original plan of 21st Army Group. At 10 a.m. on 9 June he met Montgomery and asked him to impress on 5th US Corps the importance of driving south to take Dodigny and then Caumont. Dempsey intended that 51st Highland Division, in I Corps, with 4th Armoured Brigade, would advance out of the bridgehead east of the Orne and move round Caen in a left hook to meet XXX Corps' right hook from Villers. 1st Airborne Division, allotted to him as a reserve, would be dropped between the two claws of the advance on 11 June or later. This questionable operation was arranged with Lieutenant-General F.A.M. Browning, the airborne commander, on the afternoon of 9 June.

On 10 June 7th Armoured Division moved out of Bayeux on an axis passing west of Tilly, while 8th Armoured Brigade continued to support 50th Division against Tilly itself. At 11 a.m. Dempsey met Montgomery and Bradley, and was told that 5 US Corps would send a division south to Caumont on 12 June in conjunction with 7th Armoured Division. At 5 p.m. Dempsey co-ordinated the operation with the three British corps commanders. The airborne would drop on 13 June to co-operate with one or other corps, depending on the progress that 7th Armoured Division made towards Villers.

On 11 June, 7th Armoured, having come up on 50th Division's right, ran into Pz Lehr and made little progress. In the meanwhile, 51st Highland and 4th Armoured Brigade had begun to concentrate east of the Orne when Dempsey heard that the enemy was preparing to attack northwest from Caen. He ordered 4th Armoured Brigade to stand fast west of the Orne as a precaution. Air Vice Marshal Leigh-Mallory, responsible for air support for Montgomery, objected to Dempsey's plan for 1st Airborne Division because he rightly believed it to be hazardous, if for the wrong reasons. He was worrying about the air casualties, not the write-off of 1st Airborne on the ground. Therefore, two parts of Dempsey's ambitious operation had collapsed before 7th Armoured had made any progress.

7th Armoured, with its 22nd Armoured Brigade leading, was held up by Panzer Lehr all day on 11 June. As it seems that the division could have been committed beyond the reach of Panzer Lehr, closer to the Anglo-American army boundary, a day was lost that might have been decisive. In view of the cancellation of the other parts of the operation Bucknall should have confined 7th Armoured Division's task either to taking Panzer Lehr in rear, or to forming a strong shoulder with 5th US Corps' 1st US Infantry, on the high ground near Caumont. The latter's advance had been rapid although careful for it expected German armour of Panzer Lehr or another division to appear. When it reached Caumont in the evening it found the reconnaissance battalion[4] of 2nd Panzer holding the town. It evicted the battalion on the morning of 13 June.

On 12 June, Dempsey was with 22nd Armoured Brigade soon after 11th Hussars' armoured cars reported to XXX Corps that they were in contact with 1st US Infantry, which was making good progress. When Bucknall reported this, Dempsey told him to send in the 7th behind the 11th Hussars. This move started at 3 p.m. with 8th Hussars' Sherman tanks leading 22nd Armoured Brigade. They were held up briefly at Livry in the evening, and lost two tanks on a diversion from the centre line. 'A' Company of 1st Rifle Brigade then cleared the village and the advance halted there for the night. 4th County of London Yeomanry took the lead next morning (13 June) and they were in Villers Bocage by 8 a.m. We shall leave them there for the time being. In the meantime, 50th Division had made little progress, so Panzer Lehr was able to hold the shoulder of 7th Armoured's penetration.

50th Division was 'getting tired', observed the New Zealander, Brigadier James Hargest, who was with them. He had been commanding 5th brigade of the 2nd New Zealand Division in the Western Desert when he was taken prisoner on 25 November 1941 during Crusader. Incarcerated in Italy with Lieutenant-General Richard

O'Connor, both escaped by digging a tunnel through the floor of the chapel of the ancient castle in which they were confined. Hargest and Brigadier Miles, the CRA of the 2nd Division, escaped to Switzerland, the only tunnel-diggers to get away from Italy. From there they travelled across France and over the Pyrenees into Spain. Hargest returned to the UK and was appointed as observer with 50th Division for the landings and the Normandy campaign.[5]

Hargest's comments on the 50th Division fighting at Tilly are in his 'Battle Notes on recent actions up to D+10', 'Battle Notes 13–16 June', and '13–14–16 June 1944'.[6] The division's casualties, which included two brigade commanders, eight commanding officers and over 3000 men, of which the vast majority were infantry, show the intensity of the fighting up to D+10. The figures exclude the fourth brigade, the 56th, which fought with the division, and 8th Armoured Brigade which supported its actions.

The Germans were initially overrun in several engagements between Bayeux and Tilley, but by lying low in the close bocage with its thick hedges and banks, they could re-emerge with a few tanks from woods to snipe and attack troops in rear. The close country allowed snipers to make certain of their targets, which was demoralizing. When the division tired, it could be urged forward only by the personal example of officers, among whom casualties were consequently high. Their habit of carrying map boards that glinted in the sun, indicated their rank to snipers who could pick them off at a distance of 600 yards. Later, company officers wisely carried maps folded into small squares in their pockets.

The English soldier, i.e. from the UK, differs from the soldier from the Dominions. He demands leadership by officers. I notice that as soon as men lose their officers in the thick growth they lose heart. Today, the 16th, I met several Bren gun sections coming back and in reply to my enquiries why! they said the fire was heavy and they had got out of touch. It did not occur to them to go on. Result, great loss of fire power. This is not suggesting they lack courage, they don't. This lack of independence leads to another fault – bunching together. This morning, 16th June, at a German road block which the enemy obviously registered, 8 men were killed or wounded by one mortar [bomb] – half a mile to the rear 8 more despatch riders were casualties and their machine gun destroyed by one shell burst.[7]

Bunching was as bad as ever. One other failing of the Tommy is his liability to sudden panic – not when he is attacking, but when he has gained his objective and is consolidating or has consolidated. On one occasion (10th June) at Saint Pierre, the 8th DLI captured the village with the aid of tanks (8 Armd Bde) with very little loss. That night they held it but at 0700 hours next morning, while under mortar fire, they panicked and some of them went right back to their previous start line – result very heavy casualties. They retook the place that day with little loss.[8]

The old trouble of not relying on their own weapons is prevalent among infantry here. They call for supporting fire always and often when held up whereas they might well get on alone.[9]

The guns are well served and bring down accurate fire at short call and in great volume. They are rather splendid. Their FOOs go well up and seem to know their job. The CRA is very competent.[10]

Hargest's report on an action of the 7th Green Howards of 69 Brigade, supported by tanks of the Sherwood Rangers, describes the character of the infantry fighting. At first, he wrote, the attack surprised the enemy by changing its direction.

After about ³/₄ mile his spandaus [M.G. 42s and 34s, with their intense rates of fire, gave the German infantry section between five and six times the weight of fire of the British section] came into action supported by snipers. Owing to the denseness of the undergrowth the attackers were compelled to keep close together and to offer more than good targets. This close growth – small fields and dense hedges – also prevented the tanks operating with the freedom essential to success. [The Americans fixed hedge and bank cutters, made from German beach obstacles, on the front of some of their tanks.] Our armour had to move along the main road on the axis of advance and leave it by going through gateways into fields, then out again on to the road and so on. It was slow and difficult. The enemy profited by this slowness, pushed mortars up to engage the infantry and the tanks. He cut down trees across the road as blocks and registered on them with mortars. Then he boldly brought up a S.P. anti-tank gun along the road in full view of our troops and brought it into action. All this gave him time and in a couple of hours he had sufficient troops and material on the ground to stop our attack.

The action of our infantry in cooperation with some tanks was good. They pressed in round the forward spandaus and destroyed them.

The action of our tanks on the road and adjacent to it was incredibly bad.[11]

Hargest had a low opinion of British tank units. He described how tanks of 8th Armoured Brigade, in laager above Saint Pierre, allowed a Tiger to settle in a hollow almost in the gun lines and fire for one hour without a single British tank engaging it. The Tiger drove off unmolested. On 10 June, when 7th Armoured Division was advancing towards Tilly from Bayeux, they were held up after six miles by well-hidden defences. The tank officers complained that they were in need of infantry, but although 131 Lorried Infantry Brigade was under command, there was no infantry within three miles of the front. 'The advance which had begun well ended rather dismally by being halted although there was little opposition.'[12]

On his way back, Hargest met the divisional commander, Major General Erskine, and respectfully suggested that infantry and armour could profitably work together in such circumstances. The GOC replied that he preferred to go on alone. 'The pace is too hot for infantry,' he said. 'When I suggested that they could be lorried up to the front by a shuttle service, Erskine replied that they would suffer casualties. "At any rate," he joked, he had advanced 6 miles – if he could maintain that for 30 days that would be 180 miles."' Hargest withdrew. The answer came next day, 11 June. The 7th Armoured Div advanced about a mile and the commander of 22nd Armoured Brigade, Brigadier Hinde, called urgently for infantry. On 12 June the infantry brigade, which had only two battalions at this time, was left to attack alone while the armour was disengaged for its advance on Villers Bocage. Hargest wrote:

> My conclusion is that our tanks are badly led and fought. Only our superior numbers and our magnificent artillery support keeps them in the field at all. They violate most of the elementary principles of war. They bunch up – they are the reverse of aggressive – they are not possessed of the will to attack the enemy.[13]

On 21 June, Hargest reported that the morale of 50th Division was still high after 15 days of continuous fighting, although the men were tired and wet. He wrote that in England there had been a strong feeling among them that the division should not be asked to do the assault on D-day. It had been intended that 49 Division would do it, but General Montgomery determined to use tried troops. There was a lot of resentment, especially in 69 Infantry Brigade. 'They call the C-in-C "Fling 'em in Monty."' Absence without leave became very prevalent in the New Forest area, amounting to well over 1000, and there was considerable unrest. When operations began, all this died down – but the heavy losses in officers and NCOs gave rise to new grumbling.[14]

These heavy casualties were shocking and largely unnecessary, as they were suffered in comparatively small engagements, Hargest commented. An example was 231 Brigade's action on 18 June to capture Hottot and a wood near it. 1st Dorsets was assigned the wood, 1st Hampshires the left sector of Hottot and 1st Devons the right. There were seven field and several medium regiments in support. The operation failed. 1st Dorsets found the wood strongly held and suffered heavy casualties, including 19 officers. The other battalions crossed the Hottot road but infiltration by the enemy and the appearance of tanks drove them back several hundred yards. Hargest commented: 'I feel it is a pity that these units do not hold on once they have a position. It causes great casualties to be advancing and retiring and is bad for morale. The men are very tired.' The inability of 50th Division to make significant progress around Tilly was to isolate 7th Armoured Division at Villers Bocage.

Looney Hinde, commander 22nd Armoured Brigade, earned his name early in his career because of the attention he paid to nature when he was supposed to be attending to more urgent matters. The soubriquet also suited him as a courageous, thrusting, at times incautious commander. Certainly, at Villers Bocage he drove Lieutenant-Colonel Lord Cranley, commanding the 4th CLY, himself a dashing commander with a good fighting record from the Mediterranean, beyond reason. In consequence the advance into Villers Bocage itself was incautiously pressed, despite Cranley's objections. Perhaps Cranley's tendency to imagine Tigers and Panthers in every hedgerow provoked Hinde. The 11th Hussars was not then under divisional command and so 22nd Brigade lacked close armoured car reconnaissance. The 8th Hussars, nominally the armoured reconnaissance regiment, was not employed as such in the advance from Livry to Villers Bocage and the light tank reconnaissance troop of the CLY was not in evidence either. In short, 22nd Armoured Brigade's advance-guard ran head-on into trouble.

Carlo D'Este described Villers Bocage as situated at the head of the Seulles valley, the gateway to Mont Pincon 10 miles to the south, and to the Odon valley and Caen to the east. It controlled the road network for the entire area.[15] The twin objectives of the Division were point 213, a high point north-east of the town on the road to Caen, and the town itself which was also on high ground. The drama began when 4 CLY's A squadron with A Company of 1st Rifle Brigade and its Gunner FOO, Captain Dunlop, were stationary on the road to Caen just beyond the town and short of point 213. B Squadron had moved into the town behind them. Further back the 7th Queens, 8th Hussars and 5th Tanks were between Amaye-sur-Seulles and Tracy Bocage. 7th Queens, part of 131 Lorried Infantry Brigade, was in support of 22nd Brigade and shortly to move into the town. The 6th Queens and 1st Tanks, under command 131 Brigade, were following up the centre line and the 5th Queens, which had only just landed, was moving up to join 131 Brigade.[16]

From point 213 Cranley called for an O Group and officers moved forward up the column which was, unwisely, parked head to tail. The road was lined by trees: a hedge and a high bank made it difficult for wheeled vehicles or tanks to deploy quickly off it. At that moment tanks, several Tigers and a Mark IV Special (that is, one with a long 75-mm gun first introduced in the Western Desert), were seen moving parallel to the road along a dirt track. Then all hell was let loose as the leader turned towards the column and let fly with its 88-mm gun and machine guns. After the leading vehicles had been hit, blocking the road, the other Shermans, carriers and half-tracks were brewed up one by one. The crews, which were dismounted and preparing to brew tea, were taken completely by surprise in untactical mode. A Firefly was traversing on to the Tiger when it was hit and blown up. The Tiger then trundled into the town, where it surprised regimental headquarters tanks in the main street and knocked out one Cromwell commanded by Captain Dyas of B Squadron, who had been stalking it. Sergeant Stan Lockwood, easing his Firefly into the street, saw the Tiger broadside on and pumped four shells into it. The Tiger, traversing quickly, hit the house beside Lockwood, bringing it down on him. Before Lockwood could disentangle himself, his target had gone, despite the damage it must have suffered.

The whole remarkable engagement, which so far had probably taken no more than five minutes, was achieved by the positive action of an officer of Heavy Panzer Abteilung 101, the remarkable young panzer leader *Obersturmfuhrer* Michael Wittman. He had acted on the spur of the moment without waiting for the other tanks of his unit who were in the vicinity. Intelligence had been searching for Wittman's unit, part of 1 SS Panzer Corps, but its arrival at Villers Bocage on 12 June, rather than on the Caen–Falaise sector where it was expected, was a surprise.

Wittman then left the town, in which 7th Queens and B Squadron of the CLY were buzzing with excitement and still intact, as suddenly as he had arrived. Back on point 213, A Squadron and platoons from A Company of 1st Rifle Brigade that had not been caught on the road were tending wounded, and digging hard. Survivors from the slaughter on the road had divided into two small groups which were attempting to make their way up the hill to join them. In the meanwhile Wittman returned to his base south-east of point 213, where he refuelled and rearmed. There he joined the rest of the tanks under Captain Mobius and, with some panzer grenadiers of Panzer Lehr, began an assault on A Squadron.

When Point 213 had been surrounded on three sides, Mobius's tanks reduced its defenders tank by tank and position by position. Some panzer grenadiers of Panzer Lehr brought their weapons ever closer, not without casualties. Looney Hinde, always inclined to 'swan' off on such occasions, had 'gone off the air'. Joe Lever, his brigade major, who never divulged what his master was doing, was left to manage a very untidy command, with the majority of its units west of Villers on the road to Caumont. Cranley, who may have been on point 213 at this time, was also out of radio touch. The brigade group, divided into three parts, had no commander just when it needed one to co-ordinate its action.

The men on point 213 kept fighting until about 3 p.m. The survivors were taken prisoner, although Cranley was not then with them. Thirteen of the panzers then descended again on the town, but this time they received as much as they gave in punishment, for they had left their small force of infantry behind. A dramatic incident was later captured in a Brian de Grineau sketch in the *Illustrated London News*. A Mark IV was halted in the street when a Cromwell in a side street blew out the corner of a house, exposing it to fire from a 17-pounder Firefly which knocked it out. The 7th Queens, under Lt-Colonel Desmond Gordon, had entered houses in the main street, near the station and at the entrance to the town. From there they fought the panzers with 6-pounders, PIATs and any personal arms available. Six German tanks, including Wittman's, were destroyed before the raiders retired.

Reinforcements from the rest of 22nd Armoured Brigade were now required in Villers before 2 Pz Division arrived on the scene to settle matters. Two armoured regiments, the rest of the motor battalion and elements of the S.P. anti-tank regiment were in the vicinity of Tracy Bocage. Brigadier Ekins, recently appointed commander of 131 Brigade, had brought up 5th Queens, but had been cut off after arriving with them at Amaye. The 6th Queens and 1st RTR under his command was then the divisional reserve north of Briquessard. It was placed under the command of Lt-Colonel Mike Carver, commanding 1st RTR. Carver was ordered to clear Briquessard and the road south to Amaye.

The reasons for the actions and orders of Erskine and Bucknall on 13 and 14 June are still not crystal clear. Erskine ordered Hinde, who had reappeared, not to reinforce Villers but to evacuate after dark on 13 June. After discussing the Tracy Bocage position Erskine decided that it was unsound and ordered Hinde to pull back the units there to the stronger Amaye position on the morning of 14 June. He intended to hold Amaye until the reinforcements that he hoped Bucknall would provide arrived. In the evening of 13 June 2nd Panzer started its attack against Villers. The Queens suffered casualties before evacuating the town, mounted on B Squadron tanks and those of 5 RHA.

Carver's force cleared the road to Amaye in the afternoon of 13 June. He found that 2 Panzer Division's tanks and infantry were forming a line from east to west south of it, and had strong elements to the north of it as well. 1st Tanks reported that they had knocked out two Panthers, a Tiger and several Mark IVs south of the road, and Carver's infantry secured the bridge over the river southeast of Briquessard during the night. The fighting north and south of the road at Amaye continued on 14 June until 2 Panzer launched a major attack against 22nd Armoured Brigade in the afternoon.

2 Panzer was repulsed decisively, mainly by artillery, including a substantial amount from the US position at Caumont. Before this engagement the question was whether the division should hold Amaye after being reinforced, or evacuate. The roads up which it had advanced had been cut in a few places, but Carver's actions made it perfectly possible for reinforcements to reach the fighting and, in the opinion of Erskine and Hinde, for the front to be held with them. Without re-inforcement, they thought that, in the end, they would suffer a reverse.

> Erskine's role, in short, was to represent to Bucknall that his division was out on a limb, had encountered unexpected opposition and was headed for a hiding unless reinforced or pulled back. This Erskine did with exceptional clarity and there can be no excuse for misunderstanding by his higher headquarters.[17]

Bucknall's response was to tell Erskine that he expected 50th Division to break through to Hottot on the morning of 14 June, when they would attack with substantial air and artillery support. When they failed to make progress Bucknall deemed it too late to ask for battalions of the newly arrived 49th Division, or to commit 151 brigade of 50th, the divisional reserve, to follow 7th Armoured Division's route forward to Briquessard. Consequently Bucknall ordered 7th Armoured to withdraw before it had repulsed 2 Panzer Division on the afternoon of 14 June.

The order to withdraw, Operation Aniseed, reached 22 Armoured Brigade when it was still confident of holding Amaye. Yet, after 2 Panzer had been repulsed, Major Joe Lever, responsible for the administration of the withdrawal, and expecting a further attack, thought that the position was precarious and that 'the situation could have become untenable after, say, 24 hours'. It is fair to say that opinions were divided on that subject.

The idea that the division was bound to withdraw if it did not receive reinforcements originated with Erskine. Thus he placed the responsibility for the withdrawal on the shoulders of Bucknall, who decided that he could not reinforce. That Dempsey was angry with Bucknall and Erskine after the withdrawal, although he agreed that it was necessary, indicates that a muddle had occurred. Indeed, if we compare the strengths of the two sides in the sector between Tilly, Villers Bocage and Caumont on 14 and 15 June, we must conclude that not only had XXX Corps performed poorly but that there was no need for a retreat, for the Allies were superior in numbers. The ubiquitous and tenacious Panzer Lehr managed to hold off 50th Division and 8th Armoured Brigade in front of it, while it defeated the advance guard of 7th Armoured Division in its rear, with the considerable aid of Abteilung 101's formidable heavy tanks. 2nd Panzer, except for its reconnaissance unit, did not arrive until 7th Armoured had decided to give up the battle at Villers. When it attacked the Amaye position it was repulsed, so the main body of the 7th Armoured had not been engaged at Villers and was not defeated at Amaye. As the decision to withdraw preceded that engagement, the conclusion of Max Hastings and Carlo D'Este is that Bucknall lost his nerve and Erskine should have persevered. Close to the Briquessard–Amaye position lay a strong 1st US Division at Caumont. It does not seem that Bucknall or Dempsey considered the two positions as complementary.

To criticize an operations on grounds that another conjectured course would have led to a better outcome is questionable. But Bucknall was wrong to continue to attack with 50th Division 'in the same old way' and expect it to succeed against Hottot. Panzer Lehr was bound to continue to resist in the Tilly position because it could not afford to allow a break-through while the situation in its rear was fluid. Carver, in correspondence with Alistair Horne when the latter was writing his book *Montgomery, the Lonely Leader*, argued that Bucknall had no reserves to commit. I agree that 50th was a spent force and that a brigade of 49th Division, working with 33rd Armoured Brigade, which also had recently landed, should not, ideally, have been committed to a difficult first operation. On the other hand new divisions were more successful than the veterans in Normandy. Furthermore, the power of artillery defeated every German attempt to counter-attack during the campaign. The odds on 1st US and 7th Armoured holding 2 Panzer were excellent, therefore. Had an extra infantry brigade, supported by an armoured brigade, come up the corridor, the position of Panzer Lehr should have been untenable and certainly more tenuous than that of 7th Armoured.

This was not Bucknall's operation: a member of his staff reported that he was out of touch and making little sense during it.[18] It was essentially Dempsey's plan and its over-ambitious link with Caen made it half-baked. Dempsey needed to revise its purpose when the Caen arm of it was still-born. As too often with British operations, it attempted too much for the troops committed, and the purpose was not clearly thought through. The gap on Panzer Lehr's left flank certainly needed to be exploited. The first option was to attack Panzer Lehr in rear and make its destruction the main purpose. The front would then have been significantly advanced. Certainly, the penetration of 7th Armoured Division to Villers Bocage was badly managed tactically, but its position there was bound to invite attack from three sides. It was as well that only an element of the division reached it. Alternatively, 7th Armoured could have been more closely linked to the thrust to Caumont by US 1st Division, from which it could threaten the flank of Panzer Lehr. Reinforced, it could have been part of the subsequent action of the build-up corps that attacked across the Odon in Operation Epsom. Probably the Germans would have straightened their line in the Tilly sector when threatened from the west flank.

Neither Dempsey nor Montgomery paid enough attention to what was occurring. On 14 June Dempsey noted in his diary: 'I agreed to 30 Corps' proposal to withdraw leading elements of 7 Armd Div from the Villers Bocage area to the Caumont area.' It seems from the entry that he did not intend the division to withdraw beyond Briquessard as far as the River Aurette at St Honorine de Ducy. It was probably that that angered him and convinced him that Bucknall and Erskine would both have to be removed. If Erskine had 'carried out my orders he would not have been kicked out of Villers Bocage,' he noted. 'But by this time 7th Armoured Division was living on its reputation and the whole handling of that battle was a disgrace.' Dempsey did not disclose what were the orders that Erskine had not obeyed that would have made such a difference. His own grandiose plan with 1st Airborne would have led to a disaster rather than only a missed opportunity.

While this was occurring on 14 June, Montgomery wrote to Brooke that he had decided 'to be defensive in the Caen sector' and 'hold strongly and fight offensively in the general area Caumont – Villers Bocage, i.e. at the junction of the two armies.'[19] The same day, Dempsey had asked Leigh-Mallory for Bomber Command and 8 USAAF to support an attack on the left of I Corps to take Caen – and Leigh-Mallory had agreed. Next day it was found that Leigh-Mallory had not consulted Tedder and the air force turned the idea down. Instead, Dempsey approved Bucknall's plan to attack again with 7th Armoured on the axis Caumont–Aunay-sur-Odon and with 49 Division on Cristot–Noyers–Aunay:

> This is a sound plan as it enables our overwhelming superiority in tanks to come into action on comparatively suitable ground. I told him to put the bridges over R. Orne at Amaye [actually behind the Odon] and Thury-Harcourt as objectives for strong recce forces.[20]

Bucknall's diary entry on 15 June states: 'Gen. Eisenhower & Air Marshall [*sic*] Tedder visited after lunch, with Army Comd – very nice and complimentary. Army comd accepted my plan for further advance.'[21]

This was anything but a sound plan, for 7th Armoured had just been adjudged too weak to hold on to its positions and 49th's converging attack to Aunay was beyond its capability. The competence of both men must be questioned. Perhaps Bucknall, sensing Dempsey's disapproval over the handling of 7th Armoured Division at Villers, took the hint and was sending them back into the battle. But it seems likely that this (second) impracticable operation was Dempsey's response to Montgomery's decision to concentrate on the right flank.[22]

The operation never took place. Villers Bocage had been flattened by heavy bombers while 7th Armoured Division was withdrawing. The ruins were not taken by XXX Corps until August. Dempsey's reference to superior tank strength reminds us of command thinking in the Western Desert before it faced the truth about the German's superior competence in that department. Certainly, he was thinking that he could afford to lose tanks rather than infantry. That was to be his ruling thought when he planned Operation Goodwood (Map 11) a

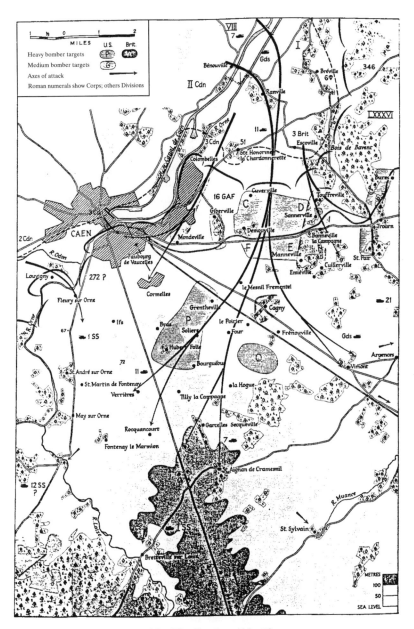

11 The Goodwood battle

month later. Had he still not acknowledged the power of German anti-tank guns to stop tanks in the open by then?

I do not think that my own division was ready for the shock of reality on 18 July, although 11th Armoured had already been through the fire on Point 112. The night before the battle tracks and wheels moved up to the Orne bridges by separate routes, as was customary. Each route was carefully marked by dimly lighted cans. You followed the differential light on the vehicle in front and hoped that no driver would fall asleep. It was a grave error for an officer or NCO to allow the column to stop for that reason. In the morning, after the 11th Armoured had passed through ahead of us and our own armour had followed it was the turn of 32nd Lorried Infantry. We saw the enormous bomb holes created by the strategic bombing previously. For this operation heavy bombers had droned over in an untidy gaggle to drop their bombs where the armour was to advance. The lorried infantry of the 11th Armoured were to take the villages that their armour would by-pass. I can remember thinking that sending in the infantry and the tanks separately was a mistake. But it was explained that the narrow entrance to the battlefield over the Orne made it unavoidable. What was not unavoidable was using 11th Armoured's infantry to clear Demouville and other villages in the open country through which their tanks were to advance round Caen, instead of accompanying them to help with the deadly anti-tank guns.

I next remember arriving with the 5th Coldstream outside Cagny in the afternoon. Over to the right tanks were knocked out and I saw crews walking back like riders in a point to point having fallen at a fence. Many tanks were on fire and I knew well enough what that meant for their crews. This was happening on the slopes up towards Bourguebus. Our own infantry had to clear Cagny which had been skilfully defended by some 88-mm Tigers and SPs. My guns were still on the move and out of radio range as well. A gunner without his guns is a vision of frustration. It was not until the evening that they came on the air, bright and raring to go. By that time we were in Cagny and the 5th Coldstream were clearing out some very young and rather frightened SS youngsters.

Next I saw the Corps Commander, Richard O'Connor, whisking into Cagny riding on an armoured car, red hat and all. We waved to each other, not that he knew me from Adam, but it showed the troops were happy and cheerful. There was an O Group and I had to make a fire-plan for the battalion to attack the next village, called Frenouville, early next morning. This village was through the woods along the railway from Caen to Vimont, which was originally our objective. Registration was achieved, a barrage laid on and bombardments of various possible targets put on call, although it was remarkable how little we actually knew about the locations of the enemy. The CO intended to walk forward behind the leading companies, which gave me a problem, for a large tank was not suitable on the march and I needed something better than a walkie-talkie to keep in touch with guns and FOOs. Fortunately I had purloined a Number 22 Set, a rather less powerful wireless than the Number 19, but one that could be mounted on a stretcher and carried forward. So that was the scheme. I forget how my FOOs functioned that day because only I had a 22 set. Perhaps they had their tanks and merged in with the 1st Armoured Coldstream, who provided a squadron to support the attack. That would have been normal, although it was the first time that we had worked with the tanks.

The village was taken without much fuss, which meant the casualties seemed light to everyone except those actually killed or wounded. Then came the lull while the enemy were discovering where we were. You then preferred to move on before they had completed the work but on this occasion we were told that Frenouville was as far as we were to go. The operation had fizzled out tamely: it was not a breakthrough. Then, as a steady stream of rustling mortar bombs fell among us with adamant bangs and whining splinters, it began to rain. The rain was by no means the reason for our halting in Frenouville It seemed a good moment to walk forward and find out where the companies were and whether the FOOs were happy and being useful.

The problem in the front of the village was sniping SPs, which were hard to identify and even harder to hit with field guns firing indirect. Their shells burst in the trees so one was better off in the open. Back in battalion headquarters my half-track (the Sherman must have been banned from the vicinity) was within a yard or two of the battalion's rear radio link to brigade in another half-track. Very suddenly a mortar bomb fell right into the rear-link, killed the occupants and started a fire. We put out the fire and my signallers took over rear-link with our 19 Set. It was just as well that gunners were obsessed with their radio communications and covered themselves two or three times over with extra sets.

It rained solidly for 24 hours. Then rumours that we were to be relieved by the Highland Division reached us. Eventually, after a few false starts, their very smartly dressed advance party arrived. The atmosphere of a relief is much the same in all theatres and wars. You have the wise, tired and probably dirty incumbents and the apparently alert, efficient, but basically ignorant newcomers who will, you think to yourself with satisfaction, very soon learn what is what. You cannot leave soon enough but duty must be served, and you tell them all you know; particular about sniping guns, warning signs and places that it is inviting disaster to visit in certain lights. You know as you leave that another operation will surely follow for you and that you will quickly forget about this unpleasant place and the Highlanders.

Back at the gun position you visit the command post and then talk to each of the eight gun detachments, who like to hear what their shells have done and where you have been. They will get an exaggerated edition later from the signallers and your drivers, who like to be knowledgeable and feel important, and appear to the gunners to be living dangerously. The gunners' faces were swollen from incessant mosquito assaults and the other batteries had been regularly attacked at last light by Junkers 88s flying at tree-top level. So they could feel they had been in the battle; and they had, for they had responded night and day to incessant fire orders from the whole of VIII Corps.

A visit to regimental headquarters followed to tell the CO what had happened and talk to Arthur Dumbrell, the Adjutant, whose brilliant performance on the wireless held the regimental net together day after day and was to do so month after month until the end of the war. After dark, with a white enamel mug of whisky held lovingly in the hand, you play liar dice. This game was particularly popular. A bottle of Dutch Bols could be held up to indicate that you disbelieved the assertion of the player on your right, although his eyes were bright with innocence.

We were in reserve for Guy Simonds' battles on the Falaise road but we were not used, although the guns continued firing day in and day out. Then came the switch to the bocage country for Bluecoat on the right flank where we fought after the American break-through on 25 July until the Falaise pocket closed.

13 Battles on the Falaise Road

The future became clear to German commanders during July. The weight of material against them was grinding down their divisions remorselessly and they would be lucky to avoid a disastrous defeat. Certainly, the Allies had missed opportunities through over-caution and tactical incompetence, but their own skill and quick-thinking, and their superior ground weapons could not delay the inevitable for much longer. General von Kluge, who replaced Rommel when the latter was wounded by fighter planes, pressed OKW to allow him to withdraw to the Seine while he was still able. Hitler's need to gain time for the V1 campaign to take effect was a reason for his refusal to agree on this occasion, but the decision continued his disastrous policy in Russia of never yielding ground.

There were a few in the highest command echelons of the allies in England and the United States who did not accept the German view of the battle. They had fallen under the malign influence of words of power like 'attrition', which they associated with lost Western Front battles on the Somme and at 3rd Ypres. They had not accepted that most campaigns were attritions by 1944 and that the defence had an advantage. Surely, the American press was beginning to prompt, the enormous amount of material that the Allies possessed should have ensured victory in July? That the Allied armies were inferior to 'the Nazis' in the field was unacceptable. There must be something wrong with the leadership. The further from the front the observer was, the less willing was he to acknowledge the limitations imposed on the Allies by their weapons, particularly their tanks, and by their training. It was not acceptable to point out that most Allied divisions were still novices, even at this stage. It was more convenient to blame their leaders for their comparative lack of success.

Veterans from the Mediterranean relearned the hard facts of combat with German soldiers. Nothing had changed. German weapons were still superior and their units seldom made mistakes. Green Allied units learned those truths after a sharp lesson or two. But all had to enter a learning curve to cope on equal terms. Retaining their morale during the experience tested their fortitude.

173

Armoured units had to deploy a troop of four tanks to stand a chance of destroying one Tiger or Panther. They had to stalk their opponent skilfully to attack his flank or rear at short range, for the Tiger was actually and the Panther virtually invulnerable from the front. German tanks could be caught in enfilade when they moved forward, but in most cases Allied tanks were advancing against a concealed opponent whom they never saw because of the high percentage of first-shot kills that he achieved. Even when Allied tank gunners scored hits, their 75-mm gun projectile did not often penetrate Panthers and Tigers. Consequently, many tank commanders were disinclined to open fire for fear of revealing their positions until they could be sure of a kill from flank or rear. German infantry in the bocage were also at an advantage with their superior, hand-held anti-tank weapon, the *Panzerfaust*, and the heavier bazooka, the *Panzerschreck*. They man-handled towed anti-tank guns into concealed positions with remark-able skill, courage and energy. Their self-propelled field-guns were devastating at short range using a telescope or laying the gun visually. The high rate of fire of German infantry machine guns (MG 34 and MG 42) gave them an advantage in the fire-fight over the Bren. the unreliable sten and the rifle. Sydney Jary, who commanded a platoon of the Somerset Light Infantry in the 43rd (Wessex) Division from the Normandy bocage to Bremerhaven, had this to say about his weapons and those of the Germans:

> Trained on the Bren light machine gun, I did not understand the use of suppressive firepower. To me, all fire was meant to hit and, with luck, kill the enemy. Doctrine and training had stipulated firing the Bren in short bursts of about five rounds. We were told that this produced greater accuracy, avoided the barrel overheating and con-served ammunition. The Germans, as I learned within a few hours of my arrival, thought otherwise. They fully understood the suppres-sive use of firepower, and the MG 34 and MG 42 were designed for that purpose. The Germans were therefore able to produce a far greater volume of firepower per man than we could.[1]

This amounted to 2400 rounds per minute from an infantry section with two belt-fed MG 42s, as opposed to the British 450 with only one magazine-fed Bren. This figure goes a long way to explaining why British infantry seemed unable to close with their enemy without pow-erful artillery and tank support and even then their attacks were halted after a short advance. The sources of the murderous fire from several German infantry sections was concealed because their tracer, unlike British tracer, started to burn some distance from the muzzle. Jary's comment that 'once you were there with rifle and bayonet, my experience was that all resistance ceased' simply underlines the point that keeping Tommy at a distance was Jerry's game, whether it was played with machine guns or tank guns.[2]

Exceptionally, the Germans found themselves at a disadvantage. At Cagny, during Goodwood, the 2nd Grenadier Guards met Tiger tanks for the first time. Sergeant White, commanding a Firefly, had a clear shot at a Tiger. The blinding flash of the cordite propellent made it impossible for the gunner to see his target until the shell had travelled at least 1000 yards. It was necessary for a neighbouring tank on a flank to report its strike over his B radio set. 'Left ten, down fifty', and so on, would come the correction. On this occasion the observer saw the Tiger fire in response and knew that the Firefly was a dead duck, for a Tiger seldom missed. Unlike our tank guns, they had flashless cordite. Although the American sighting arrangements were good on the Sherman firing APCBC (armour piercing cap with ballistic cap) the Tiger had a much better 10× magnification Zeiss telescope. Surprisingly, the Tiger missed the Firefly several times while five shots from the accompanying 75 mm Sherman bounced off its armour. The Sherman then loaded high explosive and the Tiger reversed over a ridge. It was on the Staff College tour of 1956 that Brigadier A.G. Heywood, a captain in 1944, learned from Lt-Colonel Freiherr von Rosen, then a platoon commander in 503 Heavy Tank Batallion, that RAF bombing had turned over 22 out of the 30 Tiger tanks in the battalion and that the alignment of the telescopes of the survivors was so shaken that their 88-mm guns were inaccurate.[3]

It was clear, in theory, that only by combining tanks, infantry and artillery – including anti-tank guns, of course – could battalions and brigades succeed against such competent and well-equipped defenders. In practice, joint action was not easy. In an attack through close country, tanks had to move tactically, covering each other by fire to avoid being picked off by well-concealed Panthers, Tigers, Mark IV Specials, various towed anti-tank guns and infantry weapons. On the other hand, sections and platoons and single tanks had to work together. The tank commander, with his head out of the turret to see what was going on, was often sniped. Closed down and relying on his optics, he became relatively blind and deaf to the needs of the infantry section. In open country, like that south of Caen, the long range of German guns and their penetrative power were decisive. For the infantry to get within striking distance of an enemy tank in the wheat fields was not only impossible in daylight but suicidal. Smoke and defensive shelling from your own guns could help, but co-ordinating fire was difficult. So tanks, including FOOs mounted in tanks, and infantry did not often accompany one another on the way to the objective, and if they did both were reduced greatly in numbers by the time they arrived on it.[4]

Courses of instruction in the UK, including tactical exercise with infantry or even field-firing exercises, did not ensure effectiveness in this team game. They helped, but practice in several live actions with the same units was a necessity. Every tank commander and crew needed courage and initiative and tactical sense of a high order. Small battles involving section NCOs, very young platoon officers and the crews of single tanks took place all over a battlefield. But lessons were only learned by survivors, and the wastage rate in Normandy, mainly in infantry rifle companies, was comparable to the Somme.[5]

Performance depended greatly on junior officers and NCOs knowing each other. In an independent armoured brigade like the 8th there was a tendency for squadrons and troops to change hands from day to day like library books. Prejudices had to be overcome, such as the armoured view that: 'All infantry brigadiers look the same; middle-aged, rather grim, slow thinkers and without any sense of humour.' Humour was essential. 'Arn't you under a misapprehension about the target – surely it is a cow? Over.' 'I've never seen a cow with a turret on it before. Off.'[6]

These comments about tank–infantry fighting, and the inequality between German and British arms, may serve to modify, in the mind of the reader, Brigadier Hargest's severe remarks about British armour and infantry. There is no doubt that British tank crews were intimidiated by German tanks, with good reason. But as they gained experience and with it skill, their performance improved. They learned how to look after themselves, help the infantry and be helped by them. That was not an easy juggling act to perform. Certain armoured brigades, for instance the independent 6th Guards Brigade, did it particularly well. Their team-work with the 6th Airborne parachute battalions after the Rhine was noteworthy. But armour remained cautious until the end of the war.

In Goodwood the setting of the battle placed armour at a disadvantage. Separating the infantry from the armour was an obvious weakness in the plan. The tactical air support against the German anti-tank screen broke down because of casualties to communications and key personnel. A third factor was that a proposed second phase air assault was thought likely to delay the assault on the Bourguebus Ridge and omitted. If the advance had gone well, cancelling it was believed impracticable, and dangerous if the message failed to reach the air force in time. A result was that the German anti-tank screen was outside the first bombardment zone and was intact when 11th Armoured met it on the ridge. In the meantime, the artillery was unable to pass through the traffic congestion and the armour had no artillery support at a crucial time.

We have learned that Simonds' 2nd Canadian Corps was consigned to continue the battle on the Bourguebus–Verrières Ridge on the Falaise road while the Americans mounted Operation Cobra. Simonds had his two infantry divisions and the Canadian armoured brigade with 7th Armoured Division in support and Guards Armoured in reserve. Called Operation Spring, the attack was mainly by infantry. Except for 2nd Canadian Infantry's disaster at Dieppe, Spring was the bloodiest Canadian operation of the war. The Corps gained some ground, but the armour was demoralized by the long-range, accurate fire of German anti-tank guns firing from hull-down positions at the edge of villages. Some squadrons lost half their tanks without firing a shot. The 3rd Division had been in the assault on 6 June, was tired and disgruntled at not being granted a prolonged rest. Its commander, Major-General RFJ Keller, was almost sacked and Major-General Charles Foulkes commanding 2nd Division, whose performance was undistinguished, was lucky to avoid the same fate. Their attacks on narrow fronts led to muddles when fresh units passed through, and allowed the defence to concentrate against the attackers. When their communications broke down, divisional, brigade and sometimes battalion commanders showed a lack of grip and sense of what was probably happening and what to do about it. Simonds persevered with the attack longer than his orders made necessary.

The Canadians were at a disadvantage in Spring because the high ground west of the Orne, particularly Point 112 which had featured during Epsom, gave the Germans an excellent view of the battlefield from the flank. Better co-operation between the 12th Corps and 2nd Canadian to deny the Germans that advantage might have helped 2nd Infantry Division's advance on the right.

The errors made in Spring were similar to those in many previous battles in Normandy that fell short of expectations. The Canadians were not markedly worse, although morale problems in Second Army, owing to fatigue and lack of success, came to a head at this time.[7] Divisional and brigade commanders made plans off the map without

looking at the ground with their battalion commanders. They underestimated the time taken to issue orders, reconnoitre, feed the men and
march up to a start-line. The start-line was often not secured so that
casualties were suffered during forming up. Tanks occasionally arrived
late and were strangers to the units they were supporting. As a result,
neither element knew what was expected of it. Patrols often failed to
reconnoitre the ground to locate the main enemy positions. The
Germans surprised second-phase attackers by reoccupying positions
after they had temporarily abandoned them to avoid a preliminary
bombardment. Villages reported cleared were later found occupied
because troops had not searched basements and had not prevented
infiltration. On one occasion the Germans made use of mine tunnels
to reoccupy parts of a village behind the leading Canadians. Too often
objectives were taken in the first instance and lost to well-organized
panzergrenadier counter-attacks from dead ground.

It was a common occurrence in Normandy for ground taken initially
to be lost to an immediate counter-stroke, particularly if the Germans
had withdrawn temporarily to avoid the barrage or bombardment that
preceded the attack. Defensive fire tasks laid on before the battle
added to new ones arranged on reaching the objective were supposed
to be a drill with the artillery, and when they were called down they
were nearly always decisive. But things sometimes went wrong. The
gunner observation officer might have been killed and, more important, his wireless communications destroyed: perhaps infantry wireless
was not working either, so no fire was called for on the German
counter-attack. Slow defensive reorganization on the objective, particularly failure to get anti-tank guns forward immediately, was a
common fault. But it took courage to drive guns forward under fire
and to find the right location for them in open country. 'Straggling',
which had been common on the Western Front, meant that only a
small percentage of attackers initially reached the objective. Others
joined after the dangerous part of the attack was over. It made reorganization on the objective difficult and gave the impression to those who
had reached it that the position could not be held for lack of men.
Inadequate radio communications hung over the whole performance,
particularly in the evening when attacks often came in and radio interference was at its worst. Lack of curiosity and of aggression by men
who were not anxious to enquire too closely where the enemy were
and what they were doing, was common. Poor map reading, unobser-
vant and noisy infantry and lack of rigour in choosing and concealing
positions were frequent criticisms. The flow of information during the

battle was nearly always deficient. Although routine reports have to follow a proforma and can be irritating when bureaucratically enforced, demands for information spur troops to find out what the enemy is doing. Failure to receive information ought to provoke commanders to despatch liaison officers or to go forward themselves to find out what is going on.

These are the comments of an experienced sceptic, not a cynic. After Normandy, most of the errors had been corrected, to the extent that they were no longer committed through ignorance, seldom through idleness, and far less often through a desire for a quiet life. The Second Army ran a tighter ship. Probably, also, the German Army was not as formidable after Normandy.

Goodwood and Spring taught Simonds useful lessons. In open country attacking tanks and infantry were vulnerable in daylight to long-range fire. He calculated that in darkness and smoke it ought to be the defending anti-tank guns that would be at a disadvantage. In practice, apart from overcoming the technical problem of orientation while advancing in darkness, the tanks had to be persuaded to discard their custom of closing down operations at night. While at the Staff College in 1936 and 1937, Simonds had given thought to how the infantry could keep up with tanks on the way to their objective under shell-fire. He concluded that mounting them in armoured carriers was a solution. Despite the experience of Spring he still believed in attacking on a narrow front, but that could help armour to keep direction in darkness. His observation of heavy air support suggested that it ought to be used only on the flanks to avoid making craters and inflicting casualties through shorts. Noting a lesson from Goodwood, he considered using it in both phases of a two phase attack.

Ideas are useless unless they can be applied and here Simonds exploited the ingenuity of his Canadian engineers and signals officers. He removed the guns from the 105-mm self-propelled 'Priest' field guns, used in the beach assault, and used them as armoured carriers for the infantry. They were called 'defrocked' priests. The apertures left when the guns were removed were filled by armour plate scavenged from the beaches. Searchlights beamed on cloud-cover gave artificial moonlight to enable columns to keep direction in the dark. Bofors guns fired tracer and illuminated markers on the ground indicated the flanks. A version of the signals device used by aircraft to keep within a radio beam were used by some guiding vehicles.

These were the ideas that Simonds used for Operation Totalize that was intended to sweep away opposition on the Falaise road at night on

8 August, the anniversary of the great Canadian and ANZAC victory in 1918. In the first phase two armoured brigades and parts of two infantry divisions were to overrun the opposition that had held up 2nd Corps in Spring, while infantry followed to mop up by-passed villages. The startline for the second phase would be established by daylight on the following day and a deep and final advance would then take place on a front of two armoured divisions behind another air bombardment. The model for the plan was the flanking movement of the Second New Zealand Division and the 8th Armoured Brigade at El Hamma in Tunisia. They had advanced without losing direction, through dust and smoke that confused enemy guns and tanks, behind a rapidly moving thin barrage, a cab-rank of Kittyhawk fighter-bombers overhead.

The main objective of Totalize was Falaise and the object was to meet the Americans and close the trap on the German armies. As in Goodwood, it had to be decided whether or not to dispense with the second phase of the air attack. If it were laid on it could not be cancelled subsequently without the risk of some air formations failing to receive the message, as had happened in the cancelled first attempt at Operation Cobra: if it were not laid on it could not be demanded subsequently. A very successful first phase would call for an immediate advance in the morning before the enemy recovered from the surprise of the armoured night attack; a second air attack would then be counter-productive. Informed that German armour was holding the second line in strength, as they had in Goodwood, Simonds decided to have American heavy bombers plaster them.

Simonds' innovation of a night attack with armour and infantry, despite a degree of chaos owing to dust and mist, was successful. Brigadier (later Major-General) Elliot Rodger, Simonds' Brigadier General Staff, commented to the author:

> I well recall his O Group before Totalize when the several div comds sat in a circle under the pine trees (all much older than GGS and some with desert sand in their ears) to whom he opened, 'Gentlemen, we will do this attack at night with armour.' Their jaws dropped noticeably. Prior to then I believed that not I nor any of the Corps HQ brigs knew of this plan. Perhaps he had some prior discussion with Clark (Chief Signals Officer) on the considerable plans needed to help the tanks and defrocked priests keep direction in the dark. But the whole plan poured forth complete and crystal clear.[8]

The 4th Canadian and Polish Armoured Divisions, which were to execute the second phase, were novices. The Poles were only included in a revised version of the plan when it was decided to carry the second phase through to Falaise without a pause. The front was broadened to include them but was still only 1000 yards wide, narrower than the divisional commanders wished, for it prevented their manoeuvring to avoid physical features, or resistance which was to be taken on by the 3rd Canadian Division following behind. Another important change was caused by the success of Ritchie's 12th Corps which had forced the Orne on the right, drawing German units from Simonds' front. Consequently, Totalize started on 7 August instead of the 8th. Better intelligence about the weakness of the German front would have suggested the cancellation of the American air attack even at that stage. Simonds let the plan stand.

There is still dispute over Simonds' decision. The phase 2 start-line was secured by units from phase 1 by 8 a.m. on 8 August, although the armoured divisions for phase 2 did not pass through the first battlefield until later. With hindsight, valuable time would have been saved had the phase-1 units gone ahead. As it was Kampfgruppe Waldmuller with a Tiger force under Captain Wittman, of Villers Bocage fame, from the 12th Corps front, seized high ground at St Aignan de Cramesnil by 11.30 a.m., which delayed and confused the Poles. Kampfgruppes Krause and Wunsche went to a bottleneck at Potigny between the Laison and Laize streams. The air attack missed these troops, who were able to play an important part in subsequent operations, and also caused many casualties in 2nd Corps. It contributed nothing to the operation.

The permanent integration of particular armoured regiments with infantry battalions, and the interchangeability of the roles of armoured brigade and infantry brigade headquarters, normal by now in other armoured divisions, had not been adopted in the Polish and 4th Canadian Divisions. That is, perhaps, an indication of the inexperience of these two divisions and may have contributed to the want of drive and aggression that brought the advance to a halt by the end of the day. Simonds and Major-General George Kitching, 4th Armoured Division commander, then took the Canadian commanders by the scruff of the neck and ordered them to continue the advance after midnight on 8/9 August. In fact, most of the armour, in the manner habitual to them, had retired to night laagers. The 28th Armoured Regiment with the Algonquin infantry battalion, directed on Point 195 about five miles down the Falaise road and a mile to its right, was the exception. Unhappily it lost direction by about 90 degrees arriving on point 140 left, instead of right, of the Falaise road where it was surrounded, attacked and annihilated by Waldmuller, Krause and Wunsche and their Tigers and Panthers.

When operations came to a standstill intense pressure was applied by Montgomery at the top and by Simonds as corps commander on the 11th. Falaise had to be captured 'quickly'. Simonds delivered 'a very tough and unpleasant briefing of all armd regt C.O.s. He blasted armoured regiments for their lack of support for infantry – he quoted the heavy infantry casualties of the past month compared to armour.'[9] There was to be no more closing down after dark. The result was Operation Tractable in daylight on the 14th, which meant another delay to arrange it. The APCs were used again: the start was like the Grand National with smoke and dust as well. Unfortunately Army intelligence had reported the Laison river to be fordable 'everywhere'. On the bank the scene was reminiscent of Becher's Brook as tanks milled up and down looking for crossings. Two hours were lost and the chance of a break-through with them. When Brigadier Booth commanding 4th Armoured Brigade was killed on the first morning he was not replaced until the evening. Lt-Colonel Scott, his replacement, broke his ankle and command simply ceased for the rest of the day. There was another delay before Robert Moncell, from Corps headquarters, took his place. Yellow smoke used by the artillery for target markings was also used by the RAF for the bomb safety line. The result was 400 Canadian and Polish casualties. Air Vice-Marshal Arthur Coningham, visiting the fighting to observe the air bombardment, was caught in a quarry and very nearly became one of them. Unkindly, no tears were shed on his account.

Falaise did not fall until 18 August, in the meantime the thrust line of the Corps had been redirected towards Trun.

The battles on the Falaise road have been considered less than successful – if not downright failures. In that they contributed to the destruction of the German armies in Normandy that judgment is too harsh. However, German commanders have enjoyed pointing out how they held up the advance with negligible forces and a critical school of thought on the allied side has embraced their views. Kurt Meyer, who commanded the redoubtable 12th SS (Hitler Youth) Panzer Division, was incarcerated in Dorchester Penitentiary in New Brunswick, Canada after the war, where he was interviewed extensively. Some of his comments fittingly summarize British operations in Normandy:

Every opening phase of a Canadian operation was a complete success and the staff worked a mathematical masterpiece. The staff always succeeded in burying the enemy under several thousand tons of explosives and in transforming the defence positions into a cemetary. The Canadian Army never followed up their successes to reach a complete victory. Every one of the Canadian attacks lost its push and determination after a few miles.... British and Canadian planning was absolutely without risk; neither Army employed its armoured strength for which it was created. In both armies the tank was used, more or less, as an infantry support weapon. Armoured warfare is a matter of using given opportunities on the battlefield, therefore the division commander belongs in the leading combat group to see for himself, to save precious time, and to make lightning decisions from his moving tank.... The British and Canadian forces executed the operation in an inflexible, time-wasting method. Never once did 'speed' as the most powerful weapon of armoured warfare, appear.[10]

14 Montgomery's Reputation

Montgomery's reputation was at its zenith on D-day. In October, after a rapid Allied advance to the Low Countries and the German frontier had ended in tough fighting and an almost static front, he had been eclipsed. By then Eisenhower had held supreme command for more than a month. He had intended that Bradley and Montgomery should manage operations jointly, under his own supervision. They had worked together after Patton and his Third Army took to the field in the last stages in Normandy and Bradley became commander of 12th Army Group. Eisenhower would have preferred a ground forces commander to manage operations but neither Montgomery nor Bradley was acceptable in that role and no one else was suitable. So the command arrangements were a compromise which might have worked had the three principals agreed over operational policy or had Eisenhower taken control of operations himself. Neither condition was fulfilled.

Although it was largely a media idea that attracted more attention after than before 1945, the perception that the Americans had pulled his chestnuts out of the fire in Normandy undermined Montgomery's reputation. But his decline sprang from the natural feeling that the time had come for the Americans, who commanded larger armies, to take charge of operations. It followed that unless Eisenhower commanded operations, Montgomery would find himself marginalized or indirectly controlled by Bradley. In that event, Montgomery would not tolerate bad operational decisions at American hands. His unfavourable reaction to Eisenhower's compromises with Bradley after the Seine was seen as an attempt to keep the direction of Allied strategy in his own hands. Finally, Montgomery's failure at Arnhem at the end of September, an operation that diverted resources from Bradley's army group, spoiled Montgomery's standing with his allies beyond repair.

In coalition warfare it is important to reach agreement over operations without quarrelling. It is also important to conduct operations professionally, preserve lives and win battles. These aims may be mutually exclusive, although Montgomery managed to reconcile them in Normandy. Afterwards, when he was in a subordinate position, and he observed that no one was in control, they were not reconciled. Montgomery was an autocrat. He worked well with his colleagues provided he was boss and the policies followed were his own. The post-Normandy story is about the struggle of a didactic Montgomery, who was no longer the boss, to dictate what he was sure were correct operational decisions. His questionable behaviour in trying to get his way has overshadowed the argument over whether he was right or not. In turn that has led to his earlier conduct of operations in Normandy suffering the same treatment.

Montgomery was still widely admired although he stumbled when his status changed after Normandy. An explanation of his fall from grace starts and ends at the same point; his personality. Montgomery's 'lack of concern for truth in his make-up,' as Max Hastings described it, was one of his faults. Hastings offers as an example Montgomery's fishing expedition to the Spey before D-day which yielded him nothing. On his return he wrote to the Reynolds family, his son's guardians at school: "'I have just got back from Scotland and I send you a salmon – a magnificent fish of some 18lb. I hope it will feed the whole school." The implication was as obvious as the intention to deceive,' Hastings commented.[1]

An analogy between this incident and Montgomery's insistence that he applied his master plan in Normandy virtually without change as examples of his dishonesty, is unconvincing. His contemporaries were much to blame for suggesting that Montgomery intended to deceive over his plan and their historical case against him is unproven, at best. The RAF 'barons' as they were known, had only agreed to the D-day bombardment at the last minute.[2] They were obstructive throughout the campaign, during and after Normandy, for they were of a generation that had resolutely opposed army co-operation, except on their own terms, in the 1930s. They genuinely, if mistakenly, believed that the air force was the main instrument for the overthrow of the enemy. Tedder and Coningham felt that Montgomery had stolen the limelight in the Mediterranean and claimed more than he had achieved. Neither of them had troubled to master the concept, as opposd to the details of Montgomery's Normandy plan that affected them. So when the tactical plan miscarried, they chose not to understand that the simple strategic idea of holding on the left and striking on the right had not. Nor did they grasp that the Germans were bound to hold the eastern hinge of their position and that unless it was displaced southward in the first few days, British resources were not sufficient to force it later. The undoubted tactical failures of the army catered to their prejudices, which in Tedder's case stemmed from his experiences as an infantry officer on the Western Front. Furthermore, because Tedder was instrumental in obtaining RAF and USAF support for Eisenhower, against the resistance of the strategic air commanders, he was vulnerable when the ground actions they supported were indecisive.

At Montgomery's level of command many decisions were political and he was quite prepared to treat the RAF barons as they, in fact, were treating him. His responsibility was to the ground forces so it was the other side of the inter-service coin that concerned him. His army was smaller than the American, and he wanted it to shine. His own standing in the Allied hierarchy depended, in the longer run, on his being a successful head of an elite British force, that would, inevitably, contract in size absolutely and relatively compared to the American. He had already felt political pressure being exerted on him in July, when his success was still in the balance. Had the campaign failed he would have been held responsible: when it succeeded he saw no reason not to claim the credit simply because his own command was smaller than the American. He did not accept that politics should cause the eclipse of his military influence after it was over. As Hastings discerningly pointed out, his soldiers depended on him to reassure them, by his attitude and remarks from time to time, that his plan was working, as it had in his previous campaigns. Morale was a delicate flower and it depended heavily on Montgomery's personality. So in justifying his own reputation by spinning the truth, he protected the reputation and morale of the British Army as well. In such a life and death situation truth was relative.

The question of morale was particularly vital because there was no glory to be gleaned for the British in their role on the left of the line. Montgomery's argument that the enemy could be as well destroyed by *attrition in situ* as further inland was not only unappealing but not quite true; for it was not what was intended and it was harder to achieve. The morale of British divisions suffered from battles that brought small territorial gains and many casualties. Like the soldiers in the field, Eisenhower took territorial gain as the chief measure of success. Montgomery was sensitive to this fact, which his staff and commanders reported, and was as disappointed as they by the failure of his divisions to gain space. But he had to conceal his concern by making little of it.

When the Americans had decided the campaign at St Lo, they were unwilling to have their success diluted by acknowledging the contribution of their ally in grinding down the German divisions in June and July. Montgomery's cautious gathering of resources, his set-piece battles and small advances were like the battles of attrition on the Western Front. They had been examples of unmitigated incompetence, for which Sir Douglas Haig's assertion that the victories of the Last Hundred Days were won on the Somme and at 3rd Ypres, seemed an excuse. Like their fathers in 1918, Americans claimed to have rescued the 'slow' British by their fighting advance.[3] There is a small element of truth in both ideas. General Patton justifiably used them to kick-start the morale of his Third Army, for it initially lacked the natural superiority of the First Army which had actually achieved the break-through. Americans associated Montgomery with British caution.

Eisenhower was disinclined to accept Montgomery's methods when they led to battles of attrition. Montgomery could have pointed out that most battles with the Germans would turn out that way unless the allies were greatly superior at the point of attack. Were he to deny that his methods were the cause he would have had to admit that the tactics, weapons and leadership of his soldiers were to blame. But you could not impugn his soldiers' courage or skill, or those of Bradley, and nothing could be done about their weapons at that stage. It looked as though their leaders had to take the blame in the time-honoured fashion – and that meant himself. So he fought back, relying on his reputation for winning and always being right, by insisting that everything was working according to plan, despite the tactical set-backs the Allies were suffering. Of course he laid himself open to his critics at the time, and the far greater number who attacked him after the war.

While confidence, even when it was not warranted, was expected of Montgomery during the battle, after the war his critics took him to be an egotist, which he was, because he was incapable, even then, of admitting his mistakes. The battle of Normandy had not gone according to plan, they asserted, although the flawed British official history, without documenting its case rigorously, supported Montgmery's view that his master-plan had been strictly followed. Montgomery weakened his own case by refusing to allow his archive to be released in its entirety. Ellis did not follow Playfair's method of allowing senior and middle-piece officers a free hand to write their critical comments. It was easier for Playfair because most of the Western Desert commanders before Montgomery had been sacked or had failed. It seems that, when he was CIGS after the war, Montgomery exerted pressure on

Ellis to stifle the debate that would have resulted had Ellis opened it up. But the story of Normandy became part of a seamless whole with the period of Eisenhower's command afterwards, during which Montgomery was more justifiably criticised. Montgomery never surrendered a position unless he had worked out all the implications. And Normandy was his vital ground.

Ellis' volumes are not up to the standard expected by modern historians. Carlo D'Este, whose book is arguably the best account of Normandy, supports the views of Eisenhower, Bradley and Martin Blumenson, the official American historian of the 'Break-Out' volume, that Montgomery deceived himself if he thought the campaign went according to plan. Montgomery himself disagreed, of course. After the war he wrote:[4]

> My master plan ... was so to stage and conduct operations that we drew the main enemy strength on to the front of the Second British Army on the eastern front, in order that we might the more easily gain territory in the west and make the ultimate break-out on that flank – using the First American Army for that purpose. If events on the western front were to proceed rapidly it meant that we must make territorial gains there.
>
> On the eastern flank, in the Caen sector, the acquisition of ground was not so pressing; the need *there* was by hard fighting to make the enemy commit his reserves, so that the American forces would meet less opposition in their advances to gain territory which was vital in the west....
>
> I never once had cause or reason to alter my master plan. Of course we did not keep to the times and phase lines we had envisaged for the benefit of administrative planning, and of course, too, we didn't hesitate to adjust our plans and dispositions to the tactical situation as it developed – as in all battles. Of course we didn't. I never imagined we would. But the fundamental design remained unchanged .... We did not capture Caen, for instance, till the 10th July. It had been my original intention to secure the high ground between Caen and Falaise as early as possible, as being a suitable place for the construction of airfields: but this was not vital, and when I found it could not be done in accordance with the original plan without suffering unjustified casualties, I did not proceed with that venture.... It was indeed a fundamental object of my strategy on the eastern flank to establish a force strong in armour to the south-east of Caen in the area about Bourguebus; this was the key

to ensuring that we kept the bulk of the German armour on the eastern flank, and thus helped the American expansion on the west. We did not get on to this high ground until Second Army launched Operation Goodwood on the 18th July, with armoured forces. As soon as the armoured advance came to a standstill because of determined enemy resistance, and also because heavy rain turned the whole area into a sea of mud, I decided to abandon the thrusts. Many people thought that when Operation Goodwood was staged, it was the beginning of the plan to break out from the eastern flank towards Paris, and that, because I did not do so, the battle had been a failure. But let me make the point again at the risk of being wearisome. There was *never* at any time any intention of making the break-out from the bridgehead on the eastern flank. Misunderstandings about this simple and basic conception was responsible for much trouble between British and American personalities.

D'Este picked up some of the remarks of Montgomery's better known post-war critics. It is not surprising that they failed to serve his case against Montgomery. Indeed, the plan was so simple, based as it was on a topographical fact and the necessity for the Germans to hold their right flank pivot, that Montgomery was backing a certainty. His plan was the wrong target for his opponents. They deserved to lose their case. British defects were tactical, as were American – although we still have to read a good American tactical history of the campaign. The failure to take Caen early was inconvenient, caused casualties and restricted the space available for manoeuvre. But it did not prevent the plan working. Certainly it made it harder and more expensive to achieve. Only if the intention, as Eisenhower wrongly believed, was to break out to the south-east was it significant for the general argument. Certainly the timings of the initial parts of the plan were over-optimistic, but the implications of the front being 'glued' in the bocage and around Caen were foreseen in May. Bradley was right in saying that not enough attention was paid to getting inland quickly. But that pointed to lack of drive, inadequate training and poor equipment, not to planning at the level of 21st Army Group. He said that no alternative plan was ready when Caen did not fall on D-day. On the contrary, the alternative drive towards Villers Bocage was ready, but it failed tactically and was badly commanded. The same may be said of Epsom, where there was command failure as well.

D'Este argues that Montgomery lost the initiative when the front 'glued up'. The cause was a 'second flaw ... gross under-estimation of his opponent.' He was holding too long a front with too little depth. He had to resort to limited operations when the build-up corps were ready. These statements of D'Este's are some of the results not the causes of the failure to take Caen. They are the results of tactical failures, of which Montgomery was well aware. D'Este does not analyse these failures. The causes of the 'gluing' of the front and the lack of depth were self-evidently tactical. Rather than under-estimating the enemy, the British failed to exploit German mistakes in the field in the first few days through over-caution.

The category 'operations' has been omitted by the critics who have confused it with 'planning' *qua* military strategy. In order to be con-vincing, the argument against Montgomery must concern and relate tactics and operations. An explanation must be given for an evident fact. That, despite shortcomings in allied tactical training, equipment and even perhaps morale, which accounted for less than successful operations and German resistance continuing until Cobra, dogged pursuance of the aim by Montgomery resulted in the success of his strategy.

D'Este quotes a comment by Patton that might have dealt with this point, but fails to do so. 'One does not plan and then try to make cir-cumstances fit those plans. One tries to make plans fit circumstances. I think the difference between success and failure in high command depends upon the ability, or lack of it, to do just that.' This is a remark frequently made by senior officers to their staff college audiences, which makes the latter smile indulgently. But of course! But Patton's remark is directed to the wrong level of command and the wrong stage in the armies' careers. By the time the fighting started in Normandy the mistakes had already been made, in Patton's army as well as Montgomery's, in their preparation. D'Este says Patton would un-doubtedly have argued that Caen was a prime example of unsound planning. If he is making Bradley's point that not enough attention was paid to getting inland quickly, surely we must agree. But the need was for better general and special training for an operational task specific to all landing operations. And if that was inadequate the blame may be laid not only at Montgomery's door, but also at those of Eisenhower, Bradley and all corps and divisional commanders.

Bradley's is an important criticism but it should not be directed to Montgomery's conduct of the battle specifically but rather to the tacti-cal inability of both allies to fight a professional opponent as effect-ively as they would have liked. Some soldiers, unwilling to admit their amateur status, have resorted to arguments about 'planning' to explain why the fight was so tough. In fact, 'Planning' was one of the Allies' strong-points in bringing men to battle. When they got there they had to rely on their commanders' having prepared them for the fight before hand. Perhaps they were simply less well-served there.

Why is it necessary, we should ask, to criticise a great victory, and the commanders who won it, because it was ultimately won by using the advantages of superior fire-power and the obvious strategy of holding by the nose and kicking in the backside?

15 The End or Another Beginning?

When we entered Brussels on the evening of 3 September, the crowds that showered us with flowers and fruit and embraced us without restraint believed the war was over. At that moment we had the same impression. We had crossed the Seine on 30 August and advanced, with hardly a pause for sleep, across the battlefields of the First World War (Map 12). On Vimy Ridge members of the Imperial War Graves Commission staff waved as we passed the gates of their cemetery. They ignored the bombs from a single 81-mm mortar which were dropping on the road outside the gates; a reminder of 1917. After a brief rest to maintain our vehicles at Douai, and to attend a dance given for *Les Liberateurs*, we set out for Brussels, 90 miles away, early on 3 September. That evening we deployed our guns on the Champs de Manoeuvres and posted minimum detachments. Everyone else was ordered to report next morning at 6 a.m. Surely, there would be no firing that night!

In the cellars of the Palais de Justice, a venerable building with its roof ablaze, the work of the Gestapo, I inspected the Gestapo's wine stocks. There were a few inches of wine swilling about on the floor so I wore rubber boots. Flicking the beam of my torch over the labels I chose a section of 1929 Chambertin and packed a dozen bottles into a box. On the way back to my tank I saw a guardsman of the Recce Welch sitting to attention in the driving seat of his Cromwell. He was being plied with wine by a pretty girl when he suddenly keeled over. Fatigue rather than drink was his problem. It had been a long day and we had beaten the other brigade-group, travelling on a parallel centre line, in the race for the city.

I found a smartly dressed woman standing by my Sherman. She introduced herself as Madame Pirotte and enquired if I would like to join her family for the night. I gratefully accepted, noted her address and phone number and gave it to the adjutant in case something unforeseen blew up. That night I slept in a bed with cotton sheets instead of wrapped in my silk parachute taken from the Orne bridges battlefield. The Pirottes remained friends in the years ahead.

In the morning, small, busy children gathered round the guns, sat on layers' knees, squinted through dial sights, handled ammunition, and tripped over tannoy wires as they chased each other over the gun positions. Soldiers were fine ambassadors, and they enjoyed the admiration of young women in bright summer dresses. Later I addressed the battery and told them with as much conviction as I could muster that the war was NOT over, whatever they had thought the night before. As I finished, the order 'Take Post!' came from the command posts. Target data to engage 88-mm guns on the airfield followed. Dick Eames, 439 battery commander, was directing fire from the roof of a block of flats having risen to his observation post by a lift. The crowd around the guns scattered.

In the meanwhile the Household Cavalry had continued the advance, passed the Royal Palace at Teruvain, and reached Louvain. We 'ceased firing' limbered up and were soon on the way through Louvain to Diest which we reached on the evening of 5 September. The Americans on our right were at Liege. The bridges over the Albert Canal had been blown and the Irish Guards assaulted across it to take Beeringen – immediately named 'Beerengine'. That unpleasant little battle was followed by others like it before we reached a bridge over the Escaut Canal on the road to Eindhoven. It was captured by the Irish and named Joe's Bridge after Lt-Colonel J.O.E. Vandeleur commanding the 3rd Battalion. It was from there that the advance to Arnhem began on 17 September.

In Brussels we were told that our enemy consisted of 'category units', the chronically sick, the deaf, the halt and the blind. They seemed to be quite capable of using their weapons. On the Escaut we were up against the Hermann Goering Division and were resigned to the daily grind with its permanent undertone of fear and half-sleep nights of a few hours, the radio headset music of morse-stammer and mush only arrested by: 'Hullo One Five, fetch officer, over.' If your signaller did not answer almost instantly, you woke up and answered for him.

From Joe's Bridge we punished a Herman Goering counter-attack with target Uncle 220. A battalion was caught in the woods forming up and they must have been slaughtered by scale 20 from the whole division. Our shells burst in the trees so that the air was filled with steel splinters. Second Army had suffered so much in Normandy that it gave me grim satisfaction to pay back the enemy in kind.

Church towers, factory buildings, embankments and black, lowering woods which contained the invisible enemy, dominated our lives. I remember a particular church tower, its huge bell suspended over my head, from which I searched for enemy movement. There was not

194

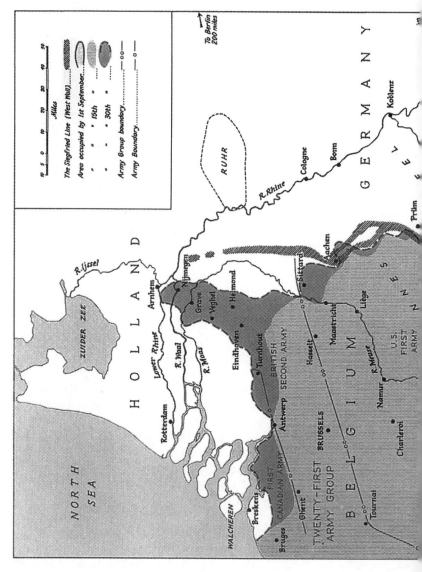

12 The September adv

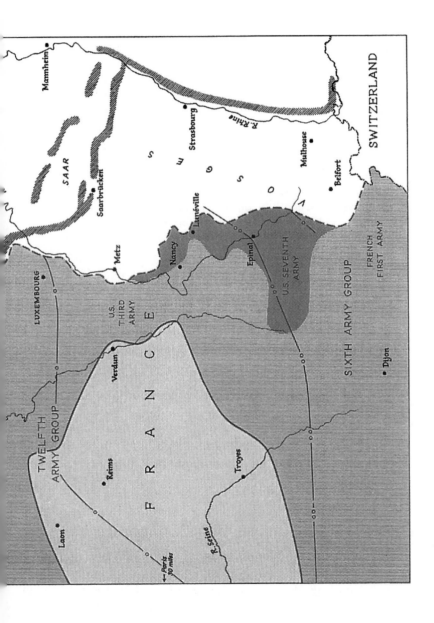

much of that, for the Germans were experts at hiding and the battlefield usually appeared to be empty. There was a hole in the back wall
of the church through which you could drive a truck. My signaller,
whose nickname was 'Bach', played the organ to entertain us while
the battle progressed outside. The music suddenly stopped. 'Bach's
footsteps approached up the twisting steps to my platform. Finally,
panting and grinning, he stood there in his leather jerkin with the
semi-quavers painted on the back. 'The Church Warden says we
must stop the war. He has to lock up the church at six o'clock.' It was
less amusing when an 88-mm armour piercing shell rang the church
bell overhead and followed it with HE. We had cleared the decks by
then.

The fighting had become less congested. There were gaps between
units and even larger ones between divisions. You knew where the
rest of the division was fighting but not what was happening in West
Holland, on the Scheldt, or on the German frontier around Aachen,
where the First US Army was grappling desperately with a more concentrated enemy. When we received orders for the great advance over
the canals betwen us and the Maas, over the Waal at Nijmegen and on
over the lower Rhine to Arnhem and Appeldoorn, we were obviously
going even further into the wide blue yonder. The operation was to be
called 'Market-Garden'.

What individuals, like myself, remember about the rest of the war is
a pastiche which can be only loosely related to its general history. The
battle of Normandy was compact and tidy. It was not difficult to
understand the way its parts were related, even at the time. But the
northern front in the autumn and winter was another matter. We
advanced up the road through Eindhoven and on to Nijmegen and the
Island between there and Arnhem, where we fought for a week or two
in what became a bridgehead. But parts of the division had to turn
round and help the Americans to clear the road south of the Maas
when the Germans cut it. The Nijmegen front faced north, on the
Island, towards Arnhem, east towards the German Reichswald and
south on the east bank of the Maas. In the autumn we moved down to
Sitard in the Dutch appendix near Maastricht, where we first entered
Germany. Loot in the form of cattle was taken there, each animal
marked on its flanks with the divisional sign, the ever watchful eye. At
Christmas the Ardennes battle required us to take up positions at
Namur and across the Meuse in the hills. The 5th and 6th Panzer
Armies that fought there did not reach us. In January 1945 we moved
back to Nijmegen to fight in the great battle called Veritable which

was designed to clear the Germans from the wet farm lands between the Rhine and the Maas. Of that battle more anon.

I have read the literature of the campaign widely since then, but at the time I was aware of its outline only. My memories are impressionistic and intermittent. Some of us may be convinced that had different strategy been followed, and even tactics, victory would have been ours sooner than May 1945. But conjecture is a poor guide. On the other hand the belief that what happened was bound to happen does not satisfy. We should record the mistakes made, even if their effect may be uncertain. They are part of the history of the campaign. In this respect the book, *A Bridge Too Far*, about Operation Market-Garden, seems like a work of fiction. The personalities of Lieutenant-Generals Boy Browning and Brian Horrocks, the Airborne Corps and 30th Corps commanders, and Major-General Alan Adair, my divisional commander, each of whom I had met, were depicted in the film of the book as actors playing Hollywood's impression of British general officers. The film's director assumed, at the beginning, what he wanted to demonstrate: that the operation could never have succeeded. That was not our opinion at the time nor, after reflection, have I changed my opinion.

Although I am professionally qualified to describe how operations were usually managed, and can describe events in which my battery was concerned, I admit that my knowledge of events beyond the division is entirely artificial, built of post-war literature and what the leaders themselves subsequently revealed. The value of my own recollections of those last months of the war depends on the context provided by other historians; a sort of cumulative and dynamic re-manufacturing of memory. What I can depend upon is the *colour* of my memories. The discomfort, the fear, the lack of sleep, the adrenalin surges and the snap-shots of moments of stress, and humour, and comradeship. Those the official history cannot provide. It does set these memories in context, so its accuracy and honesty – the truth, the whole truth and nothing but the truth – is essential.

As I have remarked previously, Major L.F. Ellis' official history volumes compare unfavourably with those of Major General Playfair. The contributions of senior commanders enabled Playfair to correct major errors in his drafts and to offer explanations for what, at first glance, appeared to be commanders' mistakes. The divisional, corps and army staff officers, and the middle piece commanders who were extensively interviewed by Playfair's team, provided the guts of the desert histories. They had the inside track at the level of generality at which official histories are written. As staff officers, their objectivity and ability to interpret what they knew of the detailed fighting sensitively, particularly if they had commanded units earlier in their careers, was invaluable. As a result, Playfair created an objective and critical history which is a cornerstone for the history of the British Army in the Second World War.

Ellis's files of correspondence are very thin compared to Playfair's. His is not a critical history and does not provide later historians with a completely reliable base. Indeed, although its form is different from Edmonds' volumes on the First War campaigns, it suffered, as did Edmonds', from the shadow of 'the great commander'. For Douglas Haig read Bernard Montgomery. The shadow of the strategic argument about the broad front versus the single thrust in late summer 1944 and autumn 1944, and the disagreement over strategy between Montgomery and the Americans, hangs over Ellis' work. I shall record that matter in the next chapter.

Those of us who were immersed in the minor engagements of operation Market-Garden and the subsequent campaign knew nothing about the strategic misunderstandings between our senior commanders that were building in the background, and would continue to do so for the rest of the war and into the peace. Indeed, nearer to home we were not to know why the 101 US Airborne Division had not taken the bridge at Son on the way to Nijmegen until we read the story after the war. We only knew that the failure cost our division hours in the race to reach Arnhem (Map 13). At Nijmegen we found that 82nd Airborne was too heavily committed to hold the high ground around Groesbeek, on the German frontier looking across into the Reichswald, and to take the bridges over the Waal on the road to Arnhem as well. This caused another delay while the Grenadiers and the 82nd Airborne between them rushed the bridge. Americans still argue that our tanks could have advanced towards Arnhem immediately the bridges were taken. But it was infantry that was needed not tanks at that stage. In fact the 43rd Infantry Division was not committed soon enough to clear the route to the Lower Rhine. Then their infantrymen asserted that they were held up by our tanks, which could not leave the road because of the soft ground. They could have moved faster on their feet. As a measure of the confusion on both sides at this time, the column edging to the Lower Rhine below Arnhem contained not a few German vehicles also unable to escape from the road.

Too many vehicles took part in the advance from the Escaut to Nijmegen. Many could have been left behind. Orders to carry

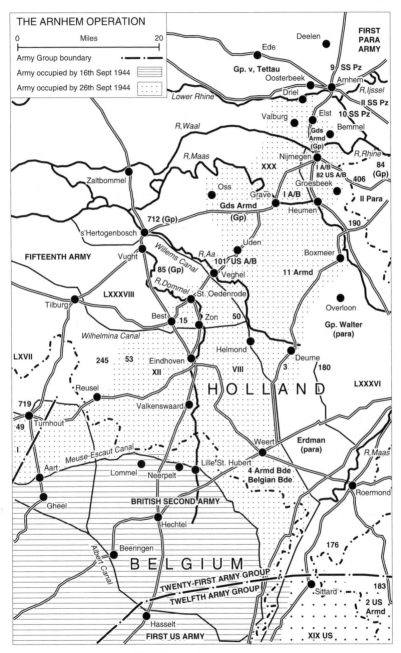

13   The Arnhem operation

ammunition and weapons and to leave behind all the comforts were not issued. We could have mounted infantry on our tanks instead of swelling the column with 3-ton transports (TCVs). I set a bad example myself. On the Escaut, my crew captured a German Mark III SP damaged by a Coldstream Guards 6-pounder anti-tank gun. My crew jumped on to it and drove it to the gun position where the artificers on the gun position made it into an excellent command post for me. A Sherman, a Ford staff car and a jeep completed my column – rather lavish for a battery commander. On the Island I purloined an abandoned Household Cavalry Dingo scout car, which I must point out was a perfect vehicle for me since it was small, quiet and proof against rifle fire. It could also travel in reverse very fast. This acquisitive behaviour, repeated many times, helped to congest a narrow axis and consume petrol.

How can one assess the cumulative effect of a few major errors and many small ones too numerous to be recorded? Battles are won by the side that makes fewer, it is said. When General Horrocks spoke to the officers and most of the NCOs of XXX Corps in Nijmegen after Market-Garden, when Arnhem had been evacuated, he took the blame for the result. His main admission was his failure to commit 43rd Division in time, particularly on the left of the Island front. He did not doubt that the operation could have succeeded. Since then we have learned about serious errors made by the airborne and airforce side of the operation. Its control was not in the hands of Second Army, or even 21st Army Group. Brereton and his Airborne Army staff were incompetent and SHAEF had neither assigned one headquarters – 21st Army Group would have been the obvious choice – to control the operation, nor handled the job itself. It was another case, it now appears, of the unsuitability of the SHAEF organisation to manage operations in the field and the need of a ground forces commander – of which Eisenhower was aware from the beginning. Had we known about the shortage of transport aircraft and gliders, the failure of Brereton to co-operate with 2nd Tactical Airforce over air support, the mistaken decision to land so far from the Arnhem bridge and on the wrong side of the river, and the presence of elements of 9th and 10th SS Panzer Division we would not have started off on 17 September so full of confidence. But we would have gone. We were not sufficiently sceptical, perhaps, about the competence of our leaders. And we still believed that the Germans were on their last legs.

By the time that we were fighting on 'The Island' between Nijmegen and Arnhem, on the high ground facing the Reichswald Forest, and on the south side of Nijmegen near Mook and the railway line to Wesel, we had learned to handle the Germans adequately. Even if the ultimate aim of Market-Garden had not been achieved, we had come a long way and outflanked the strongest German defences facing the Americans. We needed to exploit between the Maas and the Rhine. That was indeed Montgomery's intention. Our tanks were still inferior but autumn weather reduced the effectiveness of German heavy tanks. Our infantry weapons were also inferior but we engaged their infantry on more than equal terms. Our artillery was dominant so the Germans relied more and more on mortars, including nebelwerfers which were easy to hide and move. We spent great efforts trying to neutralise them because our infantry casualties were mainly from 81-mm mortar bombs. I remember standing behind the corner of a house in a company area of the 5th Coldstream on the Island with Jimmy Robertson, one of my troop commanders at the time. Suddenly he grunted and collapsed beside me. His face had turned grey-green. A splinter had knocked off the top joint of a finger. Not a life-threatening wound but a very painful one and he had to be evacuated.

A few innovations on our side made life for the enemy more uncomfortable.The Variable Time fuse, which allowed us to fire airbursts without fuse-length adjustments necessary with the clockwork number 210, appeared. Radar was used to locate mortar positions. Artillery concentrations were heavier and even more rapidly applied. Flat trajectory weapons, heavy machine guns, Bofors anti-aircraft guns and tanks thickened them in what was called 'pepper-pot'. The profligacy with which high explosive was applied concealed its comparative inaccuracy though. Barrages were still used to neutralise the enemy during the approach of the infantry to his positions. When the infantry followed the line of shell-bursts closely over relatively flat ground, which allowed shells to land uniformly across the front, barrages were successful. The use of the armoured carrier, first tried out in Totalize, was repeated with success and the armoured vehicles of the 79th Armoured Division – fascines, flails, armoured bridges, flame-throwers and petards – were effective. Otherwise, methods were increasingly like those of the last months of the First World War. They were usually successful, nevertheless.

Analysts of a later generation criticise our reliance on high explosive. They expect more original methods to have been used. What they should have been they seldom explain. They give too little credit to the autumn and winter weather through which the fighting continued. Mud and flooding, particularly in Holland, were excellent allies for the Germans whose defenders behind natural obstacles could generate tremendous fire. Furthermore, cold and damp and the realisation that the fighting was going to continue into the Spring of 1945 was depressing. When the offensive between the Maas and the Rhine, delayed from the previous October, after Market-Garden gave us the base for it in Nijmegen, and then from January to February, because of floods below the Roer dams in the 19th US Army sector, was at last fought, the resistance of the Germans was as stern as in Normandy and casualties were as heavy from their prodigious mortar and machine gun fire. Most of us remember Operations Veritable (Map 14) and Blockbuster, fought by 30th Corps and the 2nd Canadian Corps, as more unpleasant than Normandy. In the Reichswald and the fighting south of it to Wesel, subaltern officers survived barely a couple of weeks on average. Tank support was often ineffective because of mud. We were surprised that resistance west of the Rhine was so obstinate, but German losses there made their resistance east of it less coordinated than it could otherwise have been. Nevertheless, in the last weeks east of the Rhine, the open warfare, mines, snipers and stern resistance at isolated key points led to casualties which, in the case of the field artillery, were considerable.

In his *A Distant Drum*, Jocelyn Pereira offers excellent, light-hearted descriptions of the battles fought by his 5th Coldstream Guards, in which he was the Intelligence Officer. Our battle at Mull on the way to Goch on 16 February 1945 was one of them. We were to have attacked Hassum from Hommersum, after that village had been captured by Joe Vandeleur's Irishmen. 'The trouble about this stretch,' said Joe Vandeleur as he guided Roddy Hill's recce of the start-line of the 5th Coldstream, 'is that it is overlooked.' Instantly his remark was confirmed. The erwerp! erwerp! erwerp! of the *nebelwerfers* warned of the impending crrump, crrrump, crrrrump as the avenging 60 pound canisters of explosive accelerated down around them. Clearly, four companies marching down to the startline through the Irish positions could expect bloody trouble even before they met the enemy. Fortunately, Roddy Hill had the objective changed from Hassum to Mull, a large farm complex to its right.

The approach to the new objective, at least to its startline, was concealed in sandy dunes from which we would emerge on to flat, very wet, farmland. An advance of about a kilometre would end in an exposed position between Hassum on the left and a wooded area occupied by the enemy on the right. A few thousand yards beyond the objective we could see a low ridge which was to be attacked later in the day from the right flank by the 52nd Lowland Division. We devoutly hoped that they would be on time as the ridge overlooked our new positions.

Roddy Hill had taken command of the battalion in Normandy. He was my ideal model of a CO. Always quiet, thorough and willing to explain to his superior why an operation, such as the one originally proposed at Hassum, was unacceptable; or, to his company commanders, why they had to bite the bullet and get on with it. Indeed, he was very determined and his battalion always reached its objective. He and I frequently visited companies together which gave me the chance to talk to company commanders about their fronts. The only time I remember seeing Roddy rattled was when we were both chased by a swarm of bees down a bocage lane.

This was intended to be my last battle with Roddy before returning to England to take a short course to prepare me to be brigade major for the divisional artillery. It occurred to me that, as about the only officer in the 5th Coldstream who had been with the battalion since the start and not been hit, except Jocelyn I believe, this promise of relief might turn out to be a mirage. Nevertheless, at 4 a.m., when I got out of my sleeping bag and drank a mug of tea and ate a tin plate of beans and bacon, the feeling in the pit of my stomach was no worse than usual before a battle. The guns opened on time, the two forward companies shook out behind the barrage and I joined the small tactical headquarters behind them.

There was no sign of the Cromwells of the Armoured Welch for nearly all of them had bogged down. Their narrow tracks were ill-suited to Rhineland farmland. I watched the advance from the turret of my tank. The slumped, great-coated figures of guardsmen who had been hit were not too depressingly numerous. The battalion never failed to reach its objectives, and I saw the leading companies move into the first farm buildings of Mull. The second pair of companies passed through to the final objectives. The shelling against us was intense and, not surprisingly, some of it seemed to be directed at my tank, probably one of only three visible to the enemy. I heard over the radio that Tom Smith, my leading FOO, had been hit. I directed his aide, Bombardier Shaw, to carry on until I could relieve him. To use the radio for the reshuffling of support for the Coldstream I retreated into the turret from the shell splinters flying around and reached up to pull down the lid. As I did so I was hit in the left arm by what felt like a football. I knew at once that my arm was broken. I was probably too impatient to wait for my crew to strip off my tanksuit top and jacket

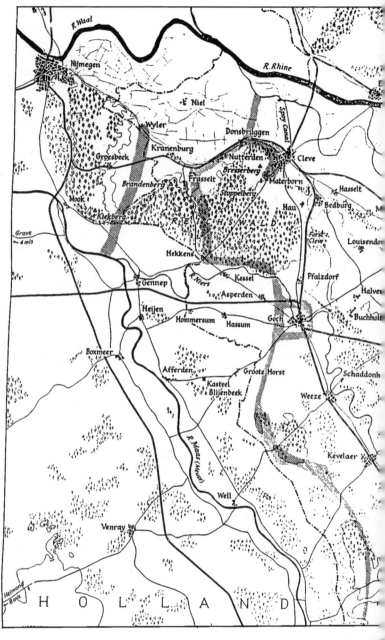

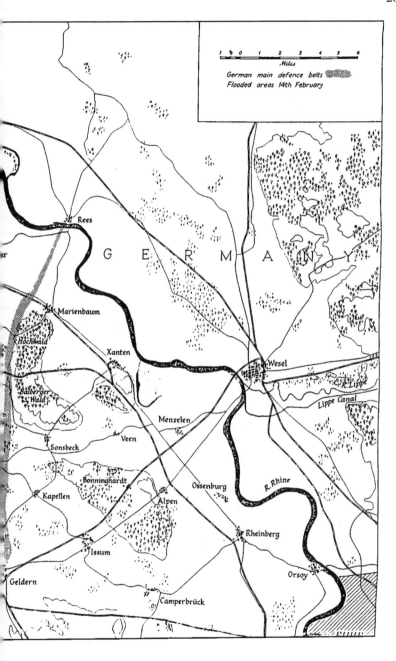

German main defence belts
Flooded areas 14th February

and tie on a first-aid dressing in the constricted space of the turret, as I remember climbing out of the turret without it. Gingerly I held on with my good arm and stepped down on to the track and then to the ground. I ran the few hundred yards to where Tom Smith's tank was hidden behind a farm building. Over Tom's tank radio I ordered Robin Peploe, my other FOO, to take my place at battalion headquarters which was being established in Mull, where he could look after the demands of Roddy Hill. Tom had already been evacuated, I think in his own jeep.

The rest of the day was taken up lying in a ditch with one of the companies directing fire through the No. 38 'walkie-talkie' radio by means of the re-broadcast system on the tank. This ingenious device I have already described. During the rest of the day I issued fire-orders over the low-power, visual-range walkie-talkie which, by the flick of a switch on the powerful No. 19 set on the tank, could be transmitted 6000 yards to the guns. I was able to move about, unencumbered, while leaving Tom's tank in the charge of Bombardier Shaw concealed behind a house. The No. 38 set was not the most reliable radio in operational conditions but on this occasion it worked like a charm, thanks to the efficiency of the tank crew. Bombardier Shaw was deservedly awarded a mention in despatches for his work on this day and previous ones.

Counter-attacks that looked as though they were developing were dispersed by the divisional artillery of 48 guns, reinforced by the 7th and 64th Medium regiments of my old friends Tony Roncoroni and Denis Duke from POW days. We had taught some of our company officers to correct artillery fire when they could see the fall of shot better than we could. They did it well on this occasion.

The winter light faded and I left the company and walked back to battalion headquarters where Robin Peploe was busy fixing up SOS defensive fire tasks for the night. A relief for Tom Smith was on the way and one for me, I hoped. Having taken leave of Roddy Hill, I walked over to the Coldstream Regimental Aid Post to get patched up before being evacuated to the Advanced Dressing Station. Ambulances could not reach the RAP so I led a convoy of jeeps and carriers with wounded on foot by a twisting track through German barbed wire entanglements. It was dark and I kept bumping into obstacles. That walk was the worst part of the day. Shock was beginning to set in and the shot of morphia Captain Menzies, the battalion MO, had given me had worn off by the time we came out on the road and found the ambulances to take us back. At the ADS Barrie Wilson, my CO, was there to cheer me on my way to the Casualty Clearing Station at 30th Corps.

I slept, exhausted but in no serious pain, on a stretcher in various corridors of hospitals on the lines of communication between the CCS at Nijmegen and a base hospital. From time to time doctors or nurses bent over me and inspected my triage label. It was a relief to be a mere parcel in the hands of a most efficient postal service and to be totally irresponsible for the first time for years. Eventually I was shifted into yet another ambulance and came to myself in a bed in a hospital at Knocke, where I had spent a summer holiday years before. I met Tom Smith there. He was preparing to return having been only superficially wounded. From there I was flown in a Dakota hospital plane in which we were loaded three deep in canvas hammocks. Blood from the man above me dripped steadily on to my blanket. From an airfield near Brize Norton a hospital train, with smart and efficient nurses, took us to an orthopaedic hospital in Worcester. A large proportion of cases there were mine casualties from Italy. After an investigatory operation I woke up in bed to find the letters LSDL scrawled on the plaster. Apparently that stood for 'let sleeping dogs lie', which meant that the bit of shell was to be left inside the wound.

I was passed fit in May and joined 5th Field Regiment as a battery commander in June. In August my arm blew up and a surgeon in the cottage hospital in Builth Wells removed the square chunk of steel. The regiment was scheduled for Japan but fortunately the Hiroshima and Nagasaki bombs saved us from that fresh adventure.

16 Montgomery versus the Americans

In the last days of August, the battle in Normandy won, the nominal control of operations passed from Montgomery to Eisenhower as Supreme Commander Allied Expeditionary Force (SCAEF). The transfer was anything but smooth. Apparently Bradley and Montgomery had agreed that the latter would make for Antwerp and the Channel ports and Bradley for Brussels and the Aachen Gap leading to Cologne and the Ruhr. To ensure sufficient force for Bradley's thrust, Patton would form a reserve on the right flank and then advance on Metz and the Saar as opportunity and the situation on Bradley's First Army front allowed. SHAEF (Supreme Headquarters Allied Expeditionary Force) planners had always agreed that the Ruhr and the ports were the prime objectives and that the main weight of the advance should be north of the Ardennes. This policy was compromised by Eisenhower.

Towards the end of the Normandy campaign the American press was asking why the US Army should be directed, any longer, by the leader of a smaller, less successful army. Of course, Eisenhower was about to take to the field but it was generally believed that Montgomery's influence would continue. Surely, it was widely believed in the American armies, the British had taken an inordinate amount of time to close the trap on the Germans in Normandy. Now a more dynamic leadership must finish the war. The Americans would advance quickly on a wide front. The time for calculation about objectives was over. It was everyone to the battle and the devil take the hindermost.

Bradley, with Patton's approval, decided to fall in with this idea which ignored the historical and geographical facts on which the original plan had been based, SHAEF's own planning staff and the logistical facts on which its plan was based.

Geography made the main axis of advance into Germany lie north of the Ardennes. Montgomery's plan with Bradley was based on that and the more specific need for the Allies to occupy the V1 and V2 sites[1] as soon as possible and to replace the Atlantic ports in the supply plan, for the Germans were defending them and their capture would take troops and time better used in the advance. When Eisenhower, bending to pressure from his American subordinates, made 21st Army Group responsible for the Channel ports, the missile sites and the Ruhr, and 12th Army Group for the Ardennes and the Saar approach to the Rhine and Frankfurt, the mismatch between resources and tasks was obvious. The result of another compromise had Bradley's First Army making for the Aachen Gap, the Ardennes and the Ruhr and his Third for the Saar; 21st Army Group for Brussels, Antwerp the Channel ports and the missile sites. Bradley's main objectives, the Ruhr and the Saar were not assigned priorities. Logically, if the Rhine were named as an objective the Saar was bound to receive priority over the Ruhr, for it lay west of the great river.

From then onwards, despite lip-service to the Ruhr objective, Bradley got his way, which was to direct his armies on a broad front towards Metz, the Saar, Mannheim and Frankfurt in the south and Cologne in the north, without much regard for his northern flank or special attention to the drive to Cologne and the Ruhr. Thus arose a chronic disagreement between Montgomery and the Americans over objectives and their priority, which festered until the end of the campaign.

The problem of logistics would have been solved by the capture and organisation of the Atlantic ports, but they were held by the Germans. Supply now depended on the Channel ports and particularly Antwerp. A logistics crisis could only be avoided if, as Eisenhower persisted in anticipating, the Germans collapsed west of the Rhine. Montgomery also believed that the Germans could be defeated but only by concentrating forces on the decisive thrust north of the Ardennes. The Ruhr could not be taken; indeed, the Rhine would not be reached unless Bradley concentrated his resources on his First Army's drive towards Cologne. Montgomery wanted the efforts of his own Second Army and Bradley's First Army to be given most of the resources and their operations co-ordinated. It was to that end, and after deciding that Bradley would not co-operate, that he proposed to Eisenhower that he undertake Market-Garden. By occupying Arnhem and Appeldoorn he would not only outflank the German frontier defences but have a base for a drive round the northern flank of the Ruhr. As well he would be able to take Rotterdam from the east. If Arnhem were not taken he could still drive southeast from Nijmegen, between the Maas and the Rhine, to take the German defences facing First Army in flank and rear. In February 1945, this became Operations Veritable and Blockbuster by the First Canadian Army and Grenade by Ninth US.

The Ruhr, without which Germany could not continue the war, was determined by the Combined Chiefs of Staff in Washington (CCS) to be the Allies' main objective. Montgomery insisted that unless Eisenhower concentrated his forces into a thrust north of the Ardennes to take it, no one would reach the Rhine, let alone the Ruhr, in 1944. Simply, his Q staff calculated that Eisenhower had neither the supplies nor the troops to reach the Rhine on a broad front.

Montgomery had intended his thrust to Arnhem to be part of a joint action by First US and Second British Armies. It was not to be pencil thin. But Market-Garden, as it was executed in late September, was only an emasculated version of the operation he first envisaged. For Bradley, attacking on a broad front with Eisenhower's agreement, denied First Army the means to support Second Army's right wing let alone to take Cologne and invest the Ruhr from the south as the CCS intended and Montgomery proposed.

In simple terms, Eisenhower asserted in his directives and his letters to the CCS that he was concentrating on the Ruhr while, simultaneously, he allowed Bradley to attack across his whole front. It was this deception that caused the dissension between Montgomery and himself. The analysis that follows may show that Montgomery was right if the argument is confined to strategy. But Eisenhower had other factors to consider.

Montgomery first challenged Eisenhower's procedure to his face on 10 September when Eisenhower and Tedder met him at Brussels airport to discuss strategy in general and Market-Garden in particular. Eisenhower had been laid up with an injured knee at his headquarters at Granville on the Cotentin peninsula in Normandy. Montgomery considered Granville a quite unsuitable location for SHAEF and made it clear that he thought Eisenhower was out of touch as a result. He was so outspoken that Eisenhower had to remind him that he was Montgomery's commanding officer.

Supply dominated the discussion. Eisenhower said that Antwerp had to be opened before deep penetration into Germany was possible. Montgomery did not disagree. By 'deep penetration' Eisenhower meant an advance beyond the Rhine, which did not apparently, include the Ruhr. Indeed, on a number of occasions Eisenhower's statements and directives give the impression that he considered the Ruhr and the Rhineland, the latter west of the Rhine, to be one and the same. At Brussels, Antwerp was not given priority over the drive to the Rhine although later Eisenhower decided that it was needed even to reach it. But in Ike-speak, 'priority' only meant that it was an item on his 'wish list'. Eisenhower refused to accept that First Army's Aachen Gap–Cologne–Ruhr axis should have 'priority', in the accepted meaning of the word, over his southern drive to the Rhine via the Saar and Mannheim, and beyond it to Frankfurt. Yet Tedder wrote to the Chief of the Air Staff, who was at the Octagon meeting in Quebec City, that the meeting would 'help to ensure that the Ruhr thrust does get the proper priority which we all feel it should have'. That Tedder, no friend of Montgomery's, should have expressed that opinion, at the very time that Bradley had told Hodges to continue his advance to the Rhine but had also ordered Patton to continue his advance on the Saar axis, suggests that either he and Eisenhower were seriously out of touch with events at the front, or that both were deceiving the CCS. The only way in which the Ruhr thrust could be adequately supported was if Bradley allotted the First Army more and Patton fewer resources. That could be achieved if General Devers' 6th Army front were extended northward into Patton's Third Army territory and made defensive. A reserve could thereby be formed for First Army. Only Eisenhower could order this step. Later he 'suggested' it so that Patton's 3rd Army could take over in the Ardennes and First Army concentrate on the Aachen gap and north of it. Bradley disliked the idea because, instead of a central strategy with Patton on the right and Hodges on the left, he would have had to work with Montgomery on the Ruhr approach. Eisenhower did not pursue the matter although it was his right and duty to order it.

Eisenhower's *laissez-faire* policy left Montgomery in the uncomfortable position of having the weakest two armies and requiring American support to initiate a drive towards the northern face of the Ruhr. One of the decisions made on 10 September was that Market-Garden, whose predecessor 'Comet', had been planned earlier, would go ahead. When Montgomery discussed it with his Q staff on the 11th, the 'consequences of Eisenhower's policy of "fair shares" were apparent'. Montgomery informed Eisenhower that, because the Ruhr axis had not been given priority over other operations, Market-Garden could not take place until 23 September or even the 26th.[2]

What followed was typical of the lack of co-ordination in the Supreme Command. Montgomery, believing that he had won his point about priority for the Ruhr axis after a visit by Bedell Smith following Brussels, signalled the VCIGS: 'The Saar thrust is to be stopped. Three American divisions are to be grounded and transport used to give (? extra) maintenance to 21st Army Group. The whole of maintenance 12th Army Group is to be given to 1st U.S. Army on my right and that army is to cooperate closely with me and I am to be allowed to deal direct with Hodges.'

Eisenhower's confirmatory telegram was not as precise and during the days that followed there was further slippage. Hodges' maintenance would be 'adequate', Montgomery was told. According to Bradley, Hodges was not short of supplies, and did not need any extras. This contradicted Hodges' own statements, as we shall see. Montgomery would be allowed to communicate direct with Hodges only if Bradley did not establish a tactical command post near him. Bradley strengthened his right rather than his left when he removed 79th Infantry from 19th Corps and sent it to help Patton who had already launched a strong attack to force a crossing of the Moselle. Bradley assured Eisenhower that Patton 'believes [he] will not only force this crossing but will open up the way for his rapid advance to the Rhine with his thrust directed on the axis Metz–Frankfurt'. With Eisenhower's agreement, Bradley told Patton to continue. The Saar thrust was not stopped, nor did it succeed as promised.[3]

It was clear to the CCS that since the Saar was west of the Rhine and the Ruhr beyond it, a broad front advance to the Rhine would reach the Saar first. Aware of this confusion of thought in Eisenhower's message the CCS, after reading the comments of the Joint Planning Staff, repeated that the northern route was more important than the subsidiary southern one without, however, demanding that it have priority.[4]

In the rush forward from the Seine a shortage of petrol imposed a choice on Eisenhower. Either he could advance with all his forces, accepting that petrol shortage would slow their advance, or he could commit fewer divisions to a well-supplied, faster advance, possibly but not necessarily on a narrower front. 12th Army Group chose the former option; 21st the latter. In the event, the armoured cars leading the 19th Corps on the left of First Army were immobilized by the side of the road to Brussels for want of petrol whereas 30th Corps, with fewer divisions, moved faster.

The original plan for Normandy envisaged a pause on the Seine during which American supply lines would switch to the Atlantic ports, as in the First World War. The rapid advance out of Normandy without a pause on the Seine, and the retention of ports by German garrisons, made this plan both redundant and unworkable. Instead, supplies continued to come over the beaches and through Cherbourg. They were moved forward in whatever road transport could be collected until the battered French railways were restored and the channel ports of Le Havre, Boulogne, Dieppe and Calais opened. This period of frantic supply overlapped the serious fighting on the frontier after the first week of September. Indeed the French railways were still in a muddle in December.

In general terms, the demand for petrol, oil and lubricants – POL – is the inverse of the demand for ammunition. During the rapid advance very little ammunition was expended. Then the battles on the Moselle at Metz on the Third Army front and in the Aachen Gap in First Army in September, demanded more ammunition than could be supplied and still required much POL. One of Montgomery's arguments for concentrating on the vital thrust lines to the Ruhr was that the supply situation demanded it. Eisenhower had taken the unexceptionable view that logistics should be a servant not a master. He thought that, when the enemy was in full flight from Normandy and obviously beaten, logistics staffs would have to improvise to allow the commanders to pursue him on a broad front. The hard fighting on the frontier which began in September and continued through the autumn, obviously indicated a new tactical phase and demanded a new logistical assessment. Eisenhower ought then to have concentrated his forces. He should have resisted, on logistical grounds alone, let alone tactical ones, the demands of his American subordinates, Bradley, Devers and Patton to be given their heads. Instead he took a political line. As he did not desire to restrict them, he made the Broad Front, on which he had advanced out of Normandy, into his strategic plan for the rest of the campaign. It was indulgence and *laissez-faire*, not a military strategy. His directives and statements, which continued to express the opinion that the enemy was beaten and could be driven back to the Rhine, justified the broad front. At the same time he declared the Ruhr to have priority.

The historical dispute over Eisenhower's strategy continues to this day. Several obstacles still impede its resolution. First, the broad advance out of the bridgehead was orthodox. When the front started to congeal in early September and orthodoxy demanded concentration, a Supreme Commander prepared to take charge was essential to form reserves and apply them to the vital sector. In May 1944, Eisenhower had noted in the margin of a draft policy statement about inter-allied operations that it should not be stated that he would take charge of operations as a ground force commander.[5] He tied his own hands thereby and allowed his subordinates, like medieval barons, to hold fiefdoms in a system in which only saints would have behaved properly. Bradley, Patton and Montgomery were not saints.

A corollary was that SHAEF was not designed to take the field, or even to direct operations at arm's length through a tactical headquarters. So Eisenhower was making a virtue out of necessity. Eisenhower's excellent chief of staff, General Bedell Smith, was dissatisfied with the system but was powerless to alter it because Eisenhower never intended to command in the accepted sense. In particular, Eisenhower was unwilling to control the administrative chief for the American Forces in Europe (ETOUSA – European Theater of Operations, USA) General J.C.H. Lee. Lee wore several hats. He was Deputy Supreme Commander of American forces, so that he was senior to Bradley in the chain of command. He was directly responsible to Eisenhower in his role as commander of the Communications Zone (COMZ), which made him the equivalent of an army-group commander. On the other hand Lee's chief of staff was a deputy chief of staff to Bedell Smith. In effect, since Eisenhower did not direct Lee as he should have done, no one else did, to Bedell Smith's irritation. By treating Lee as a commander responsible only to him, instead of a staff officer receiving orders through Bedell Smith, Eisenhower repeated the muddle that had occurred in Pershing's staff over logistics in 1918.[6]

The results, rather than the details of the COMZ muddle, concern us here.[7] On 6 September, General Hodges, commanding the US First Army, noted that 'given ten good days of weather ... the war might well be over as far as organised resistance is concerned.' By 10 September, the day Eisenhower and Tedder met Montgomery at Brussels airport, his lack of supplies had clouded his optimism. That day his G 4 (logistics) revealed at a staff conference that:

> there were no large reserves and they were scraping together enough to issue every twenty-four hours. Trains are running to Soissons but he cannot obtain any accurate information ahead of time as to what they are carrying or when they will arrive. [The first train was filled with PX goods, not the last instance of insanity in the COMZ.][8]

As German resistance stiffened, an ammunition shortage was added to a gasoline famine. On 17 September, the day Market-Garden began, Hodges' staff noted in his diary: 'Supply still critical of POL, ammunition and food and we are not now even holding our own.... It is not improbable that we shall have to slow up, even altogether halt our drive into Germany and this is in the very near future.'[9]

The supply situation had worsened when George Marshall, the US Army Chief of Staff, flew into Orly airport on 6 October in his plane, 'The Sacred Cow', to visit the Allied forces. Marshall was, incidentally, responsible to the Combined Chiefs of Staff for operational liaison on the Continent. Hodges told him that Collins of VII Corps and Corlett of XIX Corps had not the slightest doubt that, given sufficient petrol and ammunition, they could smash through to the Rhine. On the same day, Montgomery drew Eisenhower's attention to First Army's plight. He had been informed of the situation by Dempsey, who learned about the ammunition crisis from Hodges.

> Dempsey went to see Hodges today and brought back a dismal picture. First U.S. Army is, apparently, unable to develop its operations properly because it has not got the ammunition necessary. This does NOT repeat NOT promise well for our plans. Hodges' own view is that if he had the ammunition and the troops he could go right through to the Rhine easily. I considered I had better report this matter to you.[10]

The arrival of Marshall introduced politics into the ammunition crisis. Montgomery complained to Marshall that despite a directive from Eisenhower, on 13 September, which at last seemed to have made it clear that the Aachen–Cologne–Ruhr axis was to have priority in 12th Army Group, and that Patton was to stand fast, Patton had continued attacking and consumed the supplies that ought to have gone to Hodges. Although the Ruhr strategy had been agreed by the Combined Chiefs of Staff in Washington, Eisenhower was allowing each army to attempt to reach the Rhine on its own. There had to be an overall commander on the Ruhr axis. If it was not himself it should be Bradley. This information displeased Marshall and he blamed the messenger. On 13 September, he had circulated a message to twenty-one of his senior commanders:

> While cessation of hostilities in the war against Germany may occur at any time, it is assumed that in fact it will extend over a period commencing any time between September 1 and November 1.[11]

To discover that an ammunition shortage was holding up his armies, that the war was by no means over, and that Montgomery was lecturing him about the situation, angered him. In 1956, when time might have shown him that Montgomery had been justified, for the logistics muddle had caused himself and his staff much trouble, he remarked:

I came pretty near to blowing off out of turn. It was very hard for me to restrain myself because I didn't think there was any logic in what he said but egotism.[12]

The revelation did not stop Marshall sending a telegram to Alan Brooke when he returned to Washington in which, Brooke wrote, 'he seems to consider that if we really set our heart on it we ought to be able to finish the war before the end of the year.'[13]

By the time that he expressed this thought, Marshall had directed his logistics chief, General Brehon Somervell, to despatch Major-Generals Lucius Clay and Henry Aurand to sort out Lee's administrative empire. Neither succeeded, and when Somervell's senior trouble-shooter, LeRoy Lutes, arrived in December, just before the German Ardennes counter-stroke, things were little better. The ammunition shortage had extended to tank and infantry mortar rounds, cigarettes, and winter clothing. Bradley was complaining bitterly, Lutes recorded, saying that

the British would not consider an attack on only 60 rounds of 105-mm ammunition per diem. He said that normally they would have 150 and that he wants 150–200 rounds per gun per diem for his offensive operations.[14]

Bradley had not spoken out on those lines when he was sending his divisions into battle through October and November with inadequate artillery support. No doubt it would have been politically unwise.

The Germans attacked in the Ardennes on 15 December. American mishandling of the campaign became public when Montgomery had to take command of the First Army front because Bradley was at Luxembourg on the other side of the bulge in his line. Bradley's pride was badly hurt. However, the details of the ammunition muddle revealed by Aurand, Clay and Lutes were concealed lest it blow the dispute between Eisenhower and Montgomery on to the front pages of the newspapers. Its exposure would have indicated that Montgomery's repeated warnings about the shortage of resources, the need to concentrate allied offensives on the routes to the Ruhr and to coordinate command and strategy, had been justified.

By early December, their losses left American divisions gravely short of men. Replacements were not immediately available. The Ardennes offensive worsened the situation. The implications for Marshall were serious from several points of view. First, Eisenhower's policy of fighting the campaign centred on Bradley's front, so that control was in American hands, had his approval. If the Ruhr had really been given priority the centre of gravity would have shifted northward, and Bradley would have had to co-operate with Montgomery in a joint operation. Marshall had been a senior operations staff officer at all levels in the First World War and, like other American commanders, including Pershing his boss, regretted the subordinate role the Americans had had to play until the end. They had depended on their allies for most of their weapons and equipment, their training, their horses and shipping to transport them to Europe. As a result they had to be intransigent to retain a measure of operational independence. The experience made them determined never again to enter a war unprepared and beholden to their allies, as they had in April 1917. Now that the British were the subordinates Marshall intended that Eisenhower should, by one means or another, keep operational control in American hands. That was not unreasonable when they were so superior in numbers of divisions and so well equipped. It was another matter if it should be revealed that between the field commanders and the War Department, the Americans had made a hash of operations and supplies.[15]

Later, in the spring advance from the Rhine, the Ardennes behind them, Marshall ensured, through Eisenhower, that it would be Bradley, not Montgomery with the 9th American Army under command, that met the Russians over a prostrate German Army when the war ended. But before the spring the ammunition and personnel shortage had penetrated the political centre in Washington. In 1943, in North Africa, congressional representatives, determining that ammunition was being wasted, reduced funds for its production. In April 1944, scales of ammunition in Italy were found to be inadequate. When General Sir Harold Alexander, the C-in-C, appealed and obtained larger stocks, he was warned that ammunition for his American divisions had to be restricted to build up American supplies for Overloard. In the autumn of 1944, it turned out not only that Lee's supply system had failed, but that ETO scales of ammunition were too low and that stocks in depots in the United States were depleted. It was ironic that when the Battle of the Atlantic had been won, there were ships aplenty but not the cargoes for them.

In the year of the presidential elections in November 1944, this matter would have reflected badly on the administration had it become public knowledge. A major problem was that the Pacific war had been more successful than had been expected. Army and Marine demands from the Pacific were competing with those from Europe, particularly in mortar and field gun ammunition, and supplying them undermined the understanding that the European war was to have priority. Nor was that all. Eisenhower was dangerously short of infantry. Washington had misjudged the casualty rates and Eisenhower was in the same state as the British and Canadians by December. This was a result of his attacking across the front for too long. In the spring of 1944, War Secretary Stimson had advised Marshall of his unease about the availability of army reserve units and replacements. He feared that by the end of the summer American divisions would be on a par with the Germans, and by November would lack the margin of superiority required to finish the war, which might be prolonged into 1945. His anxiety proved to be well founded. Marshall, unwilling to stir up competition with the Pacific by asking for a larger slice of manpower, pressed theatre commanders to comb out *bouches inutiles* and avoid wasting manpower.[16] These events between September and the Ardennes crisis in December occurred while Eisenhower was acknowledging CCS policy on the Ruhr but not enforcing it. He agreed, as he was bound to, that if the Ruhr and the Saar–Frankfurt axes could not both be supported in sufficient strength, the former should have priority. He also acknowledged that as there were no vital objectives in front of Devers' 6th Army Group it could take over front from 3rd Army to create a reserve. Although one directive would appear to acknowledge these facts Eisenhower's subsequent actions would deny them: he would reverse a policy in the next directive or water it down so that it became ambivalent. Such inconsistency exasperated Montgomery.

The inability of London and the refusal of Washington to insist that Eisenhower reconcile his contradictory directives with their plan, and control the conflicting actions of his subordinates, became a central feature of the campaign. It offended the professional Brooke in London and provoked Montgomery's insubordination in the field.

When that has been said, it was unlikely that the CCS, meeting three thousand miles away at the Octagon conference in early September and subsequently in Washington, would or could direct their commander in chief in the field to take this or that action. If it appeared to Eisenhower that Patton might obtain a bridgehead into the Saar and that his prospects were, for the time being, better than those of Hodges, chiefs of staff away from the scene would not overrule him. George Marshall certainly would oppose any British attempt to impose action that appeared to be inspired by Montgomery whose military ambition he abhorred and misunderstood. A critical examination of the vacillation and inconsistency in Eisenhower's thinking, to Brooke and Montgomery proof that the campaign was being ill-directed, could not be sustained in the CCS over its American and probably not its RAF and RN members.

At Brussels airport on 10 September, it had been agreed that Antwerp should be opened. It was not made a priority by Eisenhower at that time but Montgomery soon pressed General Crerar to undertake the operation even before he had completed his capture of the Channel Ports. His reason was that he was already needing its port capacity himself. In his Market-Garden directive on 14 September, in which he said *'Our real objective therefore, is the Ruhr,'* he remarked obscurely, 'But on the way to it we want the ports of Antwerp and Rotterdam, since the capture of the Ruhr is merely the first step on the northern route of advance into Germany.' He meant that a deep penetration into Germany required those two ports to supply it, as Eisenhower, himself, had stated. The Canadian Army was assigned the task of clearing the Scheldt estuary in October and the port was opened towards the end of November.[17]

The Scheldt, clearing up Western Holland and defending the Island between the Waal and the Lower Rhine over-extended Montgomery. Hodges had inadequate forces to attack through the Aachen Gap and to cover the ground between his left and Second Army's right on the Maas. The Anglo-American drive between the Maas and the Rhine envisagd by Montgomery had to be postponed. Although It was clear that the Allies were already over-extended Bradley continued to attack through October and November on both his fronts.

It is arguable that Bradley's aggression worsened his administrative position, left him over-extended and helped the German attack in the Ardennes. Yet the Germans had no hope of breaking through to Antwerp as they intended. To the south Patton was able to redeploy divisions to form a reserve to attack the German left flank and hold his main front with the rest. Montgomery did the same and, in fact, the Second Army divisions that moved south together with 6th Airborne Division from England, had little fighting to do. It was redeployed American divisions, the northern flank of which were under Montgomery's general direction, that halted the Germans and eventually threw them back. The counter-operation showed that had the Allies earlier held the front with fewer divisions they could have formed a substantial strike force for the drive to the Rhine. That would have been Montgomery's procedure had he controlled the front.

But for Montgomery, those days were over. The power to direct operations was never in his hands after Normandy. He never controlled Market-Garden's airborne force, nor the air operations connected with it. His own force was inadequate to complete Market-Garden. Except during the Ardennes emergency he never directed First U.S. Army on his right, although Simpson's 9th Army joined 21st Army Group for Grenade in February 1945. Although he attempted to persuade Eisenhower to let him control the front north of the Ardennes he was allowed to do that during the German break-through simply because there was no other course. Bradley had lost control. During the Ardennes his American subordinates were happy with his operational actions. Unfortunately, his immodest and tactless comments at a press meeting afterwards offended Bradley, Patton and Eisenhower. His lack of power first reduced Montgomery to military arguments and then, when they did not prevail, to frustrated bluster. That he was probably right on operational matters was neither here nor there when the Americans were determined to manage the campaign themselves. He could not undertake decisive operations with his own forces. If this were not obvious when he was trying unsuccessfully to settle the plans for breaking out of Normandy, it certainly was after his failure to reach Arnhem. His influence as a winning general, was then lost.

Montgomery suffered a final blow in the last phase of the campaign. Churchill, Brooke and Montgomery understood that the main objectives in Germany beyond the Rhine would be investing the Ruhr and then taking Berlin, Schlesvig Holstein, Hamburg and Bremen. 9th Army would continue to fight with 21st Army Group, which would drive for the Elbe crossings and go on to Berlin. That had been part of the understanding of the British Chiefs of Staff and the CCS. For Berlin, Vienna and Prague were to set the political seal on victory over Germany and they should be shared, at least, with the Russians. Prague was the centre of Europe and Churchill was already thinking of the post-war settlement in which there was bound to be a struggle with the Soviet Union.

Eisenhower thought that he saw clearly into the future beyond the temporary military situation of March 1945. Roosevelt was dying and Marshall knew that provided Eisenhower offered military reasons for his actions Churchill would have to accept them. It was unimportant, at that late stage, that his reasons would not be approved after the war by directing staffs in military colleges who would point out that the time really had arrived for a broad front advance. Surprisingly, he argued that a tactical advance to cut the German Army in half was necessary. So, he informed Stalin and the Russian High Command, by way of John R. Deane at the American Military Mission in Moscow, that he intended to drive on Leipzig and Dresden and not Berlin. When his order was questioned in London he said that he intended to prevent the Germans forming a redoubt in the Alps. Berlin was only a political objective and not worth the 100 000 casualties that Bradley, curiously, stated would be the price to pay. He removed Simpson's army from Montgomery and gave it back to Bradley for a largely defensive role. Accused of changing his plan at the last minute, Eisenhower simply denied it. Indeed, it had been understood that if the Russians could reach Berlin first he would re-direct his armies on Leipzig. Montgomery would drive on the other northern objectives with British resources alone.

The Cold War affected our view of this event. When he heard from Eisenhower, Zhukov shifted his own drive from the Dresden direction to the area just south of Berlin. Later Zhukov told Marshall that he regretted having done so without informing Eisenhower of his intentions. Eisenhower decided on the change when taking a few days leave with Bradley in the south of France. He told Bradley that he intended to give him the main role of meeting the Russians with the three northern armies under his control. One purpose was to restore Bradley's morale. He also anticipated the amicable occupation of Germany with the Russians. A race for Berlin, with the risk of clashes between the armies, was not the best introduction to post-war international relations. Further, the war with Japan had to be finished, and Russian co-operation there was essential, he then believed. The fewer casualties the Americans suffered the better.

In this light the complaints of Montgomery and Churchill appear petty, but understandable nevertheless. American actions underlined the decline of Britain. Britain, though, was part of Europe and should have had her say in its fate. In the longer run, her actions in 1940 and 1941 had saved Europe, and, by fighting on, perhaps the Soviet Union as well. She had certainly given the Americans time to arm. The future of Europe could not be left to the United States alone, for she had left Europe in the lurch once before and might do so again.

Within a short space the Iron Curtain came down and Churchill's Fulton Missouri predictions in 1946 became a fact. Eisenhower and

Marshall were later criticised and Marshall was a target of the McCarthy campaign during the Eisenhower presidency. Years later, Marshall would endorse Eisenhower's actions as 'understandable at the time, which implied regret,' wrote David Eisenhower. And Eisenhower remained sensitive to criticism on the subject.[18]

Reflections

In the middle of the war it seemed that all my life had been spent fighting it. When it ended, most of my friends returned to familiar places and picked up their lives where they left them in 1939. I continued to serve in a regular army that was shrinking around me and making do with ageing equipment and wartime methods. Except for an enjoyable tour helping to initiate the new Royal Military Academy, I was steered into orthodox channels which were professionally boring. I was given none of the more or less dangerous assignments throughout the world to which the Army was committed. Ironically, I seemed to have been self-directed in the war but not in peace. In search of a more challenging career, I retired in 1958 and migrated to Canada.

Of course I was thankful to have survived the war without serious injury. Battle had been a lottery. Had my head been where my arm was at Mull on the 16 February 1945, I would not be writing this on a fine May evening in North Yorkshire. Had my halftrack been parked a yard or two to the right, the mortar bomb that hit Battalion rear link at Frenouville would have disposed of me. Had I not been taken prisoner in July 1942 I might have been killed at Alamein like Pip Beale and other regimental friends. And might not the Italian guard at Chieti prison camp have seen me lying helpless in the wire a yard from his foot and bayonetted me? Often, happenstance must have saved me from death or more serious wounds than I suffered in Norway and Germany.

At moments of immediate danger I promised that if I were spared I would live a useful life thereafter. I have not kept my promise. But who can tell how often I would have offended had I not shared so many experiences with men and women, in war and peace, who remained my friends for life? Peace, like war, is shared experience. I feel a bond with my wartime enemies too. I love the Italians, exasperating though I find them over things that we northerners regard as important. But they sheltered me, fed me, and wished me no harm when I was a prisoner on the run, although I had been their enemy engaged in destroying their beautiful country. I never experienced the nastier side of the German nature and never hated their soldiers, although I feared them for my own good. Their views on race saved the British from the treatment they meted out to Slavs and Jews and Gypsies. We were compromised by the distinction. Had I been a prisoner of the Japanese, I might still feel enmity towards them, as many do. But the Japanese believed that all prisoners had disgraced themselves. Through ill-treatment they might be redeemed.

In prison camp I learned that many prisoners had, indeed, given up without a struggle. When they were captured they were relieved that, for them, the war was over. I wondered how they had performed in battle; what kind of soldiers they had made. Others had disobeyed orders to surrender and withstood the general demoralization of their companions that had often preceded their capture. As prisoners they proved to be rebellious questioners of authority; a disproportionate number being regular soldiers keen to shine in their careers. Others, civilians with intellectual ability or skill with their hands, exceptionally imaginative and strong-minded, engaged in helping escapers or escaping themselves.

The majority of those with whom my father and I fought were civilians for whom the war was not a professional experience. In obvious ways it changed most of their lives, none the less. They hoped it should change the country socially and economically as well. That was their desire when so many of them voted Labour in 1945. They regarded the redistribution of wealth as their just reward. The prevention of another Depression was uppermost in their minds. The efficient actions of the state in war could be continued into peace, they believed. They understood less clearly that the pauperising of the country for the second time in the century would delay more fundamental changes, and that time was needed to overcome the prevailing class-war obsession that would frustrate reform measures.

Some clues to what was needed, beyond egalitarian measures, lay in the shortcomings of the army's weapons, equipment and fighting performance. Only in relatively recent writing, by Correlli Barnett for instance, have those deficiencies been noted, let alone associated with the relative economic, industrial, political and social decay of Great Britain since the turn of the century. The excellent administration during the war, particular as regards feeding, conditioned people to consider state intervention in their lives as right and necessary. As I write, a new government and a new political party has come to power half a century after 1945. In its search for a synthesis between personal responsibility and a humane State it is exposing the extent of the task of reform and repair and undertaking it without the bitterness of earlier decades. The relative decline of the nation is being exposed and admitted in less class-ridden terms than in earlier decades. We seem to have reached the end of the post-war era at last.

The European Union is at the centre of the new era. We are at last focusing attention on the achievements, ideas and history of continental nations. Comparisons are being made between Britain and continental Europe without disparaging the latter. Europeans were overrun in 1940 and had to pick themselves up in 1945. Their economies were ruined: physical destruction in Germany was infinitely worse than in the UK. We had grown too used to declaring their faults to appreciate their achievements, without envy, let alone their suffering. All of them had skeletons to disinter and consign somehow and somewhere. Is it not ironic that the war's victors were the last to recognise the extent of the work that they, themselves, still had to undertake? Not really. Victors seldom face up to their failures and the price of victory in both wars was economic ruin. Politics determined that the first task after the war was to correct economic and social injustice. It proved to be beyond the capacity of the country to undertake, simultaneously, a root and branch reform of the economy and industry and education.

Nevertheless, much progress has been made since 1945. Now is the turn of the Constitution, the legal system, the education establishment, several parts of the country's infrastructure and many problems common to other western countries, such as national health, to receive special attention. These have to be tackled within the spirit of the Union although the letter of its edicts should sometimes be resisted, for they are sometimes wrong-headed.

Here it is necessary to return to a point in my introductory paragraphs. We must understand our historical connection with the Continental powers. We must also grasp the philosophical, legal, social and political differences between us and them. Their desire to avoid another civil war, to form a strong economic unit against the American free trade area and the 'Eastern Tigers', should not lead us into losing the fundamentals of our own national history, many of which are admired by Continentals. We need to relearn what they are and what we are or we shall lose our souls without knowing it.

Notes

1 THE ARMY PREPARES

1. Fisher was 1st Sea Lord from 1904 to 1910 and again in 1914–15.
2. The opposition in Campbell Bannerman's cabinet until 1908 and in Herbert Asquith's thereafter saw to the economy theme and dubbed Haldane 'Minister for Slaughter'. Haldane considered the Chancellor, David Lloyd George, who was expected to oppose British involvement, 'an illiterate with an unbalanced mind'. See A.J. Anthony Morris, 'Haldane's Army Reform, 1906–8: the deception of the radicals', *History*, vol. 56 (1971).
3. Quick-firing meant a high rate of aimed fire owing to the gun's stability, maintained by the buffer and recuperator system. Only minor and rapid aiming adjustments were required between rounds. The gun could be fired from pits in advanced positions or from behind a steel shield on the gun without the detachment having to leap clear from the recoil of the carriage. 75-mm and 18-pounders fired 'fixed' ammunition – the cordite propellent and the explosive shell were in one piece. The howitzer had 'separate' ammunition.
4. 'Army Administration', a lecture given by Lt General Sir H.S. Miles at the Royal United Services Institute in November 1922. See also the chapter 'The Still and Mental Parts' in S. Bidwell and D. Graham, *Fire-Power: British Army Weapons and Theories of War, 1904–45*.
5. Minutes of the Staff Conference of 1910 at the Staff College Library, Camberley. Bidwell and Graham, op. cit. pp. 51–2. Director of Staff Duties and co-ordinator of the 'G' branches. Kiggell became Haig's chief of staff in France at the end of 1915 where he did not cover himself in glory.
6. Quoted by Leon Wolff, *In Flanders Fields* (New York, 1960) 44; quoted in Bidwell and Graham, *Fire-Power*, p. 66.
7. Winston Churchill, *The World Crisis* (abridged and revd edn) (London, 1931) p. 641; also quoted in Bidwell and Graham, *Fire-Power*, p. 66.

3 POLITICIANS, COMMANDERS AND BATTLES

1. The Haig Papers are in the National Library of Scotland, Edinburgh.
2. *History of the Great War: Military Operations, France and Belgium 1914*, Appendix 8, p. 499, compiled by Brigadier-General Sir James Edmonds (London, 1937).
3. The Rawlinson Papers, Churchill College, Cambridge.
4. Bidwell and Graham, *Fire-Power*, p. 80.
5. David French, *British Strategy and War Aims*, 1914–16 (London, 1986); Keith Neilson, *Strategy and Supply: The Anglo-Russian Alliance, 1914–17*

(London, 1984); Kathleen Burk 'The Mobilization of Anglo-American Finance during World War 1', in N.F. Dreiziger (ed.) *Mobilization for Total War*; Barry Hunt and Adrian Preston (eds), *War Aims and Strategic Policy in the Great War* (London, 1977); Michael Howard, *The Continental Commitment* (London, 1972); Norman Gibbs, 'British Strategic Doctrine, 1918–39', in Michael Howard (ed.) *The Theory and Practice of War* (London, 1965).

6. Information about the development of machine guns in the British and German armies in the G.M. Lindsay papers in the Imperial War Museum Horne Papers. Lindsay was active in the Machine-Gun Corps. This subject is discussed in some detail in Bidwell and Graham, *Fire-Power*, pp. 122–3.

7. For the changes in defence layouts, practising how to follow a barrage, see Bidwell and Graham, *Fire-Power*, pp. 119–20; also Major-General R.B. Stephens, commanding 5th Division, on the new conditions; Lt-Colonel L.L.C. Reynolds on training a battalion; and the development of bombers, rifle grenadiers and Lewis gunners from being specialists to all-rounders in sections, p. 126.

8. Observation at a conference on 28 December 1916, IWM Maxse Papers.

9. Stephens, Reynolds, Bruce Williams and Heneker papers are in the IWM, Haldane's in the National Library of Scotland. Watts of 7th, Deverell of 3rd and Furse later MGO were each active.

10. Bidwell and Graham, *Fire-Power*, p. 129.

11. The captured document that spelled them out was circulated on 7 August 1917. Plumer had told GHQ what they needed to know before Messines.

12. IWM, Maxse Papers, XVIII Corps, No. G.S. 70, 21 August 1917.

13. See D. Graham and S. Bidwell, *Coalitions, Politicians and Generals*, pp. 105–21. The errors in the official account are explained in pp. 92–3 ns 1, 2 and 3.

14. Maurice was Director of Military Operations at the War Office. Later he accused Lloyd George of fiddling with reinforcement figures and denying the BEF reinforcement before the German offensive in March 1918. After the war he became a distinguished military historian.

4   NECESSITY KNOWS NO LAW

1. Dominick Graham, 'Observations on the Dialectics of British Tactics, 1904–45', RMC of Canada, 1984, in Ronald Haycock and Keith Neilson, (eds) *Men Machines and War* (Wilfrid Laurier, 1988). The word dialectic refers to the contest between orthodox and progressive soldiers out of which tactical doctrine and practice in the British Army emerged.

2. Edited with an introduction (Cassel, 1937).

3. For example, T.H. Travers, *How the War was Won: command and technology in the British Army on the Western Front, 1917–18* (London: Routledge, 1992); John Terraine, *White Heat: the New Warfare, 1914–18* (Guild Publishing, 1982).

4. Examples of the literature are Martin Middlebrook, *The First Day on the Somme* (Allen Lane, 1971) and Lynne Macdonald, *Somme* (Michael Joseph, 1983).

5. Chapman (ed.), *Vain Glory*, Introduction and *Sunday Times* review by Siegfried Sassoon, 25 July 1939.

6. Statistics of casualties are slippery. Western Front casualties were suffered by over 60 divisions and each of 12 (only in 1918 were they reduced to nine) battalions of rifle companies. 700 Scottish Riflemen went over the top at Neuve Chapelle out of a battalion strength of about 800. Your chance of survival in a Normandy rifle company was about the same as it would have been on the Western Front. In Normandy, rifle companies were usually no more than 120 strong, often less, and in their three platoons, 90 or less. Casualties were shared among fewer divisions, with fewer battalions each with fewer 'cutting edge' sub-units. Operations continued for longer and rests were rarer. Noise and the lethality of weapons was greater. RAF and Dominion air force killed and missing over Normandy totalled 'only' 8536, but they were of 'officer grade'.

7. Up to May 1944, 52 000 civilians had been killed and 63 000 seriously injured. The first V1s landed on 13 June. 33 442 civilians were killed or severely wounded by V1s and V2s by the end of the war.

8. Chapman (ed.) *Vain Glory*, p. xii

9. Chapman (ed.) *Vain Glory*, 'Sacrifice to the Past', Otto Braun (aged 17), p. 1079.

10. John Baynes, *Morale: A Study of Men and Courage*: The Second Scottish Rifles at the Battle of Neuve Chapelle 1915, pp. 51–82.

11. Ibid., p. 73n.

12. Ibid., p. 73–4, quoting John Betjeman's collected poems, p. 643.

13. Ibid., p. 74.

14. The story that the late arrival of 6-inch howitzers was responsible for the wire fiasco is nonsense. They were not used for wire cutting but they may have been used against the trench behind the hedge, which they did not hit. But as their own infantry were so close it is probable that the battery did not fix the bottom of the bracket.

15. Baynes, *Morale*, p. 75.

16. Ibid.

17. High explosive for the 18-pounder was first tried at Ypres in October 1914 but it took months to build up stocks for the shrapnel round was still required.

18. Bidwell and Graham, *Fire-Power*, pp. 75–6.

19. *Official History (OH)*, *1915*, vol. 1, p. 151; Baynes, *Morale*, p. 84.

20. L/Cpl J.J. Cousins, 7th Bedfords, in Middlebrook, *The First Day on the Somme*, p. 184.

21. Middlebrook, *The First Day on the Somme*, p. 250.

22. Private A.R. French 7th Royal West Kents Middlebrook, *The First Day on the Somme*, p. 250.

23. Sgt H. Benzing, Grimsby Chums Middlebrook, *The First Day on the Somme*, p. 251.

24. As I remarked earlier, casualty figures in the Official History are accurate within certain limits. Comparisons between armies are difficult because they record casualties differently. For example, the periods to which the statistics refer may differ. The Germans recorded a casualty only when the man was evacuated beyond a certain point in the system. For years after the war British figures were challenged. However, the *OH* is probably correct in its conclusion that from 1 July to the end of November 1916 British and French casualties totalled about 600 000 and that the German were much the same. In the two German offensives on the Somme and the Lys from 21 March to 30 April 1918, British casualties were 22 000 killed, 96 000 wounded and 42 000 prisoners, for a total of about 160 000 on the Somme and 50 159 killed and wounded and 31 881 missing, totalling 82 040 on the Lys (*OH*, 1918, vol. 3, p. 4 fn 1). In these open operations there were many prisoners, whereas on 1 July 1916, there were few compared with the dead and wounded. German casualties were probably 348 000 against total allied casualties of about 332 000. In the Aisne and 2nd Marne German offensives in May and June 1918, in which the British took a smaller part, British casualties were 28 700, French 145 000 and German 130 000. From 21 March to 20 September 1918 British and overseas forces casualties were 27 470 officers and 584 216 other ranks. German prisoners taken were 5300 officers and 223 222 other ranks (*OH*, 1918, vol. 4, p. 518). In August and September British and overseas casualties were 190,000. (*OH*, vol. 5, p. 597–8). The total German casualties between 21 March and 1 October were 40 722 officers and 1 181 577 other ranks. There were many prisoners (*OH*, 1918, vol. 5, p. 584). Of the wounded 64 per cent returned to the line and about 18 per cent were fit for rear duties. Of the 704 803 killed in the war 40 per cent died of wounds.
25. Captain D.G. Browne (Tank Corps) on his way over Pilckem Ridge. His tank was bogged in the Steenbeek valley (Chapman (ed.) *Vain Glory*, pp. 451–620.
26. 20 September 1917, Ex-private X (63rd Naval Division). Chapman 464–6. 20 September was one of Plumer's successful battles fought in dry conditions. The 63rd were not engaged on the 20th and this incident probably took place on 26 or 30 October, unsuccessful XVIII Corps operations in deep mud in the Lekkerboterbeek.
27. Captain D.G. Browne, 20 November, 1917 (Chapman [ed.] *Vain Glory*, p. 493).
28. R.H. Kiernan, 8th Leicestershire Regt (Chapman [ed.] *Vain Glory*, p. 609).
29. H.R. Williams (Chapman [ed.] *Vain Glory*, pp. 649–50).
30. Lt-Colonel F. Lushington (Chapman [ed.] *Vain Glory*, pp. 683–4).

6 THE DESERT CAMPAIGN 1941–2

1. Major-General I.S.O. Playfair, *History of the Second World War: The Mediterranean and Middle East*, vol. I, p. 349.

2. Ibid., pp. 223–34.
3. Ibid., p. 334.
4. Ronald Lewin, *The Chief: Field Marshal Lord Wavell, Commander-in-Chief and Viceroy, 1939–1947* (Hutchinson, 1980), p. 81.
5. Playfair, *History*, vol. I, p. 340.
6. Ibid., p. 341.
7. Ibid., p. 377.
8. Lewin, *The Chief*, p. 82.
9. Playfair, *History*, vol. I, p. 369.
10. Playfair, *History*, vol. II, pp. 2–4.

7 THE ARMOUR PROBLEM

1. Vice-Admiral Sir Geoffrey Blake, one of Playfair's readers, remarked: 'The account of this [The Winter] battle reads very like the accounts of naval actions: Jutland, for example, or the chase of the Bismarck. Low visibility, scattered forces, failures of reconnaissance, errors in signal positions, breakdown in wireless communications and the dangers and benefits of wireless silence ....' (CAB 103/331).
2. Page 68 of the despatch and p. 247 of the draft of vol. III in CAB 44/98 during the Gazala battle.
3. Draft of vol. III, p. 248.
4. *History*, vol. III, p. 436.
5. Ibid., p. 435
6. Ibid., p. 437.
7. Ibid., pp. 435-6.
8. Ibid., Appx 8, p. 438.
9. Ibid., p. 30.
10. General Willoughby Norrie had been appointed corps commander to replace General Pope who had been killed in an air crash. He had been commanding 1st Armoured Division in the UK. Herbert Lumsden, also from the UK, replaced Norrie. The main body of 1 Division arrived at Suez on about 1 December.
11. Diary, WO 169/1123 pt 2, p. 3.
12. WO 169/1123 p. 29.
13. CAB 106/719.
14. 30 Corps figures are 456 initial recoveries, 231 repaired and 50 in course (CAB106/881).

8 THE GAZALA BATTLE

1. CAB, 140/134.
2. CAB, 106/662, 106/671 and 106/661 respectively.
3. When 8th Armoured Division arrived in the following July things were no better.

4. F.H. Hinsley *et al.*, *British Intelligence in the Second World War*, vol. II, pp. 330–6. Playfair vol III, pp. 97, 137, 139, 156, 159.
5. Playfair, *History*, vol. III, pp. 139, 145.
6. CAB, 106/66/1 p. 6 referring to early February.
7. Playfair, vol. III, p. 197.
8. Lt Gen. Sir George Erskine's evidence concerning the situation and opinion about Tobruk in Gott's XIII Corps, in which he was then a staff officer, is in CAB 106/698. See Playfair, *History*, vol. III, pp. 245–9.
9. Agar Hamilton to Playfair, CAB 140/137 May 1957.
10. Ibid.
11. Sir Alan Brooke was Chief of the Imperial General Staff from 1941–6, becoming Field Marshall in 1944 and Master Gunner in 1946. He was raised to the peerage as Viscount Alanbrooke in 1945. CAB 105/1219. Documents from official sources in Playfair files. First file in box, Report of Conversation with Brooke on the replacements of August '42, on 30 July 1956.
12. Hamilton wrote to Playfair: 'After Consultation with General Pienaar, General Gott allowed this operation to be whittled down to a raid.' CAB 140/137, 11 May 1957.
13. Hinsley *et al.*, *British Intelligence*, pp. 383 and 722 et seq., Appendix 16. 'Intelligence on Rommel's Dispositions before the Gazala battle'.
14. Ibid., p. 360.
15. Ibid., p. 358.
16. Playfair, *History*, vol. III, p. 218.
17. Ibid., pp. 213–4.

9   FIGHTING

1. Michael Carver, who was on Norrie's staff, wrote the best detailed account of these battles in his *Tobruk* (Batsford, 1964).
2. H.G. Knight, Signalman (From *The Royal Artillery Commemoration Book, 1939–1945*, p. 187 (London, 1950).
3. Cyril Joly, *Take These Men* (Penguin, 1955). From P.D. Mehta in *Early Indian Religious Thought: An Introduction and Essay*, Luzac, London 1956, pp. 110–13), retold by Dr Edward Hulme in a lecture in North Yorkshire.
4. *Keith Douglas: A Biography* by Desmond Graham (Oxford University Press, 1974) p. 216. Published in *Selected Poems* in 1942. Graham reports that 'Revisiting the "nightmare" where earlier he had engaged the gun that had knocked out his tank Douglas saw a dead gunner "sprawling in the sun" like a sunbather."'
5. Ibid., p. 216.
6. Ibid., p. 191. Desmond Graham writes that Douglas wrote 'Gallantry' in hospital and slipped it, unsigned, into a book lent to a friend by a hospital sister.
7. 'Major-General Rea Leakey, Second World War Memoir', Liddell Hart Centre for Military Archives, Kings' College, London. Chapter on Tobruk and conversation with the author.

8. *Royal Artillery Commemoration Book, 1939–1945* (London, 1950) pp. 184–5.
9. Leakey, ibid., and conversation with the author.
10. 'A few recollections of Jock Campbell' by Brigadier George Davy, Liddell Hart Centre for Military Archives, King's College, London. (15p)
11. Davy, ibid.
12. Davy, ibid.
13. Sergeant Raymond Ellis, Memoir, Imperial War Museum, interviews, tapes and typescripts of the Second World War.
14. Ellis, ibid.
15. Ellis, ibid.
16. Leekey Memoir, Chapter on battle of Gazala, pp. 123–9.

11   THE CONDUCT OF THE NORMANDY CAMPAIGN

1. Tactical instruction 14 April printed in *The Memoirs of Field-Marshal Montgomery* (London, 1958), pp. 234–6.
2. PRO WO 205/118, quoted by Sir Charles Richardson in *Flashback.*
3. Carlo D'Este explains the various interpretations in his *Decision in Normandy*: 'The Normandy Myth', pp. 476–501. Richardson was head of the 21st Army Group planning staff.
4. *OH*, pp. 329, 330; press comments on the report that Second Army had 'broken through', pp. 352–3; SHAEF reaction p. 353; Eisenhower's reaction to not being taken fully into Montgomery's confidence. His misunderstanding of Montgomery's campaign plan, pp. 354, 356, 357; Montgomery less than honest about the result, p. 356.
5. CAB 106/1061: Colonel Jackson's interview with Sir Miles Dempsey, 8 March 1951.
6. Interview Jackson-Dempsey on 6 March 1951 in CAB 106/1061, and 'The Airfield Controversy, the Capture of Caen, Montgomery's intentions and Relations with SHAEF' in CAB 106/1120. On Goodwood see also Dempsey's instructions to BGS 8 Corps 18 July in CAB 106/1041. April 1944 diagram I, showing forecast for the development of the battle in Ellis, *Official History* (*OH*), p. 357.
7. Tedder's views are reported in CAB 106/1120 'The Airfield controversy, the capture of Caen, Montgomery's intentions and relations with SHAEF'. In particular, f 26. 'General Eisenhower, his deputy Air Marshal Tedder ... and most of Shaef seemed to have formed the impression that Goodwood was to be the decisive breakthrough in the east. They ignored the fact that as before operations on the eastern flank were still designed to assist the western flank, they misunderstood the significance of the close synchronisation between Dempsey and Bradley's operations. And in f 34 Tedder is quoted: 'All the evidence indicates a serious lack of fighting leadership in the higher direction of our armies. From this criticism I specifically except General Bradley and his Commanders' 'Performance'.
8. M. 502, 18 June.

9. CAB 106/1120 from M. 505.
10. CAB 106/1061. Colonel Jackson, Official Narrator, interview with Sir Miles Dempsey on 8 March 1951.
11. L.F. Ellis, *History of the Second World War: Victory in the West, Vol. I, The Battle of Normandy* (HMSO, 1962) p. 386.
12. *OH*, pp. 447–8. German casualties in June were about 80 000. *OH*, p. 308n; by 16 July about 100 000, and by the end 200 000 killed and wounded and 200 000 missing, *OH*, pp. 323; D'Este, *Decision in Normandy*, pp. 456–8 and 517–18.

12 FIGHTING EXPERIENCES: TILLY-SUR-SEULLES, VILLERS BOCAGE AND OPERATION GOODWOOD

1. 'Notes for my address to senior officers', nd. Letter to Army Commanders, 14 April 1944, in Dempsey papers WO 285/2.
2. Author's experience as a battery commander. Dempsey papers WO 285/2. 'NOTES for Air Chief Marshal Sir Ralph Cochrane from Air Chief Marshal Sir Harry Broadhurst on The Tactical Air Force Operations in Normandy. At Crerar's First Army headquarters the system broke down through the latter's inexperience. CAB 101/332.
3. F.H. Hinsley, *British Intelligence in the Second World War*, vol. III, p. 181.
4. The reconnaissance battalions of the German panzer divisions were here there and everywhere and were an example to the British.
5. His report on the fighting was sent to the official historians in London by Major-General Kippenberger, the chief New Zealand historian and commander of the 2nd New Zealand Division at Cassino, where he lost a leg. (Letter dated 9 May 1951, CAB, 106/1060).
6. CAB 106/1060.
7. Hargest, CAB 106/1060, Battle Notes on recent actions up to D+10.
8. CAB 106/1060, Battle Notes 13–16 June.
9. Ibid.
10. Ibid.
11. Ibid. Tanks – Notes 16-6-44.
12 Ibid. 17-6-44 Notes – Tanks contd.
13. Ibid. Tanks 16-6-44 contd.
14. Ibid. 21 June 44 – Notes.
15. D'Este, *Decision in Normandy*, p. 177.
16. The integration of lorried brigade and armoured brigade units was first effected in this operation. It was to become standard procedure later in all armoured divisions. The headquarters of the brigades were then interchangeable.
17. Major-General Geoffrey Armitage, quoted by Carlo D'Este, *Decision in Normandy*, p. 185. Christopher Milner, MC, an officer in A Company 1 RB, has collected letters from Mike Carver to Alistair Horne, a French account of the battle entitled *La Bataille de Villers Bocage*, correspondence with one of his platoon commanders on point 213, and his own impressions of Wittman's attack on the column below point 213. Milner was one of the very few survivors of the CLY fiasco.

18. F-M Lord Carver (Mike Carver) was told by Victor Balfour, GSO I XXX Corps, 'there was almost total confusion at the time, and they had little idea at Corps HQ what was going on as Bucknall was totally out of his depth, always swanning about and never letting his staff know what he had said to anyone'.
19. M 501, referred to in D'Este, *Decision in Normandy*, p. 191.
20. WO 285/ 15.
21. IWM 80/30/1 (8) quoted by Carver to Horne.
22. WO 285/9.

13 BATTLES ON THE FALAISE ROAD

1. Sydney Jary with Carbuncle, 'Firepower at Platoon and Company Level', *British Army Review*, n. 114 (December 1996).
2. Conversation with Jary.
3. RAC Bovington Museum Library, Interviews and Transcripts.
4. The country on the Falaise road south of Caen reminds me of High Wood and Delville Wood on the Somme. Villages are 'hull down' with churches showing out of trees. Wheat fields concealed hidden 'draws' which were death traps for attacking infantry, particularly when the corn caught fire.
5. Total allied army casualties until the end of August were 209 000 (OH, p. 493). The 3rd and 2nd Canadian Infantry Divisions, in that order, suffered the heaviest casualties in Second Army and First Canadian Armies.
6. T.M. Lindsay, *The Sherwood Rangers* (London, 1952).
7. William MacAndrew and Terry Copp, *Battle Exhaustion; soldiers and psychiatrists in the Canadian Army, 1939–1945* (Montreal: McGill–Queen's University Press, 1990).
8. Dominick Graham, *The Price of Command: a Biography of General Guy Simonds* (Toronto: Stoddart), pp. 138–57.
9. Major-General George Kitching in a letter to the author.
10. Graham, *The Price of Command*, p. 156.

14 MONTGOMERY'S REPUTATION

1. Max Hastings, Overlord: D-day and the battle for Normandy 1944 (London: Michael Joseph 1984) p. 142.
2. General Sir Charles Richardson, *Flashback: a soldier's story* (London: William Kimber 1985) pp. 174–6.
3. First Army headquarters documents refer to the 'slowness' of the British and then to their surprise that after the Seine they advanced with greater speed than they themselves.
4. *The Memoirs of Field Marshal Montgomery* (London: Collins 1958) pp. 254–5.
5. D'Este *Decision in Normandy*, p. 483.

16 MONTGOMERY VERSUS THE AMERICANS

1. V1 was the flying bomb. V2 the ballistic missile.
2. 'The "Broad Front" versus the "Narrow Front Controversy", Phase One', CAB 106/1106, pp. 37–8. A historical account of the controversy.
3. On 8th September, during Octagon, the Joint Planners concluded: 'The main Allied advance should be directed North of the Ardennes on Berlin and the area Bremen – Hamburg – Kiel. The advance south of the Ardennes should at first be subsidiary; in due course it will be augmented by the Allied army advancing from the south.' This paper was followed by one from Eisenhower, 'a more sober estimate than his previous ones and he noted the stiffening of German resistance.... still doubted whether the enemy could reinforce the Siegfried Line in time and in sufficient strength to oppose our advance. His intentions were to press on with all speed to the Ruhr and the Saar. The 1st operation was to break the Siegfried Line and seize crossings over the Rhine. In doing this the main effort will be on the left. Then we will prepare logistically and otherwise for a deep thrust into Germany.' CAB 106/1106.
4. CAB 106/1106, pp. 30–1.
5. The Nevins Papers, Military History Institute, Carlisle Barracks, Pennsylvania. General Eisenhower's Comments on Command, 18 May 1944.
6. Graham and Bidwell, *Coalitions, Politicians and Generals*, ch. 8.
7. A detailed account is in Graham and Bidwell's chapter 'Logistics: Neglect and Mischief', in *Coalitions*, pp. 255–76.
8. Graham D. and Bidwell, *Coalitions, Politicians and Generals*, Brasseys, London, 1993, p. 234 (quoting Hodges Diary, Irving Papers Reel 8.)
9. Graham and Bidwell, *Coalitions*, pp. 234 and 250.
10. Montgomery to Eisenhower, M 260, 6 October 1944, quoted in Graham and Bidwell, op. cit. p. 254, Pre-presidential Papers, Box 83.
11. Graham and Bidwell op. cit. p. 233.
12. Nigel Hamilton, *Monty: the Field Marshal* (London: Hamish Hamilton, 1986) p. 133.
13. Ibid., p. 108.
14. Graham and Bidwell, *Coalitions*, p. 267, quoting from Lutes' report to Somervell.
15. Ibid., pp. 146–9, and the chapter 'The Man with the Cudgel', pp. 178–196.
16. Forest C. Pogue, *George C. Marshall: Organizer of Victory 1943–45* (Viking, 1973) pp. 361–4 and 488–504. Lieutenant-General Ben Lear was sent over to ETO to sort out the manpower situation in January 1945. Lutes' comments in December 1944 in Graham and Bidwell pp. 275–6.
17. CAB 106/1106, p. 40.
18. David Eisenhower, *Eisenhower at War, 1943–45*, pp. 729–45.

Select Bibliography

Barclay, C.N., *On Their Shoulders: British Generalship in the Lean Years, 1939–42* (London: Faber, 1964).

Baynes, John, *Morale: A Study of Men and Courage* (London: Cassell, 1967).

Behrens, C.B.A., *Merchant Shipping and the Demands of War* (London: HMSO, 1955).

Bidwell, Shelford and Graham, Dominick, *Firepower: British Army Weapons and Theories of War, 1904–45* (London: Allen & Unwin, 1982 and 1986).

Carver, Michael, Lord, *Tobruk* (London: Batsford, 1964).

——, *Harding of Petherton; a biography* (London: Weidenfeld & Nicolson, 1978).

——, *Dilemmas of the Desert War: a new look at the Libyan campaign 1940–42* (London: Batsford, 1986).

Chandler, Alfred and Louis Galambos (eds) *The Papers of Dwight D. Eisenhower* (Baltimore: University Press, Johns Hopkins).

Chapman, Guy (ed.) *Vain Glory: A Miscellany of the Great War, 1914–18*, written by those who fought in it on each side and on all fronts (London: Cassel, 1937).

Charters, David Marc Milner and J. Brent Wilson, *Military History and the Military Profession* (London: Praeger, 1992).

Churchill, Winston, *The World Crisis*, abridged and revd edn (London: Thornton Butterworth, 1931).

Copp, Terry and Bill McAndrew, *Battlefield Stress: Soldiers and Psychiatrists in the Canadian Army, 1939–45* (Montreal: University Press, McGill-Queen's 1990).

Douglas, Keith, *Alamein to Zem Zem* (London: Penguin, 1969).

Edmonds, Brigadier General Sir James (ed.) *History of the Great War: Military Operations France and Belgium* (London: HMSO, various dates).

Ehrman, John, *History of the Second World War. Grand Strategy*, vols V and VI (London: HMSO, 1956).

Eisenhower, David, *Eisenhower at War, 1943–45* (New York: Random House, 1986).

Ellis, Major L.F., *History of the Second World War: Victory in the West*, vols I and II (London: HMSO 1962 and 1968).

D'Este, Carlo, *Decision in Normandy* (London: William Collins, 1983).

French, David, *British Strategy and War Aims 1914–1916* (Oxford: Clarendon, 1986).

——, *The Strategy of the Lloyd George Coalition 1916–1918* (Oxford: Clarendon, 1995).

Gibbs, Norman, *History of the Second World War. Grand Strategy vol. I* (London: HMSO, 1976).

Graham, Desmond, *Keith Douglas, 1920–1944: a biography* (Oxford University Press, 1988).

Graham, Dominick, *The Price of Command: a biography of General Guy Simonds* (Toronto: Stoddart, 1993).

——, and Shelford Bidwell, *Coalitions, Politicians and Generals: some aspects of command in two world wars* (London: Brassey, 1993).

Hamilton, Nigel, *Monty: Master of the Battlefield 1942–44* (London: Hamish Hamilton, 1983).

——, *Monty: The Field Marshal, 1944–76* (London: Hamish Hamilton, 1986).

Haycock, Ronald and Keith Neilson (eds) *Men, Machines and War* (Waterloo: Wilfrid Laurier University Press, 1988).

Hinsley, F.H., *British Intelligence in the Second World War*, vols 2 and 3 (London: HMSO, 1981 and 1988).

Joly, Cyril *Take These Men; The Campaign of the Desert, 1940–1943* (London: Penguin, 1956).

Kitching, George, *Mud and Green Fields: The Memoirs of General George Kitching* (Langley, British Columbia: Battleline Books, 1985).

Martin Middlebrook (ed.) *The First Day on the Somme* (London: Allen Lane, 1971).

Montgomery, Field-Marshal B.L., *The Memoirs of Field Marshal Montgomery* (London, 1958).

Neilson, Keith, *Strategy and Supply: the Anglo-Russian Alliance 1914–1917* (London, 1984).

Howard, Michael (ed.) *The Theory and Practice of War* (London: Oxford University Press, 1965).

——, *The Continental Commitment* (London, 1972).

Leighton, Richard and Robert Coakley, *Global Logistics and Strategy, 1940–43* (Washington: Office of the Chief of Military History, 1956).

Lewin, Ronald, *The Chief; F.M. Lord Wavell, Commander-in-Chief and Viceroy 1939–1947* (London: Hutchinson, 1980).

Matloff, Maurice, *Strategic Planning for Coalition Warfare 1943–44* (Washington: Office of the Chief of Military History, 1959).

Playfair, Major General I.S.O., *History of the Second World War: The Mediterranean and the Middle East*, Vols I–III (London: HMSO, 1954, 1956 and 1960).

Pogue, Forest C., *The U.S. Army in World War II: The European Theater of Operations* (Washington: Office of the Chief of Military History, 1959).

——, *George C. Marshall: Organizer of Victory, 1943–45* (Viking, 1973).

Scarfe, Norman, *Assault Division: A History of the 3rd Division from the Invasion of Normandy to the Surrender of Germany* (London: Collins, 1947).

Stacey, C.P., *Official History of the Canadian Army in the Second World War. Volume III, The Victory Campaign. Operations in North-West Europe 1944–1945* (Ottawa: Queen's Printer, 1960).

Terraine, John, *The Road to Passchendaele* (London: Leo Cooper, 1977).

——, *White Heat: The New Warfare, 1914–18* (London: Guild Publishing, 1982).

Travers, Tim, *How the War Was Won: Command and Technology in the British Army on the Western Front 1917–18* (London: Routledge, 1992).

——, *The Killing Ground* (Allen & Unwin, 1987).

Wolff, Leon, *In Flanders Fields* (New York: Ballantine, 1960).

Wynne, G.C., *If Germany Attacks: The Battle in Depth in the West* (London: Faber, 1940).

Index

Arms, definition of and description of individual arms, 5

Atkinson, J., librarian, Bovington Tank Museum, acknowledgement, xii

Bidwell, Brigadier Shelford, acknowledgement, xii

Birch, General Sir Noel, Senior Gunner under Rawlinson in Fourth Army and under Haig on the Somme, warns of inadequacy of artillery for Somme, 34

Brooke, Sir Alan, relations with colleagues, 3

Brüchmuller, Colonel Georg, his artillery methods, 39, 40

Budworth, Major-General CED, as 4th Corps and Fourth Army Gunner under Rawlinson, the Loos and Somme plans, 33, 34, 59

Cambrai, 61

Chapman, Guy
his anthology, *Vain Glory*, x
morale, 52
comment by Siegfried Sassoon on *Vain Glory*, 53

Coverdale, Terrence, acknowledgement, xii

Davidson, Brigadier John, Haig's chief of operations, circulates paper about German methods at Ypres, 38

Education and physique
British and German soldiers compared, 6
and character of British soldier, 6
Brigadier Hargest's comments, 159

Fire-power
comparison of German and British, 5, 160, 174–5
McMahon and pre-war debate, 17–21
see also under Haig

Foch, General Ferdinand, conception of a break through on the Somme, 33–5

French, Sir John, relations with Kitchener and Joffre, 30

Gough, General Sir Hubert
organisation of platoons on the Somme, 37
his problems making the 3rd Ypres plan, 45

Haig, Sir Douglas
outstanding commander of the First World War, 1
authoritarian, 1
unsuitable tactics in 1917, 1
inadequate ability to communicate ideas as C-in-C, 1, 2
amiable relations with French commanders, 2
opinion about making peace in 1918, 2
comparison with Montgomery, 2, 3
comparison of status of senior commanders in the wars, 3
and the General Staff, 16
and pre-war fire-power, 20
Winston Churchill's description of him, 21
the Somme plan and his relations with Rawlinson, 33, 34
changes in command methods after departure of Joffre, 41
desires more British Army influence on strategic decisions, 41
Nivelle fails, 41